LAST WORD

Works by Mark Lane

BOOKS
Rush to Judgment
A Citizen's Dissent
Arcadia
Chicago Eyewitness
Conversations With Americans
Executive Action
Murder in Memphis
The Strongest Poison

SCREENPLAYS
Executive Action
Arcadia
Plausible Denial

PLAYS
The Trial of James Earl Ray

DOCUMENTARY FILMS
A Rush to Judgment
Two Men in Dallas

LAST WORD

MY INDICTMENT OF THE CIA IN THE MURDER OF JFK

MARK LANE

INTRODUCTION BY ROBERT K. TANENBAUM
WITH A CHAPTER BY OLIVER STONE

A HERMAN GRAF BOOK
SKYHORSE PUBLISHING

Skyhorse Publishing books may be purchased in bulk at special discounts for sales promotion, corporate gifts, fund-raising, or educational purposes. Special editions can also be created to specifications. For details, contact the Special Sales Department, Skyhorse Publishing, 307 West 36th Street, 11th Floor, New York, NY 10018 or info@skyhorsepublishing.com.

Skyhorse® and Skyhorse Publishing® are registered trademarks of Skyhorse Publishing, Inc.®, a Delaware corporation.

www.skyhorsepublishing.com

10 9 8 7 6 5 4 3 2

Library of Congress Cataloging-in-Publication Data is available on file.
ISBN: 978-1-62087-070-9

Printed in the United States of America

In remembrance of the victims.

Those more than fifty thousand Americans who died in Vietnam. The Vietnamese prisoners of war tortured and executed by the CIA in Vietnam. Those Americans who suffered in abusive experiments and those who died at the hands of the CIA in their own country.

And John F. Kennedy.

Contents

Introduction

Throughout American history, heroic individuals committed to the core principles of American exceptionalism have championed the unpopular righteous cause. They witnessed injustice and sought to correct it. They experienced intolerance and refused to accept it. They encountered evil and struggled to defeat it.

During many of these confrontations, they risked their reputations and were subjected to public scorn. Yet, they endured not because they reveled in unpopularity but because they understood that momentary public censure borne of ignorance and prejudice was the price paid for a pure soul and the cost of virtuous ethical conviction.

Mark Lane is such a man and *Last Word* is incontrovertible corroboration. Throughout his professional career, Lane has used his brilliance in and out of the courtroom to represent the underdog. Time after time, he challenged the government to present trustworthy evidence in the numerous cases he tried. He always spoke truth to power. He was so committed to exposing injustice, it can be said that he was willing to march into hell, to pursue a heavenly cause.

Lane's *Last Word* reveals his courageous challenge to the Warren Commission report and his scathing critique of unconscionable CIA outrages. The penetrating accuracy of his reportage may be measured by the personal attacks he endured that were orchestrated by upper-echelon rogue CIA operatives. In fact, to obfuscate and diminish the credibility of Lane's critique of the Warren Commission findings, the CIA created and disseminated false and defamatory impressions of, about and pertaining to him. CIA media assets were willing purveyors of this smut.

Mark Lane had the courage to enter the marketplace of ideas and challenge the government's version of the Kennedy assassination. Those who truly support the principles expressed in our founding documents, the Declaration of Independence and Constitution, believe fervently that the public square must always be open, democratic, and welcoming. The notion is that the best, most rational, compellingly truthful ideas ought to prevail. Participation is to be encouraged, particularly when it may be deemed unpopular.

In a free and open democratic society, certainly no government official or agency has the right to engage in defaming any individual simply because his views are critical of those in officialdom. As a result of the CIA's vitriolic calumny directed at Lane, he suffered public scorn and disgrace. Yet, like others whose path was righteous, he has persevered and has been ultimately vindicated.

Two other examples of courageous profiles come to mind: John Adams's legal representation of the British soldiers and their commanding officer Captain Thomas Preston in the case historically recorded as the Boston Massacre. On March 5, 1770, close to the Boston Custom House, a British sentry was confronted by an angry mob. Violence ensued, shots were fired, and five in the unruly crowd were killed. Patriots were outraged and sought a public hanging of the loathsome redcoats. No lawyers except one would represent the British soldiers. When asked to do so, John Adams accepted. As a result of his challenge of the government's case and ability to penetratingly search for and reveal the truth at trial, the British captain and six of his men were acquitted. Adams chose to honor the principles of a fair trial and render competent counsel to the accused. For so doing, he was publicly vilified.

In 1784, Alexander Hamilton chose to represent a Tory in a highly celebrated civil case, *Rutgers v. Waddington*. The plaintiff, a sympathetic patriotic widow, Elizabeth Rutgers, owned a brewery and alehouse on Maiden Lane located in the lower portion of Manhattan near Wall Street in New York City. During the British occupation of New York, she abandoned her property in 1776. At the urging of the British, Joshua Waddington ultimately took possession and became its operator.

The civil complaint lay in trespass seeking damages for the fair rental value of the property.

During the post–Revolutionary War period, Tories were routinely oppressed. Hamilton's sense of justice was offended. He also believed that the case had legal significance. On June 29, 1784, he argued Waddington's cause in the Mayor's Court in New York City. At issue was the right of a high appellate court to void a legislative act. Hamilton's legal brilliance carried the day with the court rendering an opinion favorable enough to Waddington that ultimately resulted in an amicable settlement between the parties. However, the case will long be noted for Hamilton's vision of the doctrine of judicial review, which became the law of the land in 1803 when the U.S. Supreme Court led by Chief Justice John Marshall decided *Marbury v. Madison*.

Adams and Hamilton were vilified for choosing to enter the public arena and representing vigorously an extremely unpopular cause. In so doing, they became the predicate to the Mark Lane narrative. These three intrepid advocates have enriched in perpetuity our justice system. All three understood that America would always be special if the strong were just, the weak secure and the marketplace available and welcome to all.

In early 1977, I first met Mark Lane. At the time, I was deputy chief counsel to the congressional committee investigation into the assassination of President Kennedy. During the course of the investigation, I set aside an afternoon every week to listen to individuals who had information they wished to share with me and the committee. On one such afternoon, Mark Lane came to see me. Before that, I had never met or spoken to him. When he entered the office, I stood to welcome him and asked him to be seated. He refused. Instead, he handed me a sealed envelope. I asked him if he had any suggestions or thoughts about its contents. He said, "When you read the contents, I believe you'll know exactly what to do." Immediately, he left. I never spoke to him again during the course of the investigation and for more than a decade thereafter.

The document in the envelope was a memo dated November 23, 1963, from FBI Director J. Edgar Hoover to all bureau supervisory personnel. In substance, it stated that the FBI agents who had questioned Lee Harvey Oswald for approximately seventeen hours had listened to a tape of a conversation between an individual who identified himself as "Lee Oswald" and an individual in the Cuban embassy. The conversation had taken place inside the Russian embassy in Mexico City by this faux alleged Oswald who telephoned the Cuban embassy. The call was made on or about October 1, 1963, just about seven weeks before the assassination. The Hoover memo noted that the agents categorically concluded that the voice on the tape was not that of Lee Harvey Oswald. Based upon the evidence adduced during the investigation, I had reason to believe that David Phillips, the third-ranking member of the CIA in charge of Western Hemispheric operations, employed a nom de guerre, Maurice Bishop. Bishop had significant involvement with anti-Castro Cubans and Lee Harvey Oswald.

I had Phillips subpoenaed to appear before our committee in executive session. I asked him under oath where we could locate the tape of the so-called Oswald conversation of October 1, 1963, while inside the Russian embassy in Mexico City. Phillips stated that it was CIA policy at the time to recycle the tapes every six or seven days and it was no longer in existence after the first week in October 1963. I then handed him the Hoover memo which, according to the FBI director, clearly revealed that the tape was evidently available in Dallas on November 22 and 23, 1963. Phillips read the memo, then folded it, placed it in his jacket pocket, arose, and walked out of the meeting.

I immediately urged the committee to recall Phillips and advise him to obtain legal counsel so that he be given an opportunity to purge potential criminal charges of contempt and perjury. Also, there were many more questions that he needed to answer. I further advised the committee of the urgency of the matter and gave them legal options. They chose to do nothing. Thereafter, our staff phones were denied long distance telephone access, "franking privileges" were withdrawn, and staffers' pay was withheld.

Prior to my assignment with the Congressional Committee, I served as an assistant district attorney in the New York County District Attorney's Office under legendary D.A. Frank Hogan. While there, I tried hundreds of cases to verdict. I was Bureau Chief of the criminal courts, ran the Homicide Bureau, and was in charge of the training program for the legal staff.

From experiences as a prosecutor, I knew well that there is no political way to investigate a case. There is no liberal or conservative way to gather evidence and there is no Democratic or Republican way to evaluate it. Unfortunately, the congressional committee played politics with our investigation and subverted it. The members breached the trust reposed in them by the American people. They assured me that whatever the facts revealed would be forthrightly presented to the public. Regrettably that was false.

Ironically, Mark Lane was a major moving force to have the committee organized and come to fruition. He supplied compelling evidence that should have energized the congressional probe; instead, ultimately this evidence led to its demise in terms of credibility and integrity. Recognizing that the committee was less than sincere in its search for the truth, Chief Counsel Richard Sprague and I tendered our resignations.

Whether one agrees with Mark Lane's conclusions or not, everyone should read *Last Word*. His courageous efforts, his scholarly research and remarkable advocacy are a tribute to his enormous capacity to seek the truth. We are all a better people because of all that he has done.

—Robert K. Tanenbaum

LAST WORD

BOOK ONE

THE ASSASSINATION

The Journey Begins

I began this improbable journey almost a half century ago. After John Kennedy was murdered, events sped by in whirlwind disorder. J. Edgar Hoover, perhaps the most distrusted official in the country, quickly proclaimed that the assassin was a young man who was guilty beyond all doubt and that there was no possibility that anyone else had been involved. Walter Cronkite, at the time said to be the most trusted man in the country, agreed. Then Lee Harvey Oswald, the *alleged* assassin (how rarely was that cautionary word employed by the media), was shot to death while Americans observed the murder on national television. Oswald was shot in the Dallas Police and Courts Building while surrounded by police officers by an old and dear friend of many of the cops, including those on duty that day. That Jack Ruby, the murderer, had worked for the FBI as an informant and had been previously employed by Congressman Richard M. Nixon, who was looking into subversive actions by his fellow Americans, was among the many facts suppressed by local and national police and their loyal assets in the news business.

I had known John when he was a senator seeking to become a president. I supported him for the Democratic Party nomination that took place that year in Los Angeles. I was active in efforts to wrest control of the Democratic Party in New York, led by Carmine DeSapio, from its established leaders, most of whom had substantial connections to organized crime. The founders of our Reform Movement were Eleanor Roosevelt, former governor Herbert Lehman, and many young people who, as in my case, were naïve enough to believe that change is possible. I still hold to that vision in spite of the existence of all evidence to the contrary.

Murray Kempton, a very clever writer for the then somewhat liberal and somewhat crusading *New York Post,* observed that the Reform Movement was "mostly comprised of young lawyers seeking to become old judges." I told him that I was in touch with my colleagues every day and that he was barely acquainted with them. In reply he smiled and nodded. As it turned out he knew them better than I did.

Both John and his brother Bobby, as well as some of his advisors from Massachusetts who came to New York to look over the political scene, were wary of the regular organization and not quite sure about the reformers either. They suggested a compromise regarding the campaign. Each of the warring branches of the Democrats would select a person to manage the campaign in crucial New York, and they would hopefully work together to get Kennedy elected. They asked that I be the reform designee and the reform leaders, who much preferred Adlai Stevenson as their nominee in any event, were willing to comply.

I was also nominated by community groups in Yorkville and East Harlem to be their candidate for the New York State legislature. Senator John F. Kennedy endorsed me; I helped to run his campaign locally, and we were both elected. It was during that period that I was able to meet with John and Bobby and discuss political events.

I had been practicing law in a storefront office in East Harlem for less than ten years. Much of my work had been as a defense counsel in criminal cases. I believed in due process, the presumption of innocence, and the other pillars of our judicial system. I saw them all traduced moments after President Kennedy had been assassinated. Doubts about Oswald's guilt, or his lone guilt, arose when the evidence was even superficially examined. I thought then, as I do now, that our system of justice was on trial and was not faring too well. There was also the consideration that if Oswald was either innocent or had acted with others, the murderers of a man I knew and respected went unpunished. I could not understand why those believing in law and order were not similarly concerned.

I began to look into the facts surrounding the assassination and that inquiry resulted in the first book I had ever written, *Rush to Judgment.* It immediately, to my great astonishment, became a best-selling book. Establishment polls concluded that it had changed the perception of the Warren Report and resulted in America's developing a credibility gap about unproven governmental assertions.

I never meant to devote a major part of my life to this one subject. I thought that after writing *Rush to Judgment*, I would move on to other matters and let this one sort itself out. Now, these many years later, I am still here due to the fact that the defenders of the myth, their reputations in tatters, nevertheless tenaciously hold on to a demonstrably false version of history and enjoy the support of their apologists in the media. The CIA has become increasingly more influential, now even commanding its own air force and making policy, while influencing the media, and its assets have become more servile.

The Investigators

After years of the Eisenhower Age, with foreign policy dominated by a reckless and relentless John Foster Dulles rendering a compassionate domestic approach a concept forgotten or repudiated, the lights were burning again at night in the White House, where a young and energetic leader and his family were in residence. In our country, people, many, but not all, young, were asking what they could do for their country. For some the answer was the Peace Corps, for some a new commitment to equal rights for all, and for others various ways to reshape their careers.

The new administration was not the sudden reappearance of Camelot and its policy was for cautious rather than substantial change, yet it inspired hope for millions who yearned for a better day for their country. For those of us who knew him and had worked with him, his death was also a personal loss. To millions of Americans whom he had inspired, his murder created almost unprecedented apprehension and sorrow. To the world, the assassination of the president of the United States, the most powerful nation on the planet, during the Nuclear Age and a time of incipient proliferation of weapons of mass destruction, promised almost unimaginable threats.

It was a truly American scene. The president was seated next to his wife in an open limousine riding through a prominent city on a bright sunny day in mid-America as spectators smiled, waved, and applauded. Suddenly sounds of gunfire shattered that moment. Hope died that day along with Kennedy and fear traumatized the conscience of a nation, challenging our concept of national security.

In that time of national paralysis the federal police acted at once. The rush to judgment began when J. Edgar Hoover, on the same afternoon of the assassination, callously told Robert Kennedy that his brother was dead and that Lee Harvey Oswald was the lone assassin. To people who maintained their ability to reason, a question emerged. How could the FBI have reached a final conclusion without having first conducted an investigation, especially in view of Oswald's denials that he had committed any crime? Clearly, a prospective defendant's assertion of innocence is not proof, in some instances not even evidence, but in the absence of a signed confession, on what basis could anyone almost immediately claim that the case was solved, or that even if Oswald was the lone gunman, that he had not, at some time in the past, conspired with anyone?

J. Edgar Hoover, the director of the Federal Bureau of Investigation, a position he considered to be a lifetime sinecure, issued a report as the echo of gunfire from Dealey Plaza had barely faded. He determined, within twenty-four hours and without any serious inquiry, that Lee Harvey Oswald was the lone assassin. Hoover did not lack self-esteem; his agents and special agents in charge were required to officially refer to his office as the SOG, meaning Seat of Government. Hoover saw American presidents as politicians permitted to remain in office just four or eight years, or even less, as they passed through his continuing reign. Unfortunately for him, many others had begun to fear, resent, and ridicule him rather than respect his judgment.

Frame-ups are best managed from the shadows, for they confront serious obstacles if the crime is witnessed by many during daylight hours, when forensic evidence abounds, and especially if the events are caught on film. In those trying circumstances, the fabrications require unlimited respect for the investigators and unquestioning loyalty to their conclusions from the media. They require, as well, suppression of some evidence, destruction of other evidence, and a blissful ignorance of the most relevant facts and the rules of logic.

There had been calls for numerous investigations by various committees of both houses of the Congress. Those inquiries would have been well publicized and the facts they uncovered would have been widely available. The congressional committees would have been granted, and likely have used, the power of subpoena.

The new president, Lyndon B. Johnson of Texas, appointed a commission of inquiry. Its purpose, it announced, was "to avoid parallel investigations."[1] Johnson appointed a political commission to secretly investigate. The press was banned from the hearings and the transcripts were marked top secret. The formal name of the group was The President's Commission on the Assassination of President Kennedy. It was popularly called the Warren Commission and was comprised of two Republicans, one a senator and one a member of the House of Representatives, and two Southern Democrats during the era of heated civil rights differences in which Southern Democrats rebelled by often supporting Republican candidates. There was not a single strong Kennedy supporter on the commission.

In addition, Johnson appointed John McCloy, the former assistant secretary of war, notorious for his refusal to endorse bombing raids on the rail approaches to the Auschwitz concentration camp—raids that would have saved countless Nazi Holocaust victims—and for supporting Hitler at least until 1939 (he shared a box with Hitler in Berlin at the 1936 Olympics). After the war, McCloy refused to endorse compensation for innocent Japanese Americans who had been held in American concentration camps. In short, McCloy was kind to criminals, but took a strong stance against the innocent.

Johnson also appointed Allen Dulles, the former director of the CIA, who had been fired by John Kennedy for lying to him about the CIA's Bay of Pigs invasion of Cuba and for numerous other deceits. Formerly top secret documents, now available, including transcripts of executive meetings, disclose beyond doubt that Dulles ran the Warren Commission. He was, in fact, the only active member of the group.

Dulles was familiar with assassinations. Under his leadership, the CIA was involved in numerous efforts to remove foreign leaders by covert means, including CIA-led coups. His organization was responsible for deposing democratically elected Prime Minister Mohammad Mossadegh of Iran in 1953 through Operation Ajax, and President Arbenz of Guatemala in 1954, through Operation PBSUCCESS.

---

1. Warren Commission Report, p. x.

Dulles also organized attempted assassinations of heads of state who espoused policies different from those supported by the agency. His organization, the CIA, was responsible for the Phoenix Program, the selective assassinations of more than 25,000 civilians in Vietnam, many of whom were village chiefs or other elected officers.

Dulles relied upon Leon Jaworski to help suppress evidence from Dallas. The commission praised Jaworski for his role and for being "helpful to the accomplishment of the commission's assignment."[2] Jaworski was later canonized by the media for his role in Watergate. We are indebted to *The New York Times* for recently publishing a decision of the United States Army review board which demonstrated that twenty-eight black soldiers were falsely convicted of starting a riot that led to a death.[3] All were victims of a court martial during 1944, one of the largest army courts-martial of World War II. All twenty-eight were sent to prison and given dishonorable discharges. After twenty-six of the men died, the army concluded that they were innocent and that the unethical and unlawful conduct of one man was responsible for the miscarriage of justice. That man was Lt. Col. Leon Jaworski, who had in his possession important evidence demonstrating the innocence of the soldiers. In violation of relevant ethical standards, Jaworski refused to share that evidence with the defense lawyers, thus leading to what he knew would be unjust convictions. Jaworski was later chosen to provide all of the relevant evidence from Texas to the Warren Commission.

The chairman of the group, Earl Warren, was an active politician and prosecutor. He had been appointed, not elected, district attorney of Alameda County, California, when his predecessor resigned. He established a reputation for conducting his office in a high-handed manner and in arguably denying rights to defendants. He was elected governor of the state as a take-no-prisoners prosecutor, whose reputation was similar to that which Thomas Dewey had developed in New York. As governor, Warren played a pivotal role in implementing the plan to establish concentration camps in the United States in which innocent Japanese Americans were imprisoned, while members of Warren's voting blocks seized their property. In 1948, he ran for vice president of the United States with Dewey. That Republican ticket, although strongly

---

2.   Warren Commission Report, p. xi.
3.   *New York Times*, October 27, 2007, front page.

favored to win, was defeated by Harry Truman and Alben Barkley. Later Warren was appointed Chief Justice by President Eisenhower, who later said that the appointment had been a major error. In that position he organized a series of unanimous decisions that barred the racial segregation of public schools and established certain rights for those being held and interrogated by law enforcement officers.

All of the members of the commission had full-time jobs that occupied them, with the exception of Dulles, who, then unemployed, devoted his time to running the inquiry. Johnson had not put some untrained little fox in charge of the hen house. He had awarded that position to Col. Sanders.

At an early meeting, for which the minutes were classified top secret (later released as a result of Freedom of Information legal actions brought in the United States District Court for the District of Columbia with the invaluable assistance of the American Civil Liberties Union), Dulles told the members that they need not worry about anyone doubting their false conclusions. Maybe, he suggested, at worst many years will have passed before some professor might study the evidence and by then it would not matter. Albert Einstein was proven by Dulles once again to be right when he said, "Only two things are infinite, the universe and human stupidity, and I'm not sure about the former."

Predictably, the Warren Commission adopted the FBI report and concluded that Oswald had been the lone assassin. The FBI report had been relied upon almost exclusively by an old CIA hand who had been the agency's director longer than any other person in American history. The commission's report was an intelligence fabrication.

Assassination Nomenclature

For those readers not acquainted with the facts regarding the conclusions of the Warren Commission, I have prepared a glossary to assist in comprehending the tortuous path chosen by the government to fabricate its case:

The Magic Bullet

I originated the phrase in an effort to describe the official explanation in 1964; in 1966 it served as a title for Chapter 4 of *Rush to Judgment*. It refers to the unprecedented mystic and acrobatic propensities of a bullet as imagined by two junior lawyers for the Warren Commission, Arlen Specter and David Belin, two lawyers each in search of a career, who reprised the Roy Cohn and David Schine days with Sen. Joe McCarthy where dedication to the facts was also hardly a virtue. While the bullet took a most fancy flight in their inventive minds, the explanation was not a meaningless flight of fancy; it was absolutely required to save the false conclusions reached by the Warren Commission.

The bullet's formal name is CE (Commission Exhibit) 399, but not unlike Earvin Johnson it is better known to millions by its nickname. Here are some relevant facts. The evidence demonstrated that at least four shots had been fired and that one had struck a curb, causing a minor injury to a bystander. All the shots had been fired during a period of not more than 5.6 seconds, as demonstrated by a film of the assassination that served as visual evidence and as the clock for the shooting; the frames ran through the camera at the rate of 18.3 frames per second. The rifle that the commission claimed fired all of the shots was an ancient and inaccurate Mannlicher-Carcano. The weapon, with a hand-operated bolt action, was tested by experts who testified that it required at least 2.3 seconds to reload between shots, and that was without time spent in aiming the weapon.

The president was seated in the back seat on the passenger side. Seated directly in front of him, on a jump seat, was Governor John B. Connally, Jr. A bullet entered President Kennedy's throat from the front causing a neat, small entrance wound according to every doctor who had examined him at the Parkland Hospital in Dallas. Another bullet, also fired from the front, was the fatal shot. It threw him backwards and to the left and drove brain and skull matter onto a motorcycle officer to his left and rear.

Gov. Connally suffered numerous injuries, likely the result of being struck by more than one bullet. His ribs were shattered, his right wrist severely injured and his left thigh was penetrated. The commission was distraught since it began and ended its inquiry with the irrevocable presumption that Oswald was the lone assassin and that he had used the Mannlicher-Carcano. If one bullet had missed, as both the evidence and the Warren Commission revealed, then at least four shots (probably five or more) had been fired in 5.6 seconds. But with a weapon that required 2.3 seconds between shots, four shots could not have been fired. Three intervals, assuming that the weapon was fully loaded before the first shot was fired, would have taken, at an absolute minimum, 6.9 seconds.

Another problem was that Connally, after studying the film, was able to locate the frame at which he was first struck by a bullet. It took place 1.8 seconds after Kennedy had been hit. The commission concluded that Connally probably never noticed the "glancing blow;" Connally said he had "noticed" the bullet that smashed his ribs and turned splinters into missiles as they exited.

Specter and Belin were asked to invent some explanation. Neither lacking ambition nor imagination and not bound by rules of logic or adherence to the truth, they created the Magic Bullet Theory.[4*] Satire permits us to offer this as a summary:

Oswald was at a sixth-floor window of the Texas School Book Depository as the president's limousine slowed to turn onto Elm Street. He was so close that he could have thrown the rifle at the president. Apparently, being a sport, he waited until the car gained speed and was a considerable distance from him. The president's back was then the only target available. Oswald fired the first shot, which struck the president in the back. The bullet rose upwards and exited through the president's throat leaving behind a small, neat entrance wound. The bullet hung in midair for 1.8 seconds until it noticed Connally. It regained speed and entered Connally's back, shattering ribs. Connally did not notice the glancing blow, which almost killed him. The bullet then made a right downward turn and entered Connally's right wrist. Soon it emerged from that contact and entered Connally's left thigh. The bullet, almost in pristine shape, having quite mysteriously left behind in Connally's wrist more metal than it lost (when weighed and examined by the commission's experts), was discovered at the hospital under the mat of a stretcher that had had no contact with Connally, as if it had been placed there. Therefore, one bullet having accomplished all of the many wounds suffered by Connally and two wounds suffered by Kennedy, it is clear that only three shots were fired.

Many scholars and others have difficulty in accepting the Magic Bullet Theory.

Commission Exhibit 399

How the bullet, which appeared never to have had contact with a single object as dense as bone, was found is a simple story with but one witness who came forward. Darrell C. Tomlinson, who was the senior engineer at Parkland Hospital, testified that he had found the bullet. He said he saw a man whom he could not identify in contact with a

---

4. During 1910, Paul Ehrlich, a bacteriologist, was seeking a cure for syphilis. He thought he had found it. He named the drug Salvarsan and called it the "magic bullet." That magic bullet did not work then any more than it does now, but the name was later applied to characterize hoped-for drugs. Since the Warren Report shafted the country, its solution was proven to be false, and it was offered to tranquilize the population, the name seemed uniquely appropriate.

stretcher and that when that person pushed the stretcher, a bullet rolled out. He said that it did not come from the stretcher that had been used for Connally. The only witness who testified about the stretcher was Tomlinson. The commission concluded that "the bullet came from the governor's stretcher," relying on the only witness to the event who said that it had not.

Experiments were conducted by the government's expert to determine what a bullet would look like if it shattered a wrist or struck a rib. The expert said that each test bullet did not resemble the magic bullet at all because while 399 was almost pristine, every test bullet was deformed and "severely flattened on the end."

Other government experts weighed and examined the bullet and studied Connally's x-rays. They stated that too many grains of metal remained in Connally's body to have come from 399. In all respects it was a magic missile worthy of satire—and Jerry Seinfeld and Larry David did their best to ridicule it in a very clever *Seinfeld* episode.

The Grassy Knoll

The vast majority of the eyewitnesses in numerous different locations throughout Dealey Plaza stated that shots had come from behind a wooden fence on the grassy knoll, as did the ear-witnesses, all supported by the forensic evidence, the photographic evidence, the medical evidence, and the physical evidence.

The phrase "grassy knoll" has become such an integral part of both American history and the English language that it yields many search results in Google. No need to mention JFK, the assassination, Dealey Plaza, or even Dallas—just type "grassy knoll" and Google will respond. Remarkably enough, even the word "knoll" or "grassy" standing alone will get a response relevant to the assassination.

The only Americans who appeared to have missed the importance of the wooden fence on the grassy knoll were the seven men who comprised the Warren Commission and the fifteen men who served as counsel to the commission, causing one to wonder if, had a few women had been permitted to join the men they might not have been so negligent. The twenty-two men responsible published a report with maps and photographs of Dealey Plaza from which they, through design and duplicity, excluded the fence and the knoll.[5]

For many Americans, the only mystery remaining about the location of the origin of the fatal shot was, "who named it?" While the words "grassy knoll" appear in *Rush to Judgment*,[6] I did not devise that phrase. I merely repeated it.

On February 18, 1964, I interviewed Jean Hill, a Dallas school teacher. The Warren Commission had been in existence since November 29, 1963, but I had not questioned a single eyewitness before my telephone conversation with Ms. Hill. Two weeks after my talk with her, I testified before the Warren Commission. Jean had told me that she heard between four and six shots. When I asked her where she was standing in Dealey Plaza, she asked if I was familiar with the relevant geography; and when I told her that I had never been to Dallas, she described the area and her location and said that "shots had come from behind a wooden fence on the grassy knoll." I informed the seven members of her observations. The area had been christened by Jean Hill and she never knew that she had named it. She could have said, "little hill," "small incline," or "mound," or selected a number of other descriptive terms. Instead she became a contributor to the lexicon of our time.

I met Jean for the first time at a conference in Dallas many years after the assassination. Prior to that time our relationship had consisted of the one telephone conversation. She told me then that she had not known that she had named the area where we were then standing until she read *A Citizen's Dissent,* a book I had written.[7]

In 1991, President George H.W. Bush appointed Clarence Thomas to the United States Supreme Court. During the hearings Anita F. Hill, a professor of law now at Brandeis University, testified about the actions of Thomas when Hill was working with him at the U.S. Department of Education and later at the U.S. Equal Employment Opportunity Commission. She gave details of gross sexual misconduct by Thomas, and her testimony was supported by statements made by several other women and men. I followed the matter closely as I had been counsel

5.   Warren Commission Report, Commission Exhibit 2118, page 73; Commission Exhibit 2214, page 74; Commission Exhibit 2215, page 74.
6.   *Rush to Judgment*, published 1966, Chapter 2, "Where the Shots Came From," page 37.
7.   *A Citizen's Dissent: Mark Lane Replies,* Holt, Rinehart and Winston, 1968, page 187.

for women who had suffered sexual harassment on the job and who had later filed lawsuits.[8] I was very impressed by Ms. Hill, as were several other members of the trial bar with whom I discussed the case. It is rare in such matters to secure support from other witnesses since the harassment is generally done in private and the victims are often reluctant to discuss it.

Arlen Specter, a member of the Senate Judiciary Committee, cruelly and unprofessionally cross-examined her and denounced her as a perjurer. Later Anita Hill said, "I knew his questions were both insincere and ill-informed. With every question he asked, it became clearer that despite any declaration to the contrary, he viewed me as an adversary. Rather than seeking to elicit information, his questioning sought to elicit conclusions he had reached before the hearings began."

If Anita Hill had spoken with Jean before the hearings in Washington, she may have known the type of man she would face. On one occasion I asked Jean about her appearance before the Warren Commission counsel. She said that there was a court reporter and Arlen Specter. She said that Specter did everything possible to force her to state that she had heard only three shots and that none of them came from the grassy knoll. Jean told me that Specter said that he would release the rumor that she had had an extramarital affair and that in the end she would end up looking as if she was crazy, "just as Oswald's mother had." She said that he wanted her to accept the conclusions that he had reached before he met her. She added, "He was so mean I could hardly believe it." I asked her if she could understand his anger. She answered, with a straight face but a twinkle in her eyes, "Maybe he just doesn't like women named Hill."

The Mannlicher-Carcano

Three officers allegedly found a weapon on the sixth floor of the Texas Book Depository Building on November 22 and examined it.[9]

---

8. I successfully represented Cecily Coleman in a landmark case in the United States District Court for the District of Columbia against a vice president of a major television network.
9. Sworn Statement by Seymour Weitzman, *Rush to Judgment*, p. 409.

They were joined by a captain and a lieutenant of the Dallas police who closely examined the German Mauser. One of them, Lieutenant J. C. Day, ejected a live round from the chamber while Captain Will Fritz observed. The Dallas authorities told the press that the rifle they had found was a 7.65 German Mauser and the Dallas district attorney's statement at a well-attended press conference confirmed that finding. One of the officers who found the weapon, Deputy Constable Seymour Weitzman, made a sworn statement describing the German Mauser in exquisite detail, including its 4/18 telescopic sight.

The next day, November 23, the FBI reported that Oswald allegedly had owned an Italian Mannlicher-Carcano 6.5. The Dallas police and soon the Warren Commission shared another magic moment. They decided retroactively that the weapon discovered on November 22 had, overnight, changed both nationality and size: it was Italian, not German, and it was 6.5, not 7.65. Norman Mailer reminded us sardonically that the confusing conjuration required not a rifle expert but a Zen master, while Walter Cronkite unctuously sought to reassure America by stating that "we must have faith" in the commission.

When I testified before the Commission I did so upon the condition that I be able to examine the weapon. I held it in my hands and read to the members the words clearly stamped on the rifle: "MADE ITALY" and "Cal. 6.5." I wondered how anyone who had looked at that weapon could have identified it differently. The Italian rifle became part of the foundation upon which the government built its case, but as it turns out it, too, became suspect.

Walter H. B. Smith, who was the author of several books published by the National Rifle Association, wrote in *The Basic Manual of Military Small Arms* that the Italian Mannlicher-Carcano rifles "are poor military weapons in comparison with United States, British, German or Russian equipment." *Mechanix Illustrated* found it to be "crudely made, poorly designed, dangerous and inaccurate." Jack O'Connor, in *The Rifle Book*, said that the action is "terrible" and that the weapon tends to blow "the firing pin in the shooter's face." No wonder no expert employed by the government could replicate the results that the government claimed that Oswald had achieved, in time or accuracy.

When Bertrand Russell arranged for me to speak about the issues in several European countries including France, England, Denmark, Sweden, Scotland and Italy, I made reference to the Mannlicher-Carcano at a talk in Italy as the weapon the government had credited for achieving such startling results. I spoke in English; most of those present awaited the translation as I paused. A few immediately broke into uncontrolled laughter. When my remarks were offered in Italian to the large audience, waves of derisive and mischievous howls, shrieks and laughter began and ended only when I asked for an explanation. One elderly gentleman near the back of the auditorium stood, a microphone was brought to him and he said, "We have always thought that the Mannlicher-Carcano was the reason we lost World War II."

The Zapruder Film

Abraham Zapruder, an amateur photographer, created the most important evidence available in Dealey Plaza. He stood in front of the wooden fence with a motion picture camera, a Bell and Howell 8 mm camera, and filmed the president and other occupants of the limousine while the shots were being fired. A Secret Service interview report stated that Zapruder had told the Secret Service that the assassin had fired from directly behind him. The film, according to the commission and its experts, ran through the camera at the rate of 18.3 frames per second; it was therefore not only a filmic record, but the clock for the assassination. The commission found that the time span between the first shot to strike the president and the bullet which shattered his skull "was 4.8 to 5.6 seconds." The indisputable evidence revealed that at least five shots were fired; and even the Warren Commission concluded that an expert required a minimum of 2.3 seconds between one shot and the next, demonstrating that one person using that weapon could not have been responsible for all the shots fired.

The problem with the film is that it was not available to the American people, or even to the FBI, the Secret Service, or the Warren Commission. It had been purchased by *LIFE* magazine, which declined to share it. More than three months passed before agents of the FBI and the Secret Service, together with representatives of the commission, saw the original film, although stills from the film had been published in *LIFE* one week after the assassination.

When New Orleans District Attorney Jim Garrison indicted Clay Shaw for conspiracy in the assassination, he subpoenaed the film from *LIFE*. It was a late afternoon when Jim and I were discussing a restaurant for dinner that evening. The city was filled with some of the finest restaurants in the country; but for reasons never discovered by me, Jim preferred the mundane cuisine served at the New Orleans Athletic club, where the aroma of sweaty sneakers and socks was never far away. That night I won the debate, and we ate at Antoine's. When we returned to his office, Jim stood up abruptly, pointed to a file on his desk and said, "Mark, the Zapruder film is in there." Jim left the office, adding, "When you leave, just lock up."

The next morning, for reasons that I do not wish to recall, Jim's evidence was back at his desk and I was the owner of one hundred copies of the film. I decided to share this largesse with those who might be interested. I sent copies to Walter Cronkite and other influential media grand pooh-bahs. None of them ever utilized that rare resource.

My next media interview was with a well-respected personality who broadcast nightly from a radio station. I brought an 8 mm projector and a screen to the studio. He said, "Mark, you know this is not television." I said, "Nevertheless, we are going to show the Zapruder film to your audience." He asked how that could be accomplished. I said, "I will play it, and you will see it and narrate it to your audience." On the air I played the film and he said as the bullet struck the president in the head, "Oh my God, he was hit from the right front. He was driven backward and to his left." In that manner, the first showing of the Zapruder film was accomplished on a radio station.

Subsequently, I was invited to speak at the John Jay College of Criminal Justice in New York. It is the only liberal arts college with a criminal justice focus in the United States. When the college was founded in 1964, the classes were held at the police academy and it remains a training facility for local, state, and federal law enforcement personnel. I asked the school to announce that I would show the Zapruder film to the present and future criminologists. When I arrived at the school, an attorney approached me and said that he represented Time–Life, the owners of the film, and that I was instructed not to show the film unless I could prove that I was an owner. I responded that I was an owner since I was an American, our president had been killed and we were entitled to all of the evidence. Of course, being a trained lawyer in a large Wall Street law firm, he was unable to follow my clearly logical argument. What he did comprehend, however, was that

I was going to announce to the members of the press, who were also present, that two magazines, theoretically responsible for broadcasting the news, *TIME* magazine and *LIFE,* ironically a photo magazine, were seeking to suppress the information. He left the hall. I set up the screen and the projector.

Just before I was introduced by a professor, the corporate lawyer returned to convey a message to me from his clients. "Time–Life has given you permission to broadcast our film this one time today." I thanked him and said, "Nevertheless, I'm going to show it."

Why Did the CIA See John Kennedy as Their Enemy?

The orthodox method, employed by prosecutors the world over during recent centuries to determine why a crime was committed, is to apprehend the culprit and slam him figuratively or literally against the wall until he reveals his motives and his associates. More civilized societies employ the former method; more barbaric the latter. While Bush and Cheney advocated torture, and those means have been employed by our interrogators the world round, it is a little more difficult to determine at present into which category we fall. But regrettably, fallen we have.

In the death of President Kennedy, no measures were employed since the prosecutors and their legion of FBI, CIA and local police agents declined to look for the assassins and actively sought to obscure the facts. There was, therefore, no one to question with the exception of Lee Oswald, who had been murdered in the Dallas Police and Courts Building by a friend of the local police, a man who had worked for Hoover's FBI in Dallas. Absent a confession and with much information destroyed or distorted, we are reduced to using our minds to think about and evaluate the total circumstances and seek explanations here, as we do daily when called upon to make difficult decisions. First the facts.

President Kennedy was furious with the CIA's deliberately false reports to him about prospects of victory at the Bay of Pigs invasion of Cuba. He fired its director, Allen Dulles, and later told his brother Bobby that he planned to dissolve the CIA, create a new agency and place Bobby in charge. Panic, fear and outrage reverberated through the halls at Langley.

In September 1963, Kennedy decided to end the war in Vietnam and he began to withdraw troops, then called advisors. The CIA strongly opposed those efforts and privately said sardonically, "it may be a dirty little war but it is the only one we've got."

And he was exploring an amicable agreement with Cuba, over the heated objections and acts of sabotage by the agency.

The Witnesses

In any murder investigation, an inquiry is made into those who might have motivation or who profited by it. *Cui bono,* who benefited, is the starting point. On October 2, 1963, Richard Starnes, an editor of *The Washington Daily News* and a respected reporter, wrote from Saigon that the CIA had "arrogantly" rejected orders from President Kennedy about ending the war in Vietnam. He said that if an attempted military coup against Kennedy took place, it would be organized by the CIA. He stated that Kennedy was reluctant to confront the agency head on, perhaps because he was "simply afraid they'd kill him if he tried."

On that same day, Arthur Krock devoted his daily column, "In the Nation," in *The New York Times,* to "The Intra-Administration War in Vietnam." Krock, a three-time Pulitzer Prize winner, was the nation's most famous conservative journalist and was referred to as the "Dean of Washington newsmen." He was very close to President Kennedy. Kennedy's Pulitzer Prize–winning book, *Profiles in Courage,* was drafted and written in Krock's Georgetown home. Krock wrote, quoting a "very high American official," that "the CIA's growth was 'likened to a malignancy' which the 'very high official was not sure even the White House could control ... any longer.' If the United States ever experiences [an attempt at a coup to overthrow the government] it will come from the CIA . . . ' The agency 'represents a tremendous power and total unaccountability to anyone' . . . The CIA may be guilty as charged." Starnes also reported that President Kennedy had commissioned a major inquiry into the misconduct of the CIA. The Krock and Starnes predictions were published in October 1963. Kennedy was murdered the next month.

A serious inquiry would have begun by calling Krock and Starnes and exploring the facts surrounding Kennedy's fear about being overthrown or killed by the CIA. The commission and its FBI and CIA agents stated that they had questioned 25,000 witnesses. Krock was never interviewed, Starnes was never interviewed, and Dulles, who had engaged in the misconduct leading to the threats, had become the leader of the investigation.

Who did testify? Tip O'Neill, the Speaker of the House, used his power to prevent the Congress from looking into the murder. He was confident that Oswald was the lone assassin, basing his belief upon testimony from two men, Kenneth O'Donnell and David Powers. Those of us who worked in Kennedy's presidential campaign knew that Kenny and Dave were close to John, called themselves The Irish Mafia, and became presidential assistants after the election. Both men, seated in a car directly behind the Secret Service car that followed the president's limousine, had testified before the commission and later insisted that all of the shots had been fired from the Texas School Book Depository Building behind the president.

In his autobiography, published a quarter of a century after the assassination, Tip O'Neill made these admissions for the first time.

> I was never one of those people who had doubts or suspicions about the Warren Commission's report on the president's death. But five years after Jack died, I was having dinner with Kenny O'Donnell and a few other people at Jimmy's Harborside Restaurant in Boston, and we got to talking about the assassination.
>
> I was surprised to hear O'Donnell say that he was sure he had heard two shots that came from behind the fence.
>
> "That's not what you told the Warren Commission," I said.
>
> "You're right," he replied. "I told the FBI what I had heard, but they said it couldn't have happened that way and that I must have been imagining things. So I testified the way they wanted me to."
>
> Dave Powers was with us at dinner that night, and his recollection of the shots was the same as O'Donnell's. Kenny O'Donnell is no longer alive, but during the writing of this book I checked with Dave Powers. As they say in the news business, he stands by his story.

And so there will always be some skepticism in my mind about the cause of Jack's death. I used to think that the only people who doubted the conclusions of the Warren Commission were crackpots. Now, however, I'm not so sure.[10]

And so almost a quarter of a century after the assassination, one of the leaders of Kennedy's party decided, in public, for the first time, that the issue was not settled, as Powers and O'Donnell joined the vast majority of the witnesses in Dealey Plaza who had previously sworn or stated that shots had been fired from behind the fence on the grassy knoll. Even the members of the Warren Commission, along with its lawyers and its apologists in the media and elsewhere, agreed that Oswald was not lurking back there. We also learned that Tip, Dave and Kenny knew where to dine on excellent seafood in Boston.

Has hope for the truth vanished, and do we see the darkness of a winter's night beckoning us? It is more like the spring bursting with new discoveries, for in spite of the universal and active endorsement of the false report by almost all of the means of communication in America, television networks, newspapers and news magazines, in spite of the Cronkites and their clones who acted as salesmen for a shoddy and suspect product in hours of one-sided programming, very few in our country have accepted it. Eye- and ear-witnesses to the assassination, came forward to tell the truth. Not the princes concerned for a place near the throne, but teachers, students, workers, businessmen, mechanics, doctors and hundreds of other ordinary people. In a short period of time, every national survey and poll demonstrated that the overwhelming majority of Americans rejected the conclusion of the Warren Commission that Oswald was the lone assassin.

Not one word of dissent from the commission's finding was permitted on the television networks for more than a year after the assassination, and the report was treated as sacrosanct with our opinion makers urging us to have faith in it, as if it were not a political document but rather had been handed down from Mt. Sinai; there was near universal media acceptance and approval of the report.

Perhaps the most revealing fact about the polls on this subject conducted by the traditional experts—Harris, ABC News, the Scripps Howard News Service, Time/CNN and Fox News utilizing Opinion Dynamics—is that their surveys appear to have originated in September

---

10. *Man of the House*, Tip O'Neill, Random House, 1987.

1966.[11,12] At the outset the Hoover Report—later to become the Hoover/ Warren Commission Report—was widely believed in the enforced absence of an alternative. However, one month after the publication of *Rush to Judgment* in August 1966, the first polls revealed that 46 percent of Americans suspected that there had been a conspiracy.[13]

---

11. For almost three years following the assassination the national news media was reluctant to raise any question about the validity of the official story; that embargo was almost absolute for more than one year following the murder.
12. ABC News Poll: Who Killed JFK, published November 16, 2003. Summary of ABC News, Harris and Time/CNN polls from September 1966 to November 2003.
13. Ibid.

Silent Voices

Acquilla Clemons

Acquilla Clemons was an eyewitness to the murder of Dallas police officer J. D. Tippit. The Warren Commission stated that Oswald had killed Tippit but could provide no credible evidence to support its conclusion. When I visited Dallas in search of witnesses for a documentary film, three friends, Shirley Martin and her two daughters, participated in that effort. We located Ms. Clemons, an African American woman who had been threatened by two men who said they worked for the Dallas Police Department and ordered her not to talk. At first she was reluctant to discuss the matter, fearing that we might be associated with the police. She then recognized me in my role over the years in the civil rights movement and agreed to a filmed interview, which took place at her home at 618 Corinth Street in Dallas.[14]*

She said that two men had been involved in the murder. One was "kind of heavy" and the other "was tall and thin and wore light khaki trousers and a white shirt." Oswald was certainly not heavy; neither was he tall. When shown pictures of Oswald, Ms. Clemons said that he was not one of the two men she had seen.

She said that Dallas police officers wearing guns had visited her and said that if she talked to anyone about what she had seen she "might get

---

14. The film *Rush to Judgment* includes her statement.

hurt." She also said that one of the police officers said that if she talked to the Warren Commission, she "might get killed."

She said that two men were standing near Tippit's police car and that one of them shot him. One of them then waved to the other and they ran from the scene in opposite directions. She did not know if both men had fired at Tippit.

Her statements were corroborated by other witnesses who saw men running from the scene and who stated that Oswald was not one of them. Her more specific testimony would have destroyed the case that was being fabricated. Physical evidence also supported the facts revealed by Ms. Clemons and even confounded and confused some of the Warren Commission members. Four bullets had been recovered from Tippit's body, yet the FBI stated that only one bullet was provided to it for examination by the Dallas Police Department, which asserted that it was "the only bullet that was recovered." But wait, more than a quarter of a year later, three other bullets appeared. The FBI expert stated that "it was not possible" to "determine" whether the bullets had been fired from a gun identified as belonging to Oswald.

Hale Boggs, a member of the commission, stated that he was confused by the fact that three bullets taken from Tippit's body had been manufactured by Winchester-Western and one bullet had been manufactured by Remington-Peters, and that shells from both manufacturers had been found at the scene. Rankin, the general counsel for the commission, replied, "There is a slight problem here." The commission offered several surreal "possible explanations for this variance" of course, not including the possibility that two men had been involved, since its oft-repeated mantra, *Oswald acted alone,* was inviolable.

Instead, in yet another astonishing feat of reverse conjuration, the Warren Commission made Ms. Clemons disappear. The Warren Commission did not interview Ms. Clemons and her important testimony was, therefore, never considered. While her name does not appear in the commission's report, she was anonymously dismissed in a section entitled "Speculations and Rumors"[15] where the commission gathered inconvenient evidence.

---

15. *Report of the President's Commission on the Assassination of President John F. Kennedy* (Warren Commission Report), pages 637–668.

Regarding Ms. Clemons, the report stated that there was speculation that "an unidentified woman" had seen "two men involved in the shooting and that they ran off in opposite directions afterward."[16] The commission's perplexing finding was that such a woman did not exist. It is clear that the Dallas police (a group relied upon by the commission for evidence) did not want Ms. Clemons to testify and that the FBI, the commission's primary source, knew all about her long before the report was issued.

At numerous lectures, I spoke of her observations in some detail as I did when interviewed on various local radio programs. The many hundreds of pages of FBI files reveal that special agents were always present and always recording my words and preparing copies of transcripts of every word. For example, on August 21, 1964, Hoover wrote to Rankin about my appearance on the "Barry Gray radio program over station WMCA in New York City."[17]

He wrote that I had discussed the substance of Ms. Clemons's observations, that the FBI had monitored the program and recorded it, and that he was enclosing two original copies of the tape recordings and "two copies of a verbatim transcription of the program prepared by this bureau," and that one copy of the recording and the transcription "will be maintained (by the FBI) for future reference."

Both the FBI and the Warren Commission had known of the proposed testimony of Ms. Clemons for months before the report was written and before I was asked to appear before the commission during July 1964. To accommodate the commission's request, I returned from Europe to testify. I was not asked about her observations.

During September 1964, Dorothy Kilgallen published an interview with Ms. Clemons that was featured in the *New York Journal-American*. The filmed interview that I conducted with Ms. Clemons, shown first at the movie theatre at Carnegie Hall in New York and later elsewhere throughout the country, as well as Ms. Kilgallen's independent interview, refutes the conclusions of the FBI and the commission that she did not exist.

She was a courageous woman who came forward to tell the truth about what she witnessed although her life had been threatened. Her

---

16. Warren Commission Report , page 652.
17. *Hearings Before the President's Commission on the Assassination of President Kennedy* (Warren Commission), Volume XXV, page 874.

words were dismissed without inquiry by the president's commission. Yet this discriminatory treatment was far less severe than the suffering of others who made a similar journey.

Dorothy Kilgallen

Of course I knew of Dorothy Kilgallen. She was a star of a leading national television program *What's My Line?*, and a columnist for a New York daily afternoon newspaper, the Hearst-owned *New York Journal-American*. What I was curious about was why she was calling and asking me to visit at her Manhattan town house. It was an invitation that I could not refuse. She had a drink in her hand and offered me a cocktail, another invitation I accepted. She got down to business at once. She knew of my interest in the Kennedy assassination and her own preliminary inquiries had made her doubt the official version. I was aware of the fact that the host of her program, John Daly, was the son-in-law of Earl Warren. She suggested that we share information, but not sources, about our separate investigations. I knew that although a number of volunteers were working with me and conducting useful interviews in Dallas that her resources reached to a higher and secret level that I could not begin to match. I agreed.

Dorothy said that she had reason to believe that her telephone was being monitored and would be greatly surprised if mine had not been tapped by the federal government for some time. In order to reduce the opportunity for such surveillance, she suggested that in telephone calls we use code names for the person calling, Miss Parker for her and Mr. Robinson for me, and that we only call from public pay telephones.

She said that she was aware of the circumstances; she wanted the truth to be known and the government wanted to suppress it. She was a well-known establishment figure, and her distrust of authority surprised me. She told me that after she had obtained a copy of Jack Ruby's testimony, then classified top secret, she had difficulty persuading her newspaper to publish it until she agreed to take full responsibility for any response. The *Journal-American* published the lengthy transcript as a series in August 1964. Three hours after the first article was on the newsstands, two special agents of the FBI visited her home to interrogate her about how she had secured it. Of course, she did not reveal her source, but she told the agents that a man, not a woman, had provided the document and that John Daly, then the director of the Voice of America, was not the man. She explained that she had learned that Warren was investigating an innocent secretary whom he considered a suspect and that since she knew that Daly's relationship to Warren might cause him to be considered as the source, she wanted to resolve those issues at the outset.

Dorothy was also known for her coverage of social events and entanglements, so I was not surprised when she told me that she had asked the FBI agents why they arrived so quickly when it took the Chief Justice so long to question Ruby and other important witnesses, adding, "Jackie wasn't questioned for months. Why, Warren knows Jackie very well; kisses her when they meet. No one can say that she couldn't see him. She had been seeing Marlon." In fact Mrs. Kennedy was asked a few questions by Warren and his counsel at a private meeting with Robert Kennedy in attendance for the first time on June 5, 1964, at 4:20 PM.[18] The interview lasted ten minutes. It took place more than half a year after the assassination. Years later when I met Marlon Brando, the Marlon I presumed Dorothy had referred to, discretion prevailed and the subject never came up. Jack Ruby also testified more than six months after the assassination.[19]

Dorothy and I met many times and exchanged information, including the interview with Acquilla Clemons she published in her newspaper, always by appointments made in telephone conversations that were likely overheard in spite of our inadequate efforts at disguise. She was married to Richard Kollmar, who, while agreeing with his wife's views, believed that she was endangering her life with a pursuit of the evidence. She knew that the FBI had focused its legions upon our work. She wrote in the *Journal-American* the FBI "might have been more profitably employed in probing the facts of the case rather than how I got them." Of course, it was not the facts that the FBI sought—it was instead a method to suppress them.

Her close friend, she told me one afternoon, was Florence Smith, who she said had an ongoing relationship with John Kennedy. She was a journalist "and the one person I can trust with the work we are

18. Vol. V, page 178.
19. Vol. V, page 181.

doing." After Dorothy managed to arrange an interview with Jack Ruby during 1965, she told Florence and other friends that she was about to "break the case wide open," and that, aware of what happened to others with decisive information, she had given her notes to Florence. In one telephone call to me she said that she needed just one more trip to Dallas to complete her work. Then, she said, she would share all of her findings with me.

On November 8, 1965, Dorothy died. Two days later, Florence, who had been ill, died of a cerebral hemorrhage. No notes or memoranda about Dorothy's investigation could be located. Later I met with Richard Kollmar who told me that Dorothy had died because of her efforts to investigate the assassination. He said he would not talk to me about that subject since "enough innocent people have already died." Six years later he committed suicide. The medical explanation for Dorothy's death was that it may have been caused by a moderate amount of alcohol together with an ordinary sleeping pill or a suicide. Lee Israel, a biographer and editor, wrote an excellent and well-researched biography called *Kilgallen*[20], in which she explored Dorothy's life and death. She interviewed a number of key witnesses about Dorothy's last days and her observations were based upon all of the available evidence, including, but certainly not limited to, the medical records. She concluded that Dorothy had been murdered.

Roger Craig

Roger D. Craig served in the United States Army and later joined the Dallas Sheriff's Department. One year after becoming a deputy sheriff he was named Man of the Year by that department for his work in capturing an international jewel thief. During the next three years he was promoted four times. Although the Secret Service had assured Kennedy he would be safe in Dallas and that all local police and deputy sheriffs had been integrated into the federal protection plan, Craig knew those assertions were untrue. The sheriff had told Craig and other deputies that they had no duties to perform on November 22, 1963, and that the local police also had been similarly instructed unless

---

20. *Killgallen,* Lee Israel, Delacorte Press, 1979.

they were directing traffic. That day, Roger Craig stood in front of the Sheriff's Department Building as a spectator awaiting the motorcade. When he heard the shots he ran toward the grassy knoll, from which witnesses stated they believed the shots had originated.

Roger Craig's observations on November 22 established him as an important witness in Dealey Plaza. Immediately after hearing the shots he interviewed a witness who told him that he had seen two men on the sixth floor of the book depository just before the shots were fired. Upon entering the book depository he, along with other officers, located the alleged murder weapon. He saw Lee Harvey Oswald at the scene fifteen minutes after the shots were fired. He saw Oswald enter a light-colored station wagon, driven by another person. Later, at police headquarters, he saw Oswald and identified him as the person he had previously seen. He heard Oswald make statements that were of crucial importance.

Each of these observations by a trained and respected law enforcement officer destroyed the essential presumptions and conclusions of the Warren Commission. Two men on the sixth floor at the relevant time rebutted the conclusion that any one man acting alone had fired from that position. The rifle, which Craig and others found on the sixth floor, was not a Mannlicher-Carcano, although the commission concluded it was and also asserted that it had been owned by Oswald. In fact, while this was not proof of Oswald's guilt, it was the only evidence against him.

If Oswald was in Dealey Plaza fifteen minutes after the assassination, then the Warren Commission's neatly fabricated timeline for his movements, which allowed the commission, in the absence of any credible evidence, to conclude that Oswald had killed police officer J. D. Tippit a little later that day, would have been rendered void. Oswald's statements made in police headquarters and in Craig's presence indicated not only that he was innocent but that he was secretly involved in some activity with others.[21]

---

21. After studying the record, Hugh Trevor-Roper concluded in his introduction to *Rush to Judgment*:

    Deputy Sheriff Craig gave an important and perhaps illuminating piece of evidence immediately after the assassination. If his evidence had been confirmed, the whole official story would have been suspect from the start. Why was his evidence cut short and dismissed by the police at that early stage on the grounds

No Warren Commission member ever met Craig. A deposition was taken solely by an inexperienced attorney, David Belin, who had been practicing law for just a few years. A deposition, to paraphrase *Black's Law Dictionary*, is a witness's testimony taken by a lawyer outside of the courtroom that is to be used in the preparation for a civil or criminal case. It is, in fact, a "pretrial discovery device."[22] Many experienced trial lawyers have written treatises on the subject; they often stress the need for preparation by counsel before conducting a deposition since the rules for taking testimony during a deposition are far more liberal and relaxed than those that apply at trial. After many years of practice, I also wrote an essay about techniques that may be employed in depositions.[23] There is no evidence to support the conclusion that Belin was properly prepared for questioning Roger Craig. His deposition transcript was not used as preparation by the commission since Craig was never permitted to testify before any member of the Warren Commission.[24]

In federal practice, the deposition is often a means to prepare counsel for trial and generally not a substitute for testimony before a court. The jurors are the triers of fact in most cases unless the defendant has waived a jury trial, in which case the court becomes the trier of fact. It is generally of crucial importance for those charged with determining the facts to observe the witnesses' testimony in order to determine credibility.

Craig stated that he ran up the grassy knoll into the area behind the wooden fence because police officers and others were converging on that point and witnesses were saying that the shots had originated from there. He encountered a man behind the fence who stated that he

---

that it "didn't fit with what we knew to be true"—i.e. with the immediate police version of Oswald's movements? What indeed were Oswald's movements both before and after the assassination? Mr. Lane gives reason to suppose that the official version of his movements after the assassination is quite incorrect. (*Rush to Judgment,* p. 18)

22. *Black's Law Dictionary*, 6th Edition, West Publishing Co., 1990, p. 440.
23. *Plausible Denial*, Thunder's Mouth Press, 1991, p. 157
24. The Warren Commission listed 552 persons as "witnesses whose testimony has been presented to the commission." However, 458 of them never appeared before any commission member. Some merely signed affidavits that were prepared for them; others signed statements that they did not even attest to and some were questioned by junior lawyers.

was a Secret Service agent and had the credentials to prove it. This area was not explored by Belin.

Craig, while under oath, told Belin that he interviewed two eyewitnesses, Arnold Rowland and his wife, Barbara, minutes after the assassination. He testified that Arnold Rowland told him that a few minutes before the shots were fired, he saw two men on the sixth floor of the book depository building, one of whom held a rifle with a telescopic site.[25]

Craig also testified that after he entered the book depository with two other deputy sheriffs and a number of Dallas Police Department officers, it was decided to search the building. He said he was approximately eight feet from Deputy Sheriff Eugene Bloom when the rifle was discovered.[26] He added that Dallas Police Captain Will Fritz arrived with a criminal identification man and that photographs were taken of the weapon before the weapon was moved. Belin did not ask Craig even a single question about the make and caliber of the alleged murder weapon.[27] However, when I was present at a filmed interview with Craig, he was asked to describe the weapon.[28] Craig had previously said and repeated many times that the weapon he observed was a German Mauser, caliber 7.65. Seymour Weitzman, a Dallas deputy constable, was a weapons expert who was called to the scene. In an affidavit sworn to on November 23, 1963, Weitzman described it as "a 7.65 Mauser, bolt action, equipped with a 4/18 scope, a thick leather brownish-black sling on it."

The commission, having been told that Oswald had purchased an Italian Mannlicher-Carcano, rejected the testimony of those officers who had found a weapon where it had been planted on November 22. The switch might have confounded the Central Intelligence Agency which, on November 25, 1963, in a top secret report, stated that the murder weapon was not an Italian Mannlicher-Carcano but in fact a German Mauser. Apparently the interagency coordination was imperfect.

Approximately fifteen minutes after the gunfire Craig saw Lee Harvey Oswald travel from behind the book depository building and

25. WCR, Volume VI, pp. 263–265.
26. Ibid, p. 268.
27. Ibid, pp. 260–273.
28. *Two Men in Dallas.* A documentary film by Mark Lane, 1987.

enter a light-colored station wagon that was being driven by a person waiting for him. The Warren Commission concluded that Oswald had left the scene immediately after the shots and had worked out an elaborate timeline that accommodated their false presumption that Oswald had shot Officer Tippit. That fifteen-minute delay demonstrated that the commission's version was inaccurate. Was Craig wrong? Certainly a brief observation of a man walking toward a vehicle could reasonably be contested.

However, Craig later entered the offices of Dallas Police Captain J. Will Fritz, where Oswald was being held. He entered the room, saw Oswald, and said that he was certain that it was the same man he had seen. In Craig's presence, Fritz asked Oswald to explain his entry into a vehicle. Oswald replied, "That station wagon belongs to Mrs. Paine. Don't try to tie her into this. She had nothing to do with it." According to Craig, Oswald was annoyed and said, "Everybody will know who I am now," as he rose partially out of the chair in which he was seated and leaned over the desk, looking directly at Fritz. Craig had testified that the light-colored station wagon was equipped with a built-in luggage rack on the top. Ruth Paine owned a light-colored Nash Rambler with a luggage rack on the top. Mrs. Paine was responsible for separating Lee Oswald from his wife, Marina, and moving Marina to Dallas, which inevitably led to Lee Harvey Oswald moving to Dallas. Mrs. Paine and her friend, CIA operative George De Mohrenschildt, who became the official babysitter of the intelligence agencies for Oswald, found a job for Oswald at the book depository located directly on the route selected for the presidential motorcade.

All of the observations by Craig were worthy of serious inquiry and evaluation. At the very least, Craig should have been called as a witness before the Warren Commission so that his credibility could be judged. He was not, although I was asked to testify twice before the Warren Commission and I was in New York City at the time of the assassination. The commission, under the leadership of Allen Dulles, sought to eradicate dissenting views, not to secure the facts. The commission concluded that it "could not accept important elements of Craig's testimony,"[29] although no commission member had ever talked to Craig. The commission said that Craig could not have seen Oswald

---

29. *Warren Commission Report*, p. 160.

leave the depository building fifteen minutes after the assassination, because Oswald was, according to their unsubstantiated timeline, "far removed from the building at that time."[30] The commission declined to comment on Craig's statement that the weapon found in the building was a German Mauser. Since the prosecuting authorities had photographs of the weapon that was located on the sixth floor, which were taken even before the rifle was removed from its location, that matter could have been easily resolved by an examination of the pictures. However, the pictures have not yet surfaced.

In *Rush to Judgment*, and in lectures before that book was published, I discussed the investigative work that Craig accomplished beginning just after the assassination. Later, I produced a documentary film comprised of an interview with Craig and evidence that he had uncovered.[31] Craig was fired from the sheriff's department in 1967 because he continued to discuss the facts related to the assassination. That year he was asked to testify for the prosecution in the trial of Clay Shaw, who was indicted for the murder of President Kennedy. A sniper fired a shot that grazed his head. As public attention became refocused on the subject matter, and demands were made for a congressional investigation relying in part upon Craig's observations, another shot was fired at him. During that period, he was starting his car when a bomb planted in it exploded, injuring him. Later, the car that Craig was driving was forced off of the road by two men in a vehicle parked across the highway. He was seriously injured and hospitalized for one year with a broken back, broken leg, and other injuries.

During 1974 and 1975, I participated in drafting legislation to establish the House Special Committee on Assassinations to investigate the murders of President Kennedy and Dr. King. During 1975, we organized support for the legislation and secured more than one million signatures on petitions, letters and telegrams that were delivered to the members of Congress. Craig was to be a witness to numerous events. On May 15, 1975, Craig was shot to death with a rifle. The official version was suicide. His good friend, Penn Jones, Jr., said that Craig had owned two pistols, but not a rifle. He seriously doubted that Craig had killed himself.

---

30. Ibid, p. 253.
31. *Two Men in Dallas*, 1987.

Lisa Howard

Not long after I opened my law office in East Harlem, I visited the posh Lexington Democratic Club. It had been founded in 1949 primarily by upwardly mobile, white and accentless law school graduates. Even today, its published mission states as its first listed objective the resolve to remain involved in selecting judges. In the early days, the political bosses made the selections. Often their choices lacked judicial temperament and knowledge, but abounded in unbridled devotion to those who gave them their jobs. One can note a slight improvement in the judiciary, but the fealty factor has survived. People with school-age children were willing to pay almost exorbitant sums to rent an apartment or buy a condominium in the area because the public schools there were far superior to others and even compared favorably with expensive private academies.

I met Lisa Howard at a club function. She had been an actress and a television star. She was very bright, progressive, charming and startlingly beautiful. She had become an important journalist and was the first reporter to conduct a major interview with Soviet Premier Nikita Khrushchev at the United Nations. She was hired by ABC News as a reporter and later became one of the first women to anchor her own television news program, *The NewsHour with Lisa Howard*.

We became friends; and during lunch at the Four Seasons, the first and only time I ate there, she said, "Mark, I'm worried about you." When I asked her why, she said, "Those men, the not so young anymore lawyers at the Lex Club, really don't like you." I said that it was not a matter of concern, sipped a martini, and then proved my previous lack of sincerity by asking why. She laughed and said, "You say you want to see reform all over the city, including in Puerto Rican and black communities and among the wretchedly poor. You say we are all, including the Lex Club members, obligated to participate." I asked what was wrong with that and added some members and leaders of her club said the same thing publicly. She sighed and said, "Yes, Mark. But those men think you mean it." After a moment or two of silence I asked, "What about the women?" The response was a smile.

Lisa scored another journalistic coup in April 1963 by interviewing Fidel Castro. Later she produced two network news specials that were regarded as the most substantive coverage of the revolution. In 1963, she became President Kennedy's secret intermediary to Castro. Documents released in 2003 demonstrate, in the words of Peter Kornbluh, a researcher at the National Security Archives in Washington, "that the whole history of U.S.–Cuban relations might have been quite different if Kennedy had not been assassinated."

It all began when Lisa met Castro. In eight hours of meetings he told her that he was very interested in rapprochement with the United States and made numerous suggestions about how to proceed. Lisa was asked to meet with CIA Deputy Director Richard Helms. Helms, in charge of the "dirty tricks department" (so designated by the CIA) was at that time engaged in planning to assassinate Castro. CIA Director John McCone argued to McGeorge Bundy, Kennedy's national security advisor, "that no active steps be taken on the rapprochement matter at this time." He also suggested that the Lisa Howard report be "handled" to prevent word from getting out. Lisa saw the CIA as an agency that would rather kill Castro than resolve differences with Cuba through negotiations. She rejected the CIA's demand for silence.

Instead, Lisa, in defiance of the CIA edict, wrote an article stating that in her conversations with Castro he had proposed that all issues that separated the two countries should be examined in a new light with the objective of eliminating them. Lisa said that Castro "made it quite clear that he was ready to discuss: the Soviet personnel and military hardware on Cuban soil; compensation for the expropriated American lands and investments; the question of Cuba as a base for communist subversion throughout the hemisphere."[32] Lisa had told Castro that Cuban interference with other states in Latin America was a genuine concern for Kennedy and urged Castro to make that matter the capstone of his proposals for change. She then suggested that the Kennedy administration "send an American government official on a quiet mission to Havana to hear what Castro has to say." She added that a country as powerful as the United States "has nothing to lose at a bargaining table with Fidel Castro."

I asked Lisa if she was concerned about retaliation from the CIA. She replied, "JFK is with me on this. I feel safe as long as he is around." On September 12, 1963, William Attwood, an advisor to Kennedy on foreign policy and to the U.S. Mission to the United Nations,

---

32. The article was published in a journal, *War and Peace Report,* on May 13, 1963.

having read Lisa's article, asked her if she could arrange a meeting at her apartment with him and Carlos Lechuga, the Cuban ambassador to the United Nations. On September 20, Kennedy authorized direct contacts between Attwood and Lechuga, and on September 23, 1963, one day less than two months before the assassination, Lisa, Attwood and Lechuga met in her apartment to discuss rapprochement. When Lisa told me about the meeting, I could almost imagine where they each had been seated. She had earlier arranged a much less important meeting at her place between me and Adlai Stevenson.

Events were moving quickly, both Kennedy's efforts to resolve differences with Cuba and the CIA's plan to murder Castro. On September 24, Attwood met with Attorney General Robert Kennedy in Washington. Bobby said that he believed the matter was "worth pursuing." On November 5, Bundy stated that "the president was more in favor of pushing toward an opening toward Cuba than was the State Department." Bundy directed that his assistant, Gordon Chase, be in direct contact with Howard and the White House about future meetings with Fidel Castro.

During October, Castro told Lisa that he was very eager to begin negotiations with Kennedy and proposed that he, Castro, send an airplane to Mexico to pick up Kennedy's representative and fly him to a private airport near Varadero where Castro would meet him and the two would speak alone. Kennedy agreed to send Attwood. Lisa transmitted that decision to Castro on November 14, eight days before the assassination.

On November 20, Kennedy chose a public speech to demonstrate to Castro that rapprochement was at hand, in a clever Kennedyesque manner. His coded words were meant for Castro alone: "Cuba has become a weapon in an effort dictated by foreign powers to subvert the other American republics. This *and this alone* divides us. As long as this is true, nothing is possible. Without it, *everything* is possible." Of course the CIA was listening closely. It was two days before the assassination.

In order for Castro to know that Kennedy strongly supported a new opening with Cuba he invited Jean Daniel, a prominent French journalist, to the White House, having learned through Benjamin Bradlee, vice president of the *Washington Post,* that Daniel was about to visit Cuba and interview Castro. Daniel was the founder and executive editor of *Le Nouvel Observateur,* the weekly magazine with the largest circulation in France. Daniel later wrote of Kennedy's message to Castro.[33]

Kennedy said, "I believe that there is no country in the world, including the African regions, including any and all the countries under colonial domination, where economic colonization, humiliation and exploitation were worse than in Cuba, in part owing to my country's policies during the Batista regime. I believe that we created, built and manufactured the Castro movement out of whole cloth and without realizing it. I believe that the accumulation of these mistakes has jeopardized all of Latin America. The great aim of the Alliance for Progress is to reverse this unfortunate policy. This is one of the most, if not the most, important problems in American foreign policy. I can assure you that I have understood the Cubans. I approved the proclamation which Fidel Castro made in the Sierra Maestra, when he justifiably called for justice and especially yearned to rid Cuba of corruption. I will go even further: to some extent it is as though Batista was the incarnation of a number of sins on the part of the United States. Now we shall have to pay for those sins. In the matter of the Batista regime, I am in agreement with the first Cuban revolutionaries. That is perfectly clear.

"In any case, the nations of Latin America are not going to attain justice and progress that way, I mean through Communist subversion. They won't get there by going from economic oppression to a Marxist dictatorship which Castro himself denounced a few years ago. The United States now has the possibility of doing as much good in Latin America as it has done wrong in the past; would even say that we alone have this power—on the essential condition that Communism does not take over there."

Kennedy underlined his proposed agreement with Castro indicating that the isolation of Cuba could be ended. "The continuation of the blockade depends on the continuation of subversive activities."

The president invited the journalist to return to the White House with Castro's response. Castro and Daniel met in Cuba. Castro was enthusiastic about the message from Kennedy and told the journalist that Kennedy could become "the greatest president of the United States,

---

33. *The New Republic,* December 14, 1963.

the leader who may at last understand that there can be coexistence between capitalists and socialists in the Americas." They were speaking about the future on that bright day in Cuba on November 22, 1963, when the news arrived that President Kennedy had been assassinated. Castro turned sadly to Daniel and said, "This is the end to your mission of peace. Everything has changed."

Lisa Howard, having initiated the effort, refused to abandon it. In 1964 she resumed her discussions with Castro and informed President Lyndon Johnson that Castro wished to have the negotiations continued. When Johnson did not respond she contacted her friend Adlai Stevenson at the United Nations. He served as the U.S. ambassador to the U.N. from 1961 to 1965. Stevenson agreed with Lisa and so informed the new president. Gordon Chase, in a then top secret memorandum, wrote that it was necessary "to remove Lisa" from further participation in the matter.

Lisa invited me to appear as a guest on *The NewsHour with Lisa Howard*. It was to be taped with the producer closely monitoring it as it proceeded. He began by instructing us both that while I could talk about the issues relating to the assassination, not a word critical of the Warren Commission or its conclusions could be uttered. The lights were on, the tape was rolling, Lisa and I exchanged glances and she began. "Well, Mark, is Mrs. Oswald, Lee's mother, really pleased with all the events thus far? I mean that her son is so famous now, even though regrettably dead?" I answered, "Delighted, I think would be the word .. ." Before I could continue the producer waved his hand, shrugged and said, "I give up. Do it anyway you want." And for the first time words of dissent were uttered about the official conclusions on a national television broadcast.

Lisa, undeterred by official rejection, pressed on in an attempt to have Johnson respond to Castro's peace initiatives. She met with Che Guevara and invited him and Senator Eugene McCarthy to meet with her in her apartment for the purpose of having negotiations with Cuba restarted. The State Department was furious. The death of President Kennedy had apparently not ended the episode. Lisa was a loose end and it seemed impossible to "remove her" through suggestions and warnings.

Lisa Howard, then thirty-five years old, died near her home in East Hampton, Long Island. She had rushed to a pharmacy in an attempt to save her life. The authorities said she had killed herself. Many of her friends had doubts. I am cognizant that those close to a person alleged to have committed suicide are reluctant to accept that finding even when it is supported by evidence. In this instance there seemed to be little credible evidence to sustain that conclusion.

The similar authorities had initially claimed that Dorothy Kilgallen, a conservative journalist who was on a diligent campaign to learn and publish the truth about the assassination, had killed herself and they would say it again about other inconvenient witnesses.

Some years ago a man presenting himself as a messenger from the CIA (I knew that he had held a fairly high commission in the U.S. Navy and that he enjoyed intelligence connections) said that the CIA would never attack me again if I agreed to never again raise issues about the possible role of the CIA in the assassination or referred to efforts by the agency to obscure the facts. I pondered a life free from constant false attacks from the CIA and its assets in the media and confess I seriously considered the offer. Nevertheless, much later, after comfortably not having been a CIA target for years, I was tempted perhaps beyond reason to conduct a successful trial in a federal court against E. Howard Hunt for his involvement with the CIA in the murder of the president and then wrote a book about it.[34] The CIA attacks upon me, silent for so long, were renewed with a vengeance.

I thought of Lisa and my response to the self-described CIA representative is that some things are not political. Some things are not solely based upon principle since that concept is unfortunately too easily rationalized under the pretext of reasonable compromise. Some things are irrevocably personal.

The Ominous Prophecy

It was not a prophecy, but it was ominous. During 1968, President Lyndon B. Johnson was faced with a raging debate about his policies, particularly the war in Vietnam. There were riots in America's large cities and sit-ins at colleges and demonstrations throughout the country. Johnson was unable to make major appearances, except for speeches arranged from military bases.

Senator Eugene McCarthy had entered the primary campaign for the Democratic Party presidential nomination. In March, Gene won 42 percent of the vote in the New Hampshire primary. Four days later,

34. *Plausible Denial*, Mark Lane. Thunder's Mouth Press, 1991.

Bobby Kennedy announced that he was a candidate as well. Two weeks later Johnson, aware of the repudiation of his policies, withdrew from the contest and said he would not seek reelection.

The assassination of Dr. King on April 4 of that year led to riots in almost one hundred American cities and reminded us again that John Kennedy had been murdered less than five years earlier. Jim Garrison, the New Orleans district attorney, was openly investigating the New Orleans connection to that assassination. I was living in New Orleans at Jim's request and providing factual analysis to the sometimes bizarre, often odd, information being funneled to the prosecutor's office. Later, we were to discover that a number of theories had been authored by the CIA to discredit Garrison.

Jim and I met one early evening at the Napoleon House on Chartres Street in the Quarter to discuss the case and down a couple of Sazeracs. Jim said that the establishment served the most authentic libations in the city, to which he added, "Therefore, almost needless to say, in the country, really the world, or so far as we know, far beyond." The drink was impressive, but the news was far more astounding and promising. Jim said, "Not to be repeated, Mark, through a friend of mine and also his, Bobby has communicated with me. In case you haven't figured out who Bobby is, it is Senator Kennedy." When I asked what the message was, Jim took a sip, leaned over and whispered, "He said, 'Keep up the good work. I support you and when I am president I am going to blow the whole thing wide open.'"

I asked Jim how he responded. He told me that he was encouraged but also frightened. "If Bobby is telling people privately what his plans are, I think his life is in danger. Even the White House is not a sanctuary; his brother was president when they killed him. And Bobby is much more vulnerable now; he doesn't even have Secret Service protection, not that those clowns are effective, and he mingles with crowds of people who want to touch him. He shakes hands with everybody. I told him that he should publicly announce his intentions now and that keeping them hidden from the public would provide motivation for the Company, since they obviously knew what his plans were."

Two days later Jim said that the honest broker had conveyed his views, that Bobby thought about the matter for a short time and said, "Tell Garrison that if I win the California primary I will state that I have doubts about the official version and that I will conduct a thorough investigation if I become president. If I win California I think I'll be on my way."

When frequently asked by the media why Robert Kennedy seemed to be satisfied by the Warren Report, I was honor bound not to reveal what I had learned. One evening I appeared on a PBS television program in New Orleans. Jack Anderson, the most widely syndicated columnist in the country, was in the audience since he was also to be a guest in a different segment. I was called upon to explain Bobby's silence. I began to avoid the question by focusing on the facts and then realized that the primary was at that time taking place in California and that the polls would be closed shortly. I observed that nothing I reported on a local program would reach the voters before the voting ended that night, even with the two-hour time discrepancy. I then revealed the Kennedy–Garrison dialogue in its entirety. I said that I would be heading home shortly to a television set possibly to hear Bobby's announcement about his brother's death later that evening or the next morning at a press conference.

As Bobby mingled with his supporters, those nearby were, instead of Secret Service agents there to provide protection, two maitre d's, a writer, a couple of athletes, and one FBI agent. The agent, William Barry, changed the route at the last minute. "No, it's been changed. We're going this way," Barry insisted. Bobby had just turned to his left in a kitchen corridor to shake hands with Juan Romero, a busboy, when he was shot. As Kennedy lay wounded on the floor Romero placed his rosary in his hand. Bobby was taken to a nearby hospital where extensive surgery was performed. He died nearly twenty-six hours after having been shot.

Jack Anderson later told me that he had written about my disclosures, which he had heard just before the assassination. His column, he said, bore the headline "Ominous Prophecy." There seems to be no present evidence that it was ever published.

Implausible Denial[35]

Willis A. Carto was the publisher of *The Spotlight*, a weekly newspaper associated with Liberty Lobby, Inc. The newspaper had its detractors, many of whom branded it a leading anti-Semitic publication. Others said that it was anti-Zionist, that is, it opposed the politics of the State of Israel. The paper had been sued by E. Howard Hunt and had lost. The court had awarded Hunt substantial amounts for damages to his reputation.

Liberty Lobby and its founder and CEO, Carto, operated from a building located near my home and office. He was facing bankruptcy and was in need of counsel. When Willis called, I agreed to meet him. I was intrigued by the substance of the lawsuit but cautious about the politics of the organization and its founder.

On August 16, 1978, *The Spotlight* had published an article by Victor Marchetti, a former CIA officer, who said that in his last three years with the CIA he had served as a staff assistant to Richard Helms. Almost fifteen years had passed since the assassination of the president; during that period *The Spotlight* had not published a word of doubt regarding the official explanation. Clearly, Marchetti's line of communication with his former employer was questionable. Yet the

---

35. Some two decades ago I wrote *Plausible Denial*. It is the account of a trial involving E. Howard Hunt, an officer of the CIA, and his complicity in the assassination of President Kennedy. In summarizing that work here I have drawn upon transcripts from the trial in the United States District Court and related comments. A full account of that trial is presently available since Skyhorse Publishing, Inc. has now republished the original *Plausible Denial*.

newspaper was impressed with his past credentials and his assertion that he had inside information intrigued them. While he was a fading star in the intelligence controversy, his name had some caché that might extend beyond the reach of the publication at that time, and could give a boost to the circulation.

No confirmation could be retrieved from the CIA since the agency almost always refused to comment on the subject; and when it did so, its motives and credibility were universally suspect. The House Select Committee on Assassinations, on the other hand, had been created and was authorized to investigate the assassination of the president. In the article published in *The Spotlight,* Marchetti wrote, "Chief among those to be exposed by the new investigation will be E. Howard Hunt, of Watergate fame. His luck has run out, and the CIA has decided to sacrifice him to protect its clandestine services. The agency is furious with Hunt for having dragged it publicly into the Nixon mess and for having blackmailed it after he was arrested." Marchetti added, "In addition, it is well-known that Hunt hated JFK and blamed him for the Bay of Pigs disaster." He also predicted, "In the public hearings the CIA will 'admit' that Hunt was involved in the conspiracy to kill Kennedy." Marchetti asserted, "Now, the CIA moved to finger Hunt and tie him into the JFK assassination," and "E. Howard Hunt will be implicated in the conspiracy and he will not dare to speak out—the CIA will see to that."

None of Marchetti's published predictions were realized. The CIA did not "sacrifice" Hunt, and it did not state that he had been involved in the assassination conspiracy. To the dismay of the newspaper, the most painful of the failed prognostications involved the prophecy of Hunt's assured silence. Instead, he filed a massive defamation case in the United States District Court in Florida against the newspaper and chose as his counsel Ellis Rubin, not the most talented of trial lawyers, but the one who seemed committed above all others to obtaining press coverage. The trial judge was James W. Kehoe, an experienced, fair and learned jurist.

The newspaper retained as counsel a lawyer whose lack of knowledge about the facts leading to the assassination was equaled by his lack of interest in the subject. He began by asserting in his opening statement to the jury that he was genuinely sorry that the article had even implied that Hunt was involved in any mischief that fateful day. He said, "We are not going to come forward and try to prove that Mr.

Hunt was involved in the Kennedy assassination." He then offered his personal assurances of Hunt's innocence as well as a statement from his client, Liberty Lobby, the publisher of the newspaper. "I will be candid with you, and from what I know about this case, there is no question that he was not involved. There is no question in the minds of the people at Liberty Lobby." He completed the abject surrender by imploring his adversary to accept a formal agreement to be read by the judge to the jury in the form of a stipulation about the facts. Hunt's counsel agreed and Judge Kehoe obliged, saying, "For the purpose of this trial, the defendants have acknowledged and conceded that the plaintiff in this case was not in Dallas, Texas, on the date of the assassination of President Kennedy, which was November 22, 1963."

Hunt and his counsel at that point, quite certain of victory since no serious defense had been offered, concentrated on testimony regarding damages. They each expected millions of dollars with at least a third to be retained by Rubin. The newspaper's publishers knew they faced bankruptcy. Hunt's direct testimony took a considerable period of time and 137 pages of the trial transcript. Defense counsel cross-examined Hunt for only ten minutes, comprising six pages of the transcript. With so impotent and subservient an adversary, Hunt felt free to take extraordinary liberties with the truth. He felt certain that none of the issues could ever again be raised in court, and that therefore, his assertions could not be challenged then or in the future. But then fate intervened, not just once as in *Casablanca*, but twice.

Hunt testified both at a pretrial deposition and then at the trial about the pain and suffering that he endured. He claimed his wife and his own children, then all adults, read *The Spotlight* article and believed it. They confronted him and asked if he had been involved in the conspiracy to murder the president. They asked what he was doing in Dallas that day. Why would the newspaper publish those accusations if they were untrue? Hunt testified about the "strains" in the "familial relationships." His wife was "shocked" by the accusation. Hunt, almost in tears, testified, "Being queried by my adult children, by my wife—'Is there any truth to this? Why would they say this? How can they print this if it is not true?' It's a very heavy psychological burden for me to carry, for any man to carry." At the trial, Hunt stated that even after his fervent denials his children could not reject the article and that it was "very difficult to quell."

The story was comprised of a number of predictions; it was written by a person and printed in a publication none of the family members had ever heard of, a newspaper with a limited circulation, which sold almost all of its copies to subscribers. An inquiring mind might wonder if Hunt had fabricated a potentially remunerative myth, with the expectation, soon fully realized, that he would not be challenged at the trial by opposing counsel and that the jury would, therefore, have no basis to disbelieve him.

Not satisfied that the case had been almost certainly won on the facts, counsel for Hunt apparently decided to seek an edge as to the prevailing and relevant law. As a trial draws to a close, all counsel begin to prepare their final remarks to the jury. After each side closes, the court instructs the jury as to law. For counsel to apply the facts to the law, it is necessary for the lawyers to know what the judge will say to the jury about the law before he instructs them. The anomaly is resolved in a simple, yet somewhat convoluted manner. The judge arranges for a charge conference, often in chambers, where the parties make proposals for the language of the instruction. Often, the court will require that those suggestions be made in advance and in writing. Where the parties agree, the judge will generally give that instruction, for it is the general principle of law that a party will later be precluded from appealing without having made a timely objection. Where the parties disagree, the judge will make the decision.

In this case the only hope for the newspaper was based upon an accurate instruction about the concept of "actual malice," a term of art that holds that if the plaintiff is a public figure he is obliged to demonstrate that the published document was made by a defendant who either knew it was false or acted with reckless disregard to its lack of truthfulness.

Counsel for Hunt struck again, this time with reckless disregard for his own client's best interest. He offered an instruction that violated the clear and unambiguous decisions of the Supreme Court. Counsel for the newspaper immediately, and unfathomably, joined in. The court read the agreed upon instruction.

With no facts and no law to interfere with Hunt's view of the case, the jury returned a verdict for Hunt and awarded him $100,000 for compensatory damages and $550,000 for punitive damages. Hunt was an ex-convict and had been convicted of serious crimes at Watergate.

His reputation was in ruins. He had not been accused of murder, much less convicted for having assassinated the president, so the jury, given no contrary facts or law to consider, had reached the only verdict possible; their award of damages was reasonable. The newspaper was constrained to consider filing for bankruptcy. In a last-ditch effort it considered an appeal based upon the erroneous instruction agreed to by its attorney.

Kismet and the United States Court of Appeals for the Eleventh Circuit entered the contest, a development that Hunt's counsel had not anticipated. The applicable standard is that failure to make a timely objection bars an appeal. However, at law, there usually are some exceptions for the rare and unexpected case. In this matter it is called "plain error." If the instruction is so egregiously wrong and so clearly affected the verdict so as to deny a fair trial, an appeal may be considered. The three-judge panel met. All seemed to agree that the instruction comprised error. One thought it was "plain error" and one did not. The third jurist agreed that it was "plain error" and the Court of Appeals reversed the verdict and award and sent the case back to Judge Kehoe for a new trial.

Hunt fired his trial lawyer, Ellis Rubin. The newspaper also sought new counsel: an experienced trial attorney with some knowledge about the assassination of President Kennedy.

Later, Willis Carto was to say that destiny led him to my office in Washington, D.C. If so it was an occurrence that Hunt could not have envisioned. I had not heard of *The Spotlight,* had no knowledge that Marchetti had written an article and had not known that a lawsuit had been filed and won by Hunt. I agreed with Willis only to review the trial transcript. After I read the record of the trial I said I would try the case.

I agreed to a small fee, but my other conditions could be evaluated as being somewhere between inflexible and nonnegotiable. We would defend the case primarily on the merits. Hunt had been in Dallas on November 22, 1963; he and the CIA had conspired to assassinate the president, and we would try to prove that to the satisfaction of a jury. In order to meet that test, I would require my client to pay the costs of a court reporter as I took depositions from Hunt; G. Gordon Liddy, another Watergate conspirator and ex-convict; Richard Helms, former director of the CIA who was convicted after having been charged with seeking to mislead Congress while under oath; David Phillips, who had run the Western Hemisphere for the CIA and who admitted that he had led a CIA effort that tried to destroy the reputations and livelihoods of those who sought the truth about the assassination in order to protect the agency; and all those who had contributed to Hunt's fabricated alibi. The character of the witnesses was, in my mind, not in dispute. I expected evasion and deception, but even those responses could be illuminating. I did not underestimate the challenges ahead, but the promise of questioning those villains of our time, I confess, made me look forward to the test as a child might look at a future in a candy shop.

Hunt had retained a respected and formidable law firm. Before I took Hunt's deposition I studied the record of various statements he had made under oath as to his whereabouts on November 22. He had consistently stated that he had not been in Dallas that day. He always had presented an alibi as to where he had been. However, the alibis were both contrived and contradictory. One was transparently false, since the Chinese grocery in Washington, Wah Ling, where he claimed he and his wife had shopped while Kennedy was being assassinated in Dallas, was not in existence in 1963. Hunt's wife, Dorothy, had worked for the CIA in Shanghai and later prepared Chinese meals at home. I had dabbled in Asian cuisine as well and had often shopped at the same market. I knew when it had first opened its doors.

Hunt's law firm filed a motion to have me removed from the case, stating that I would "turn the courtroom into a circus." I could not take the ludicrous motion seriously. By then I had tried cases in almost half of the states in both federal and state courts and, unlike my adversaries, I had practiced law for a quarter of a century and had never been held in contempt or sanctioned by any court. I responded to the motion by stating that I had made arrangements with the clown organizations, which I presumed my adversaries knew since they were probably members, and the tigers and lions. Even before my responsive pleading was completed, Judge Kehoe, acting *sua sponte*, expressed his outrage as he denied the motion and welcomed me to his court.

Hunt's counsel filed emergency motions to prevent me from looking into Hunt's alibi. My opposition stated that the stipulation made during the last trial survived until that trial ended but could not impact upon a future trial. That position was well based upon the law and the facts; one of the facts being the language read to the jury by the judge which began, "For the purpose of this trial . . . " and not *for the purpose of this case.* The stipulation survived for for that trial only, not for a subsequent trial. Judge Kehoe agreed with me and later so did a unanimous Court of Appeals. Now, clearly relevant was where Hunt would finally state he was on that tragic day for America.

We explored that matter in exquisite detail during his deposition. Hunt was not concentrating on a damage award before an emotionally charged jury, but trying to extricate himself from serious discrepancies. I met Hunt at his attorneys' offices at 10:05 AM on July 11, 1984, for two hours and ten minutes. Although I asked questions about numerous matters, I wanted to know the answer to but one. When the Rockefeller Commission[36] had investigated the matter it concluded, "It cannot be determined with certainty where Hunt and Sturgis were on the day of the assassination." Since everyone had to be somewhere, and just about everyone of a certain age recalled where he or she was that day, it is difficult to understand the commission's bewilderment. I asked Hunt about the matter and he told me that the commission must not have asked "the right questions of the right people."

Over continuing objections by his counsel, I asked Hunt where he had been at the time of the assassination. He had been at home with his wife, "a domestic servant" and his three children. His wife and the maid, he said, were now dead. In 1963, his daughters were teenagers, and his son, St. John, was ten.[37] His aunt, who was also with the family, had also since died.

Hunt testified that he was in his automobile in Washington when he heard the radio report of Kennedy's death. He then picked up his children from school and went home. The entire family, the maid and the aunt remained together. They stayed there in the recreation room together for forty-eight hours watching television. They never left the house. Then he paused and seemed to be rethinking his testimony and

---

36. The United States President's Commission on CIA activities within the United States, directed by Nelson Rockefeller (1975).

37. Later, St. John Hunt stated that the story about the family being home so that Hunt and his wife could cook dinner was false. St. John Hunt said that not long before his father died he confessed to him that he had been involved in a conspiracy to assassinate the president and that Frank Sturgis was part of the plot. He also said that Hunt later stated he was glad that Kennedy had been killed. The confession was published by *Rolling Stone* on April 5, 2007, and has appeared in a book and a DVD by the son.

he corrected himself. They had remained together for seventy-two hours. Surely they ate? Yes, they ordered food to be delivered.

With me at the deposition was a paralegal, Brent Whitmore, and the general counsel for the publisher, Fleming Lee. When the deposition concluded, the three of us entered an elevator. Fleming seemed a bit disappointed. He casually observed that in view of Hunt's changing alibis he thought that perhaps I might have been "more confrontational." He said, "You might have gotten much more." I was silent. When we left the building in search of a taxicab, I answered his unspoken question. "It wasn't the right audience." He asked what I meant by that. I said, "The jurors weren't there."

The jurors were present in the Miami courtroom when the case began with opening statements from each side. Counsel for the plaintiff said that Hunt was an honorable man. He had been defamed by Marchetti, who had lied about everything, even his own role in the CIA where he was a mere "gofer," little more than an errand boy. He said that Hunt was at home with his family watching television at the time of the assassination and that he and his family remained there together for days. His alibi was unshakable as the evidence would prove. I said to the jury that the evidence would demonstrate that the CIA killed their president and that Hunt was involved in that conspiracy. I observed that some of the jurors were astonished and one rolled her eyes in apparent disbelief.

The testimony began with Hunt. It had been well rehearsed and smoothly described Hunt's exploits for his country. He then repeated his assurance that he and his family were together at his home on Friday, November 22, watching television for days and did not leave the house until Monday or Tuesday.

During my cross-examination, Hunt admitted that CIA records documenting sick leave on a two-week basis revealed that he took eleven hours of sick leave in the two-week period ending on November 23. The official records disclosed that if Hunt was in Dallas on the day before and the day of the assassination, there was nothing in the agency's official records to dispute those conclusions. Hunt admitted that he had no recollection that he had been ill during that two-week period. He could not explain why he was absent from his job with the CIA in the D.C. area, or where he had been in the days just preceding the assassination. We had, of course, not proven that Hunt was in Dallas; we had established that there were no official records precluding that.

Then I focused on Hunt's alibi. I directed his attention to his testimony at the first trial. He agreed that on December 16, 1981, he had sworn that his children were very upset when they read that he had been in Dallas on November 22. He said that he tried to convince them that he had nothing to do with the assassination and that he was being persecuted for reasons unknown to him, but that they continued to believe the Marchetti accusations. He agreed that he had testified that the issue was the cause of a great deal of inter-family friction and exacerbated difficulties in the family. It seemed that neither Hunt nor his attorneys sensed the danger that was looming. I noticed that some of the jurors were anticipating the next questions, and they understood the path we were pursuing. I placed the dog-eared 1981 trial transcript on the counsel table, paused, and then asked Hunt a question that I believed he would not, could not, truthfully answer.

Quietly, in a then silent courtroom, I said, "Mr. Hunt, why did you have to convince your children that you were not in Dallas, Texas, on November 22, 1963?" Hunt's reaction was visceral; he sat up straight up in stunned silence. I asked again why his children needed to be told that their father wasn't in Texas on the day of the assassination since they were at home with him on that day.

I inquired if any of his three children were going to be called as witnesses in the case. None of them was going to testify for their father. I could have then subpoenaed them as witnesses for the defense, but I thought that they had suffered more than enough and that testifying that their father had committed perjury would have inflicted further undeserved pain. I also thought that his case was in shambles and that we had likely already prevailed. Hunt, while under oath, had lied to two juries, at numerous depositions, and before investigating committees, and it became apparent that he would not disclose where he had been on November 22.

Hunt was going to call other witnesses. I thought that they would be irrelevant to an evaluation of the case by the jury. I met with my client and told him that I wished to focus almost exclusively upon evidence demonstrating the role of Hunt and the CIA in the assassination of President Kennedy. I suggested that we call Marchetti only for a rather cursory presentation and that Carto, the main potential witness as to lack of actual malice, should not testify at all. We had probably won the case for Willis and his newspaper. We had not established the truth about the assassination, and we had a unique opportunity to make that effort.

Willis asked one question. "Have you ever been this confident about a jury's verdict in advance and been wrong?" I laughed and conceded that over the years I had made numerous errors at trial, including misreading a jury's reactions. We both knew that the plan could involve a substantial risk. Carto's sense of history overcame his concerns of the survival for his organization, and he said, "Go for it." He was on the next flight from Miami to his home to continue his daily work.

After Hunt rested, I presented the testimony of Marita Lorenz. She had been the attractive eighteen-year-old daughter of the captain of a West German luxury liner docked in the Havana harbor at the time of the Cuban Revolution. She met Castro when he paid a visit to her father's ship. Her romance with Castro continued even after her father's ship had sailed away. Later, their child was born.

Subsequently, Francisco Fiorini was named chief of security for the Cuban Air Force. It was not a significant assignment, since there wasn't much of an air force, but it was useful to Fiorini because he was employed by the Central Intelligence Agency. The CIA fabricated a story that Castro was going to kill Marita's child. That information was provided to Marita Lorenz by Fiorini, who arranged for her to flee from Cuba with the assistance of the government of the United States and the American embassy. Later in Miami, Fiorini, operating in the name of Frank Sturgis, recruited Lorenz for the CIA. Sturgis was later convicted for Watergate crimes along with Hunt, Liddy and various anti-Castro Cubans living in Miami who had been recruited by Hunt.

When I met Lorenz in New York City, she was residing in a large apartment building on the east side of Manhattan in which minor and mid-level diplomatic employees of the Soviet Union also lived. Her assignment was to examine all of the garbage and trash in the apartment building in a search for letters or other documents discarded by the Russians. Marita Lorenz told me that she knew of my work in investigating the assassination of President Kennedy and that she wanted to share detailed information with me. The information was supported by documents and implicated both Sturgis and Hunt in planning and carrying out the assassination.

When I was retained by the newspaper to defend it against Hunt, I located Marita. I asked her if she would testify at the trial in

Miami. She seemed terrified at the thought and said, "You don't know these people. They have killed and would not hesitate to kill again." I suggested the possibility that she make a sworn statement in New York City before a court reporter, thus sparing her a trip to Miami with the horrible consequences that she feared would result. She considered that suggestion, and then asked if Hunt or his representatives would be at the deposition. When I said that they would be present, she said she would not appear. At that point I created a novel concept for the deposition. I would reserve a room at a large and impersonal hotel in Manhattan directly across the street from Madison Square Garden. Hunt's representatives would meet me in the lobby and then be directed to the room. There was to be no telephone service from the room, and a representative of mine would be present when I left. The court reporter, Hunt's counsel and my representative would be locked in the room when I left to meet Marita. She agreed, and I brought her to the room to testify. I explained that Marita and I would be leaving, and they would be remaining for twenty minutes after the deposition had been concluded. I also stated for the record that any further communication with Lorenz would be through me and that her address would not be made available. The deposition proceeded.

At the trial, I offered the sworn statement of Lorenz as evidence of Hunt's involvement in the assassination. Earlier at the trial, counsel for Hunt had read a deposition into the record utilizing the standard method. That is, in a somewhat bored manner, he began each statement with "Question" and after reading the question, then said, "Answer," and read that. Before long, some of the jurors began to fidget, and others took a well-earned brief nap. That example demonstrated the weakness of a deposition as opposed to live testimony. Some lawyers ask permission to circulate copies of the deposition transcript to the jurors. That method creates an individual experience unlike a theater or a courtroom where everyone hears and sees all nuances together. In the theater and in a courtroom a communal response, laughter or horror, creates intensity. I have always considered the courtroom to be a stage for a dramatic production and that the most serious offense a lawyer may engage in is to bore the jurors, so I devised a method to both entertain and educate the jury about our case.

I asked a woman to play the part of Marita Lorenz. She was dramatically inclined and had studied her script, the deposition transcript. While I asked the questions, she was able to respond not as a reader, but as a witness. Of course, I informed the jurors that the woman was not Marita Lorenz, but that the words she spoke were the statements to which Lorenz had sworn.

Lorenz, through her proxy, testified:

Q: What is your present employment?
A: I do undercover work for an intelligence agency.
Q: Are you permitted to discuss the nature of that work, or where you work?
A: No, I am not.
Q: Is it also true that, as I have stipulated, you do not wish to give your home address?
A: No, I do not.
Q: Have you been employed by the Central Intelligence Agency?
A: Yes.

Lorenz had also done intelligence work for the New York Police Department.

Q: During 1978, did you appear as a witness before the United States House of Representatives Select Committee on Assassinations?
A: Yes.
Q: Was that in relation to the assassination of President John F. Kennedy?
A: Yes.
Q: Did you appear as a witness after the chief judge of the United States district court of Washington had signed an offer conferring immunity upon you and compelling you to testify?
A: Yes.
Q: During and prior to November 1963, did you live in Miami, Florida?
A: Yes, I did.
Q: I want you to understand, if I ask you any question which you are not permitted to answer, you may of course say that, but I will try, based on my previous interview with you, to just ask you questions which you can answer.
A: Yes.

Q: During and before November of 1963, did you work on behalf of the Central Intelligence Agency in the Miami area?

A: Yes.

Q: Did you work with a man named Frank Sturgis, while you were working for the CIA?

A: Yes, I did.

Q: Was that in Miami, during and prior to November 1963?

A: Yes.

Q: What other names, to your knowledge, is Frank Sturgis known by?

A: Frank Fiorini, Hamilton; the last name, Hamilton. F-I-O-R-I-N-I.

Q: Was Mr. Fiorini or Mr. Sturgis, while you worked with him, also employed by the Central Intelligence Agency?

A: Yes.

Q: During that time were payments made to Mr. Sturgis for the work he was doing for the CIA?

A: Yes.

Q: Did you ever witness anyone make payments to him for the CIA work which you and Mr. Sturgis were both involved in?

A: Yes.

Although Hunt had testified that Sturgis had never worked for the CIA, Richard Helms, the former director of the CIA, said he had. He testified in this case that "Frank Sturgis was an agent, an outside agent, a contract agent, of the agency." Sturgis himself had stated under oath in another case that he had been recruited by the CIA. Hunt's sworn denial that Sturgis had a CIA connection was repudiated by the testimony of all of the relevant witnesses.

On the other hand, Lorenz, who had testified that Sturgis worked for the CIA, received corroboration from Helms and Sturgis himself.

Q: Who did you witness make payments to Mr. Sturgis?

A: A man by the name of Eduardo.

Hunt had testified that he had used the alias "Eduardo."

Q: Who is Eduardo?

A: That is his code name; the real name is E. Howard Hunt.

Q: Did you know him and meet him during and prior to November 1963?

A: Yes.

Q: Did you witness payments made by Mr. Hunt to Mr. Sturgis or Mr. Fiorini on more than one occasion prior to November of 1963?

A: Yes.

In a previous meeting, Lorenz had agreed to talk about the days preceding the assassination, but her training in secrecy hindered her and her answers sounded stilted.

Q: Did you go on a trip with Mr. Sturgis from Miami during November of 1963?

A: Yes.

Q: Was anyone else present with you when you went on that trip?

A: Yes.

Q: What method of transportation did you use?

A: By car.

Q: Was there one or more cars?

A: There was a follow-up car.

Q: Does that mean two cars?

A: Backup; yes.

Q: What was in the follow-up car, if you know?

A: Weapons.

Q: Without asking you any of the details regarding the activity that you and Mr. Sturgis and Mr. Hunt were involved in, may I ask you if some of that activity was related to the transportation of weapons?

A: Yes.

Q: Did Mr. Hunt pay Mr. Sturgis sums of money for activity related to the transportation of weapons?

A: Yes.

Q: Did Mr. Sturgis tell you where you would be going from Miami, Florida, during November of 1963, prior to the time that you traveled with him in the car?

A: Dallas, Texas.

Q: He told you that?

A: Yes.

Q: Did he tell you the purpose of the trip to Dallas, Texas?

A: No; he said it was confidential.

Q: Did you arrive in Dallas during November of 1963?

A: Yes.

Q: After you arrived in Dallas, did you stay at any accommodations there?

A: Motel.

Q: While you were at that motel, did you meet anyone other than those who were in the party traveling with you from Miami to Dallas?

A: Yes.

Q: Who did you meet?

A: E. Howard Hunt.

Q: Tell me the circumstances regarding your seeing E. Howard Hunt in Dallas in November of 1963?

A: There was a prearranged meeting that E. Howard Hunt deliver us sums of money for the so-called operation that I did not know its nature.

Q: Were you told what your role was to be?

A: Just a decoy at the time.

Q: Did you see Mr. Hunt actually deliver money to anyone in the motel room which you were present in?

A: Yes.

Q: To whom did you see him deliver the money?

A: He gave an envelope of cash to Frank Fiorini.

Q: Did anyone else enter the room other than you, Mr. Fiorini, Mr. Hunt, and others who may have been there before Mr. Hunt arrived?

A: No.

Q: Where did you see the person you identified as Jack Ruby?

A: After Eduardo left, a fellow came to the door and it was Jack Ruby, about an hour later, forty-five minutes to an hour later.

Q: When you say Eduardo, who are you referring to?

A: E. Howard Hunt.

Q: When did that meeting take place in terms of the hour; was it daytime or nighttime?

A: Early evening.

Q: How soon after that evening meeting took place did you leave Dallas?

A: I left about two hours later; Frank took me to the airport and we went back to Miami.

Q: Now, can you tell us in relationship to the day that President Kennedy was killed, when this meeting took place?

A: The day before.

Q: Is it your testimony that the meeting which you just described with Mr. Hunt making the payment of money to Mr. Sturgis took place on November 21, 1963?

A: Yes.

In the original trial, the defense worked to prove that Hunt had not been in Dallas on November 22. However, Hunt was charged with conspiracy in the assassination. It was not imperative that he be there on the day, just that he have a connection to the crime. Marita Lorenz had just placed him in Dallas on November 21. Hunt had no alibi for that day.

Hunt had not prepared himself for questions about the twenty-first, and freely admitted to me that it was entirely possible that he had not been in his office in Washington, D.C., on November 21, although he was quite certain he was there on the twenty-second.

I asked Marita about Jack Ruby:

Q: Is it your testimony that the man who killed Lee Harvey Oswald is, to the best of your ability to identify him, the person who was in the room in the motel in Dallas the night before the president was killed?

A: Yes.

Q: Had you ever seen Jack Ruby before November 21, 1963?

A: No.

During cross-examination, Lorenz was able to clarify some of the details of her testimony. She was asked why she was not questioned by the Warren Commission and responded that the CIA had instructed her not to answer questions that were put to her by the Warren Commission. She did, however, testify in front of the House Select Committee on Assassinations in the 1970s.

Q: Is it your testimony today, that today's testimony is consistent with what you said before the House Select Committee?

A: That's right.

Q: When was the first time you met Howard Hunt?

A: 1960, in Miami, Florida.

Q: How was he identified to you?

A: Introduced. Introduced as Eduardo.

Q: How do you spell that?

A: E-D-U-A-R-D-O, Eduardo, E-D-U-A-R-D-O. He was to finance the operations in Miami.

Q: What language did he speak to you in?

A: English and Spanish.

Q: English and Spanish?

A: Yes.

Q: When is it that you became aware that this person you know as Eduardo was E. Howard Hunt?

A: About the same time. Eduardo was the name we were to refer to him as, when discussing things.

Q: Who did you believe he was working for at that time?

A: CIA.

Q: Why?

A: Because we were all at that time CIA members of Operation 40. We had been given instructions from Eduardo and had certain rights and permissions to do things that the average citizen could not do.

I asked Lorenz to tell me the names of the men with whom she had traveled to Miami. She refused, saying, "They killed Kennedy. I don't want to be the one to give their names; it's too dangerous." I warned her that Hunt's attorney might ask her about them.

Hunt's lawyer did. He asked her for the name of the persons in the car with her. She told him of Gerry Patrick Hemming, two brothers named Novo and Pedro Diaz Lanz.

She told me later, "If Hunt and his friends in the CIA wanted that question answered, or were too dumb or too lazy to keep their lawyer from asking it, the responsibility is theirs, not mine."

Counsel for Hunt asked her about the weapons in the car, and she identified them as handguns and automatics, rifles, "cases of machine guns, rifles, thirty-eights, forty-fives." When he asked her what happened to the weaponry after the caravan reached Dallas, she told him, "They were in the car and I presume they took them to the motel the next day, the next night. A lot of things they carried in."

Hunt's lawyer continued to question her. At one point I had to break in and remind him that she was testifying about classified subjects and could be breaking the law in order to answer his questions.

Lorenz left Dallas on November 21, 1963, because, as she said:

> "I knew that this was different from other jobs. This was not just gunrunning. This was big, very big, and I wanted to get out. I told Sturgis I wanted to leave. He said it was a very big operation but that my part was not dangerous. I was to be a decoy. Before he could go further, I said please let me get out. I want to go back to my baby in Miami. Finally he agreed and drove me to the airport."

She flew to Miami, picked up her child, and then flew to New York so that she could be with her mother in New Jersey.

Counsel for Hunt asked her if she had done anything with her information after she had found out the president had been killed and was in New Jersey.

A: Talked to the FBI.

Q: You talked to the FBI?

A: Yes.

Q: Voluntarily?

A: They wanted to talk to me anyway about certain things with my child's father and they picked me up and took me to the office.

Q: What day would that have been?

A: A few days after I arrived, after everyone got over the initial shock.

Q: It would be some time in the month of November of 1963?

A: Yes.

Q: In your discussions with the FBI, they inquired about your activities which related to Dallas and this group of seven people that took the car trip?

A: Well, they discussed my associates down there and my relationship with my daughter's father, mostly.

Q: Did they know the names of the people you took the car trip with, from Miami to Dallas?

A: Yes.

Q: Did they ask you about each of those people?
A: Yes.
Q: Did you tell them about the guns and money and about Eduardo?
A: Yes.
Q: You told them about Eduardo?
A: Yes.
Q: And the guns?
A: They know about all those associations. They didn't want to go into it. Those were CIA activities, not FBI.

Marita Lorenz clearly did not want to talk about her associations with the men in Dallas, but Hunt's lawyer pressed her further.

Q: Did you ever talk with Frank Sturgis about it, since then?
A: We are not on talking terms, Frank and I.
Q: That was not my question. Have you ever talked about it with Frank Sturgis since 1963?
A: Yes.
Q: Did he indicate to you that he was involved in the assassination of the president?
A: Yes.

Counsel finally pressed Lorenz to tell of her last meeting with Sturgis, when he told her:

"We killed the president that day. You could have been a part of it—you know, part of history. You should have stayed. It was safe. Everything was covered in advance. No arrests, no real newspaper investigation. It was all covered, very professional."

In a closing argument, Hunt's counsel told the jury members that they should have faith in our nation's leaders. I suggested that they should have faith in their own ability to evaluate the evidence. Judge Kehoe instructed the jury about the law and then, since it was late in the day, suggested that they retire to the jury room to go over housekeeping matters, look at the verdict form and take an initial look at the evidence. Soon he excused them for the day and asked them to return the next morning. At 9:30 the next morning, they resumed deliberations. Sixty-five minutes later the clerk announced that there was a verdict. To the question by the judge, "Have you arrived at a verdict in this case?" the jury foreperson responded in the affirmative. The unanimous verdict was read, "We, the jury, find for the defendant, Liberty Lobby and against the plaintiff, E. Howard Hunt." The jury also awarded costs to the victorious party to be assessed against Hunt. When questioned by the media on the steps of the courthouse, Leslie Armstrong, the foreperson, said that the evidence clearly demonstrated that Hunt and the CIA had assassinated President Kennedy and that the government should act so that those responsible be brought to justice.

Later I was able to locate Hemming in Florida. I had been informed that he had trained guerillas to kill with their bare hands when it seemed necessary for some project that the government found worthy. I also learned that he was a very large man. I checked into a well-known and adequately populated Miami Beach hotel and called him. He said, "I know who you are and what you've done. I would like to meet you." The more eager he seemed, the more my fervor for the assignment faded. I told him where I was staying, and we agreed to meet in one hour in the large and busy lobby. I informed the desk not to give my room number to anyone. A few minutes later there was a knock on my door. It was Hemming. He was approximately six feet eight and weighed about three hundred pounds. He said, "Don't worry, I'm not armed." I was less than assured. I asked how he got my room number. He laughed and said, "Piece of cake. You forget where I worked." We talked for a while, but I was not about to accuse him of murder while in the secluded confines of the room. I suggested a walk about the grounds, which overlooked the beach and ocean. He agreed. There, under a palm tree, alone but not out of sight of witnesses, I recounted for him almost verbatim what Marita had said. He watched me intensely and without changing expression. When I completed my narrative, he said, "And do you have a question?" I hesitated and then asked, "Was her testimony accurate?" He responded, "No. Not entirely. It was not a two-car caravan, there were three cars." He paused and added, "Otherwise everything she said was true."

The Real Firing Line:
The Brothers Novo and the
Brothers Buckley

During December 1966, I was invited to appear on William F. Buckley's *Firing Line*. I wondered why Buckley, who both ardently supported the Warren Commission Report and had neither read it nor examined the evidence upon which it was allegedly based, wanted to duel with me about a subject for which he was totally unprepared. This was an unprecedented break with the tradition he had established for his long-running program on public television. In advance, he advised me that we were not to talk about the details in the Kennedy assassination, but only broader philosophical questions raised by the appointment by the president of a commission to investigate a murder. Buckley also operated from a position of advantage in that he was the host, the person who proposed the specific questions as well as the general subject matter, and the debater who could respond whenever he wished to, and he often wished to.

I knew little about Buckley's background at that time; only that he was an icon of the right and respected as a responsible conservative, even by the liberal news media. I wrote briefly about that appearance in *A Citizen's Dissent*, evaluating the program as being relevant and fair. Years later I was able to make a judgment as to why the invitation had been offered to me.

During the Hunt trial, Marita Lorenz testified that two brothers, Guillermo and Ignacio Novo, were involved in the assassination of President Kennedy on behalf of the Central Intelligence Agency, a statement later confirmed by Gerry Patrick Hemming, a CIA assassin who had traveled to Dallas with Lorenz, just before the assassination. If the Novo brothers had been arrested in November 1963, a tragedy that took place in the nation's capital many years later might have been avoided.

On September 18, 1976, Orlando Letelier and Ronni Moffitt were assassinated in Washington, D.C. Letelier had served as foreign minister under Salvador Allende, whose administration was overthrown by the CIA. Ronni Moffitt was a twenty-five-year-old American woman who was involved in efforts to bring about democracy in Chile. They were murdered by Guillermo Novo and Ignacio Novo.

At the time of the murders George H. W. Bush was the director of the CIA and was informed that DINA (Departmento de Intelligencia) and its contract agents were involved in the Letelier/Moffitt murders. DINA operated as agents for General Augusto Pinochet who had seized power in Chile in 1974. Bush became an active participant in an effort to falsify the record and deny that DINA had been involved in the murders. Two intelligence-related journalists, Jeremiah O'Leary, writing for the now defunct *Washington Star*, and William F. Buckley, formerly with the CIA, led that disinformation campaign. O'Leary wrote, "The right wing Chilean junta had nothing to gain and everything to lose by the assassination of a peaceful and popular socialist leader." Buckley wrote, "U.S. investigators think it unlikely that Chile would risk an action of this kind with the respect it has won with great difficulty during the past year in many Western countries, which before were hostile to its policies." *Newsweek* asserted, "the CIA has concluded that the Chilean secret police was not involved."

In fact, in spite of the assurances from Buckley, O'Leary and the CIA, all offered within days after the two murders, DINA, likely in cooperation with the CIA, was responsible for the murders. Michael Townley, an American with contacts in the CIA, admitted in a plea bargain that he had been a professional assassin for DINA and that he and others had murdered Letelier and Moffitt. At the trial, Guillermo Novo insisted that Townley "was a contract agent for the CIA" and that "the CIA was also responsible for the murders in the nation's capital."

On March 23, 1979, Townley, Guillermo Novo and Ignacio Novo, who had been convicted of the murders, appeared before Judge Barrington Parker for sentence. Judge Parker, before whom I had appeared on numerous occasions, was an impartial, intelligent jurist and as honorable as any judge I have ever met. In imposing sentence Parker said, "In the ten years I have served on this bench, I have never presided over a trial of a murder as monstrous as this."

Before sentence, Townley had entered into an agreement with the Department of Justice, resulting in his being eligible for parole in two years and entry into the Federal Witness Protection Program. Townley and the United States Attorney's Office also agreed to omit from the public record any evidence of misconduct by DINA. Judge Parker sarcastically asked the prosecutor if he was "representing the Chilean government." Covering up for the CIA was the duty expected by the U.S. Attorney's Office which theoretically represented the United States government including its intelligence operations; however, extending that courtesy to a foreign government that had carried out murders in Washington, D.C., was extraordinary.

It became clear during the trial that the United States Attorney's Office and the FBI had agreed to prevent the most relevant evidence from reaching the jury and the judge. Nevertheless, some testimony, when examined in the context of indisputable facts, revealed both the nature of the government's conspiracy to cover up the facts and the importance of the evidence that the government sought to suppress.

For example, FBI Special Agent Larry Wack, after being thoroughly prepared by the United States Attorney, described a meeting he had had with Townley. Wack said that he had met the defendant Townley at the John F. Kennedy Airport and "proceeded under his direction to the International Arrivals building." The purpose of the testimony was for Townley to retrace the steps he took that led to the conspiracy to murder Orlando Letelier.

Wack continued, "The route we traveled was to the International Arrivals building, to the second floor to LAN Chile Airlines Office to their first class lounge and, subsequently left the airport." This colloquy followed:

Q: Who was directing the route that you were taking?
Wack: Mr. Townley was.
Q: After leaving JFK Airport, did you go anyplace else?
Wack: We went to the vicinity of Forty-second Street and Fifth Avenue, New York City.
Q: And would you tell us what happened when you got to the vicinity of Forty-second Street and Fifth Avenue?
Wack: Mr. Townley led us to the specific building of 500 Fifth Avenue.
Q: And what happened when you got to 500 Fifth Avenue?
Wack: Mr. Townley—we entered the building and we proceeded to determine what office he had visited in the building.
Q: Did there come a time when he pointed out an office that he had visited?
Wack: He did. He pointed out the office of a New York state senator on the forty-first floor of the building.
Q: Do you know an individual by the name of William Sampol?
Wack: I do.
Q: Where does he work?
Wack: William Sampol works in an office of a New York state senator at 500 Fifth Avenue, New York City, on the forty-first floor.
Q: Are you aware, sir, whether or not he has a relationship with the defendant Guillermo Novo Sampol?
Wack: William Sampol is known to me as the cousin of Guillermo Novo.

The "New York state senator" was never identified at the trial. Both the U.S. attorney and the FBI agent who testified knew that there was no office of a New York state senator on the forty-first floor of 500 Fifth Avenue. There were scores of senators in the New York State legislature; there were but two United States Senators in each state, including New York State. As the U.S. Attorney and the FBI agent knew, the office that Townley visited initially, and the FBI visited subsequently, was the office occupied by United States Senator James Buckley, the brother of William F. Buckley. Buckley had been elected to the Senate in 1970, winning 38.7 percent of the vote in a three-way race. He was defeated by Daniel Patrick Moynihan by a wide margin when he sought reelection, and then moved to

Connecticut where he again lost when he ran for the Senate against Christopher Dodd.

The meeting at Buckley's office with his employee William Sampol and Guillermo Novo and Michael Townley, two of those convicted in the murder of Letelier and Moffitt, took place just days before the killings. While it has been charged that Senator Buckley was present at the meeting in his office, that matter has not been pursued by the United States Attorney's Office. Instead, James Buckley was appointed to a lifetime position by President Reagan to serve on the second-most important court in the United States, the United States Court of Appeals for the District of Columbia.

Finally, many years after appearing on *Firing Line*, I understood why I had been invited. It was not until my book was a best seller that Buckley sought my appearance in an effort to undermine the evidence that merely demonstrated that Oswald could not have been the lone assassin. Many were asking if Oswald had not killed Kennedy, who had? It was that questioning that Buckley sought to silence.

For more than a decade, scores, then hundreds, of ordinary citizens began to research and investigate the facts surrounding the death of their president. Had their findings and the evidence they uncovered been credited by those in position to act, and had the Novo brothers been arrested as suspects in the assassination, they would have been unable to carry out the murders of Orlando Letelier and Ronni Moffitt. To those apologists for the Warren Commission Report, including William Buckley, who said during his interview with me, "I don't really much care who killed Mr. Kennedy," it should now be clear that our efforts were not merely pure research.

The question that remains is on whose behalf had the Buckley brothers worked, one meeting with the murderers in his office just before the killings took place, and the other, again covering up for his friends at the CIA as he had after President Kennedy had been assassinated. Based on the Lorenz testimony there was sufficient evidence for the federal government to consider indicting the Novo brothers for conspiracy to assassinate President Kennedy and certainly to examine the evidence about others who had acted with them.

But with the government holding to its preconception that Oswald acted alone, in the face of all evidence to the contrary, it was in no position to consider a conspiracy indictment against anyone.

The refusal of the justice authorities at the highest state and federal levels to act appropriately in 1963 and 1964 meant that the identified assassins would be free to ply their trade. The murders in Washington, years later, was the price the two victims, Letelier and Moffitt, paid for the government's refusal to act in a timely fashion against those who conspired to murder the president.

The government knew Marita Lorenz quite well. The CIA had previously sent her to Cuba on a mission to assassinate Fidel Castro, and she had worked undercover for various other federal and state police organizations. I have examined a number of those authorizing documents. Her statement that the Novo brothers were prone to commit murder was later proven to be accurate when they were convicted of committing murders in the District of Columbia. As was the case with other witnesses who had inconvenient information to offer, the members of the Warren Commission were neither informed of her previous employment by the CIA nor of her statement about her trip to Dallas with Frank Sturgis and the meetings with the Novo brothers. Of course, Dulles was well-acquainted with her prior involvement with the CIA; he was the former director of that agency. When I took the deposition of Richard Helms, a director of the CIA, I asked about Sturgis. He testified, "Sturgis I have heard of." He described the relationship between the CIA and Sturgis: "Frank Sturgis was an agent, an outside agent, a contract agent, of the agency."

The political members of the commission, the senators and representatives of Congress, however, were not permitted to hear her words. Their part in the investigation was limited in large measure to providing window dressing for Dulles and to discourage congressional committees from conducting parallel investigations.

Although CIA officials subsequently conceded that the agency had a relationship with Sturgis, an examination of the Warren Commission Report reveals that the names Sturgis and Lorenz do not appear. An examination of page 885 of the report, the relevant portion of the index of those mentioned in the report, discloses that the names Guillermo Novo and Ignacio Novo are not present.

BOOK TWO

THE MEDIA RESPONSE

The KGB and Jim Garrison

by Oliver Stone

[I recently met with Oliver Stone to film an interview with him about the repercussions resulting from his historic film JFK, *about the investigation that had been conducted by New Orleans District Attorney Jim Garrison into the assassination. Stone's films have been nominated for thirty-one Academy Awards and seventeen Golden Globes. He is considered a war hero for his service as an American infantry soldier in Vietnam and one of the country's most successful and innovative filmmakers. He told me that he thought that George Orwell's* 1984 *was apocryphal until he suffered from the relentless and cruel attacks by the media as a result of stating in his film what most Americans consider to be true, that the Warren Report's conclusions were incorrect and that there had been a conspiracy to murder the president. He said, "It was as though I had been made into a non-person." The statement below was Stone's response to a false CIA-sponsored story linking Jim Garrison to KGB material.—ML]*

Nation contributing editor Max Holland wrote an article for *Studies in Intelligence* asserting that former New Orleans District Attorney Jim Garrison was duped by a KGB disinformation operation that led him, along with most Americans, to believe that the CIA had been involved in the assassination of President Kennedy.

This spring, *Foreign Affairs* magazine published a generous review of Holland's article. As a writer of the film *JFK*, I sent a reply to *Foreign Affairs*. The editors refused to publish it. I offered to pay for an ad, but *Foreign Affairs* again refused.

For the record, here is my reply:

Dear Editors of *Foreign Affairs*:

Philip Zelikow's review of Max Holland's recent article in the CIA publication *Studies in Intelligence* is a disservice to your readers. Zelikow uncritically accepts Holland's theory that a KGB disinformation operation back in 1967 is at the root of most Americans' current belief that the CIA was involved in the assassination of President Kennedy.

Holland's thesis rests on one unproven premise: that the KGB planted a false story in March 1967 in *Paese Sera*, an Italian left-wing newspaper. The story reported that Clay Shaw, then recently charged with conspiracy to assassinate the president, was a board member of Centro Mondiale Comerciale (CMC), an organization that had been forced out of Italy amid charges that it was a CIA money-laundering front.

The problem Zelikow ignores is that Holland's only evidence to support his premise is one handwritten note by a KGB defector named Vasili Mitrokhin that "refers to a disinformation scheme in 1967 that involved Paese Sera and resulted in publication of a false story in New York." The note, supposedly summarizing a KGB document that Holland has never seen, does not mention Clay Shaw, Centro Mondiale Comerciale, Jim Garrison, or any specific New York publication.

Holland speculates that the New York publication may have been the *National Guardian*, which based an article on the *Paese Sera* series. But one short article in an obscure left-wing weekly that routinely picked up stories from the international press does not seem like much of an accomplishment for a KGB disinformation operation. There is no evidence that the *Guardian* article was picked up anywhere else in the U.S.

Rather than speculate, Holland might have tried to interview the editors of *Paese Sera* who were responsible for the articles on Centro Mondiale Comerciale, as scholar Joan Mellen has done for her forthcoming biography of Garrison. They would have told him that the six-part series had nothing to do with the KGB or the JFK assassination, that they had never heard of Jim Garrison when they assigned the story six months before, and that they were astonished to see that Shaw might have any connection to the assassination. The articles were actually assigned in the wake of a right-wing coup in Greece and were intended to prevent such a coup in Italy.

Holland says, "everything in the *Paese Sera* story was a lie." His evidence? A recently released CIA document saying that the agency itself looked into *Paese Sera*'s allegations and found that the CIA had no connection to CMC or its parent, Permindex. Holland may be willing to accept this as the whole truth, but it is unconvincing to the rest of us who have noticed the agency's tendency to distance itself from its fronts, to release to the public only documents that serve its interest, to fabricate evidence, and to lie outright even under oath to congressional committees.

Two important facts from the *Paese Sera* story remain true:

1. CMC was forced to leave Italy (for Johannesburg, South Africa) in 1962 under a cloud of suspicion about its CIA connections.
2. Clay Shaw was a member of CMC's board, along with such well-known fascist sympathizers as Gutierrez di Spadaforo, undersecretary of agriculture for Mussolini; Ferenc Nagy, former premier of Hungary, and Giuseppe Zigiotti, president of the Fascist National Association for Militia Arms.

Holland claims that the *Paese Sera* articles were what led Garrison to believe the CIA was involved in the assassination. This is nonsense. Garrison's book *On the Trail of the Assassins* describes in detail how his uncovering of various pieces of evidence actually led him to the conclusion that the CIA was involved. This gradual process began two days after the assassination when he questioned David Ferrie, a pilot who flew secret missions to Cuba for the CIA and trained Lee Harvey Oswald in his Civil Air Patrol unit. It included his investigation of a 1961 raid of a munitions cache by CIA operatives in Houma, Louisiana; the discovery that several of Oswald's coworkers at Reily Coffee Company in New Orleans now worked at NASA; the fact that Oswald was working out of an office that was running the CIA's local training camp for Operation Mongoose; many eyewitnesses who saw Clay Shaw, David Ferrie and Oswald together, etc. No doubt the *Paese*

Sera series was another piece of the puzzle for Garrison, but it was not the centerpiece of his thinking that Holland makes it out to be.

From the moment his investigation of the JFK assassination became public, Garrison was pilloried in the press. This treatment was part of an orchestrated effort by the CIA to discredit critics of the Warren Commission. A CIA memo dated April 1, 1967, never mentioned by Holland or Zelikow, outlines the strategy and calls for the Agency's "assets" in the media (writers and editors) to publish stories saying the critics were politically motivated, financially motivated, egomaniacal, sloppy in their research, supported the Soviet Union, etc. This is exactly the inaccurate portrait of Garrison that emerged in the press.

With the publication of Holland's recent article attempting to link Jim Garrison to the KGB, the CIA continues to pursue this misguided strategy of smearing Garrison and other critics of the Warren Commission. Fortunately, the American public has never bought the tired old lie that the CIA's misadventures can be written off as figments of KGB disinformation. Too bad your critic did.

[This statement was written in 2002. At the time Holland was posing as an authentic contributing editor to the Nation. *His ties to the CIA were not acknowledged or known. They are discussed here in the chapter entitled "The CIA and the Media."—MLJ]*

Contacts with Totalitarian Structures

When the CIA imposes sanctions upon a perceived opponent, whether the subject is an American or not, it is often quite unpleasant. Murder, torture, subterfuge and defamation appear to be among the chosen weapons. I have been fortunate since only the last options have been employed in my case.

Before I wrote *Rush to Judgment* the CIA evidenced little interest in me. Those halcyon days began to fade when I sought a publisher for that work. Unpublished books apparently are not a matter of major concern. Visits to prospective publishers by intelligence assets made it impossible for me to find one in the United States for some time; only after a British publisher agreed to print it did an American company acquiesce.

My journey to London to edit and revise the first book I had ever written brought me in contact with Benjamin Sonnenberg, Jr., an American living there. He had volunteered to the publisher for that task. He wanted no payment, just influence.

His efforts were destructive and I finally asked him to withdraw after I had rejected all of his counterproductive offerings. Years later he wrote his own book, *Lost Property: Memoirs and Confessions of a Bad Boy*.[38] The confession that most intrigued me was his admission that he had been working for the CIA while he sought to edit my book. He

---

38. Ben Sonnenberg, *Lost Property: Memoirs and Confessions of a Bad Boy* (Simon and Schuster, 1991).

provided details, including the name of his CIA contact and discussions that they had about *Rush to Judgment*.

Of course, the CIA was ready with a response if one was needed. Never mentioning its own role in seeking to alter and then suppress *Rush to Judgment*, it later said that the KGB was somehow involved. My history with brutalitarian organizations, including the Soviet Union, its satellite nations, and the CIA, has demonstrated my animosity towards and distrust of all of them. For their part the Soviets and their friends have been displeased with my efforts to assist those who have struggled against their lack of democracy and due process, and have made that clear on more than one occasion.

During April 1964, the International Association of Democratic Lawyers (IADL) was holding its convention in Prague. I was invited to speak about the investigation into the assassination of John Kennedy.

My government was interested in what I had to say, although I had made my case quite publicly at scores of colleges and law schools in the United States at which, on each occasion, special agents of the FBI and local police intelligence agents were present.[39] Among those reports were documents showing that the FBI, and agents of the Department of Justice and of the United States Department of State reported upon my remarks in Budapest. The legal advisor to the Department of State, Abram Chayes, sent a secret letter with copies of two telegrams, one dated "April 6, 1964 at 10:13 AM" and the other "April 7, 1964 at 11:29 AM" to the Warren Commission on April 9, 1964, about my speech. I can only conclude that not much else was happening in the world at that time.

The rivalry between the Soviet Union and China was rapidly becoming vitriolic. That year Mao stated that there had been a counterrevolution and that capitalism had replaced socialism in the USSR. Both countries were represented at the IADL convention.

A delegation of Chinese lawyers called upon me at my hotel room to warn me that I should not speak at the meeting. "The assassination of your president is an irrelevancy and we do not care who gets the credit," the spokesman said, adding that if I spoke his delegation would walk out and that I would be greatly embarrassed. I suggested that their

---

39. I received copies of their reports through our Freedom of Information requests and motions to the United States District Court.

rejection would not harm my image in the United States and provided him with the name and room number of the reporter from *The New York Times* who was covering the event.

I spoke to an attentive audience of lawyers and judges from numerous countries, including France, England, Germany and other Western democracies. A motion to conduct an international inquiry passed overwhelmingly with only the Chinese lawyers abstaining.

Before I left the United States for the conference, a lawyer from Canada had provided me with the name of a man he said was a political prisoner in the East who had been held incommunicado and denied the right to counsel. He asked me to talk with the representative of the Justice Ministry about the matter. I tried several times to talk with the official, but he never responded to the messages, which surprised me since most of the officials there had been very supportive and generous with their time.

On the next to last evening that I planned to spend in Budapest, I attended a social event for all of the delegates and speakers. I saw the official and introduced myself to him through his interpreter. He smiled, shook my hand and said that he had appreciated my speech.

He remained smiling as I began to raise the matter of the political prisoner, but when I mentioned his name, even before my request to see the prisoner was translated, the smile was replaced with a scowl. He responded that it was rude of me to talk politics at a social celebration; I agreed but said that my efforts to meet at his office had brought no response. He stated that neither I nor any other lawyer would be permitted to see the prisoner, that I had overstepped the hospitality that had been shown me, and that I had likely violated some statute. He wheeled away and left the party as his entourage followed him.

I returned to my hotel, and with the assistance of the concierge, I booked a flight to New York leaving the next morning. The FBI report stated that I had left Budapest for a "destination unknown." Fortunately the pilot and each of the passengers knew where we were headed. In fact I had never seen an airplane ticket without the name of the city where the pilot had intended to land. I thought then that the secret police of many countries had much in common.

That same year, a journalist from Czechoslovakia covering the United Nations interviewed me about the assassination of President

Kennedy. He was intrigued by the facts and asked if he could meet with me for a series of additional interviews. I had some free time since the American media was demonstrating little interest in the subject. I visited him at a modest apartment near the U.N. that he, his wife and their young son occupied. We had dinner followed by an in-depth interview that continued for hours.

Later, he called to tell me that the interview was to be published as a booklet in his country. Still later he called to tell me that he had received an award for his work. Subsequently, he was recalled to Prague.

On January 5, 1968, Prague Spring arrived, early for the calendar but not too soon for the residents who had been dominated by the Soviet Union since the end of World War II. The enterprising journalist who had interviewed me was an activist in the liberation movement led by Alexander Dubcek, who began to remove restraints upon the media, permit free speech and unrestricted travel.

During the night of August 20, 1968, the invasion of Czechoslovakia by the Soviet Union and its allies began and continued until the next day. Two thousand tanks led 200,000 foreign troops and before nightfall on August 21 the country was occupied. Later, Dubcek was replaced and his reforms abolished.

I made one visit to the country and met with a number of students who told me that I was under surveillance by the secret police. Unable to locate the address of the journalist who had interviewed me, I asked several writers for his contact information. A government official told me that he was on vacation and would not return to Prague for several weeks, long after I had left the country.

That evening an author called to tell me that the journalist I was looking for was in prison charged with a violation of the Brezhnev Doctrine[40] by suggesting that there should be "democratization." He said that the journalist's wife would like to meet with me and asked if I would be willing to see her. I said that of course I would.

---

40. "When forces that are hostile to socialism try to turn the development of some socialist country towards capitalism, it becomes not only a problem of the country concerned, but a common problem and concern of all socialist countries."— Leonid Brezhnev

Several hours later there was a knock at my door. A young man whom I did not recognize asked if he could come in. He was, he explained, the journalist's son; I had met him in New York when he was a child. He said that his mother wanted me to know that it might not be safe for me to meet her but that she was waiting a block away if I still wanted to see her. I put on my coat and he led me to her.

She embraced me and said that of all the friends they had in America I was the only one willing to see her after her husband was arrested. I told her that I belonged to no political party where I was subject to discipline. Actually I was a member of no organized political party at that time; I was an enrolled Democrat.

I asked what I could do to help. She said that some of the members of the Czech government respected the work I had done regarding the assassination of President Kennedy. Could I ask them to release her husband and could I, after returning home, ask people I knew to write to the government on behalf of her husband? I agreed to do whatever I could, but I assured her that I had little influence with any government.

The next day I met with the official who had said that the journalist was on vacation. I petitioned for his release from prison. He asked when I was leaving the country and suggested that I should not attempt to extend my stay.

The architecture, the food and, above all, the students were, in that order, historic, delicious, intelligent and curious. Nevertheless, I left at the assigned date and have not returned.

When I arrived home, I sent letters and telegrams and made telephone calls and visits to enlist influential people to join in the effort for freedom. Later, almost certainly for reasons unrelated to my efforts, I was told that the journalist had been released.

Years later, in 1972, I received an unusual request. The letter was postmarked Leipzig, Germany, and it invited me to be the one American judge at the Leipzig International Film Festival that had been held annually for the previous decades. It was the largest festival in Germany and the second largest in Europe. I thought they had made a mistake and confused me with someone else as I was not a filmmaker, not a director, and not even a regular moviegoer.

My documentary film *Rush to Judgment,* although it had won some awards, was a simple work whose strength was not in its artistry or direction; it had simply permitted the eyewitnesses to the Kennedy assassination to speak to the American people. It was that film that apparently impressed the organizers of the Leipzig festival. I accepted the invitation.

In four days the judges watched and graded more than one hundred films. Mercifully, most of them were short. I was also eager to visit the remarkable architecture of the city. I visited the University of Leipzig, founded in 1409, almost a century before Columbus lost his way to India and found America, but the rest of the time was spent in rooms watching documentary films.

We each were given a scorecard, and we each studied the films with others in their assigned categories. Then we posted our score sheets on a bulletin board where the other judges could see them. I appreciated that method for its transparency, which indicated that the judges were going to make the award decisions without political interference. My impression proved to be wholly inaccurate.

There were a number of important films shown, but the individual merits of some were lost for me since they were all compressed into a wearingly short and intensive period and projected one after the other. Thoughts of two films, though, still remain with me. One was quite political and the other seemingly without a specific viewpoint but all the more political for its exquisite simplicity.

The first was called *The Road*; it had been translated from Vietnamese to German to English. It was a remarkable bit of history. The war in Vietnam was raging, and the United States Air Force was determined to prevent supplies, including weapons, ammunition, food and medicine, from reaching the National Liberation Front (NLF) fighters in the south of Vietnam. The road, called "The Ho Chi Minh Trail," the lifeline for the NLF, was bombed and strafed daily and attacked with napalm and Agent Orange, an insidious defoliant.[41]

---

41. Agent Orange was so devastating that decades later a fourteen-member panel selected by the prestigious Institute of Medicine in the United States found that seventeen serious medical conditions still afflicted American former servicemen who had been exposed to the defoliant, possibly including Parkinson's disease and ischemic heart disease (July 25, 2009, *The New York Times*). Since those GIs were not the chosen targets one must assume that the Vietnamese who were and who survived the attacks must have suffered greatly.

At night hundreds of volunteers, most of them women, carried large rocks to fill the craters left by the bombs and then covered them with earth so that vehicles could pass. There was no single road; there were many paths through the jungle, hidden by the triple canopy of trees and other vegetation. The daily raids of napalm and Agent Orange were designed to kill those who lived in the area and to expose the paths.

Some of our finest academic institutions, including Stanford University, helped to develop the "people sniffer" used by the Chemical Corps to locate the enemy. The *Army Chemical Review* much later revealed that "the detection methods used to locate people depended on effluents unique to humans . . . Ammonia, when combined with hydrochloric acid, a particulate, is detectable in a cloud chamber. Using these processes, scientists at General Electric developed people sniffer detection capabilities for the Chemical Corps . . . the people sniffer was a helicopter-mounted configuration called the XM3 airborne personnel detector . . . used almost daily in LOH-6, OH-58, and UH-1 helicopters."

The response from the NLF was less expensive and far less sophisticated. They hung buckets or helmets of mud and urine in trees far away from their location and the American forces dropped napalm, Agent Orange and anti-personnel cluster bombs[42] on deserted areas while women repaired the Ho Chi Minh Trail.

At one point in the film the camera went far off message as it recorded trees, the earth, the sky and then nothing. The photographer had been killed by enemy fire. Within a moment another person picked the camera up and continued filming. It was a historic document and all who saw it experienced an emotional response.

I nominated it for first prize in its category. I noticed that other judges had given the film high marks in their written and posted scorecards. Before the balloting began, not secret but blatantly open, we were addressed by the East German bureaucrat in charge of the festival. He said, without explaining, that the film was not going to win a prize. He proposed another film, a well-made documentary about working

---

42. During May 2008, one hundred and eleven nations signed a treaty banning cluster bombs. The United States, at that time led by President George W. Bush, refused to participate.

people in the Soviet Union, in my view a more pedestrian subject. It became clear that the Sino-Soviet split had its implication in Leipzig. The Soviet leaders were concerned that a victorious Vietnam might become an ally of China.

I argued for the film and finally, although not another judge supported me, our official leader decided to withdraw his objection. The film was awarded a prize and most of the judges, except for a fairly well-known English author, declined to speak to me thereafter, apparently by agreement.

The author invited me to dinner. I thought he had been assigned to me as a mission. He began, "Mr. Lane, the government here said that they knew they were taking a chance with you; they knew you were an independent and not subject to any particular political discipline. But they thought that you knew how things worked."

I asked him to explain "how things worked." He said, "If you just go along you will be invited back next year as the American film judge, as we all have been several times." I answered that I did want to see more of historic Leipzig, but the price was too high.

He then went directly to the point. "We are both authors. We know that the Soviet Union and its allies do not abide by international conventions regarding copyright laws. They publish my books in the Soviet Union and several of the other countries. True, I cannot negotiate advances or royalties but they are fairly generous and they keep on printing my works. They support my work and they do it quite legitimately, and I am willing to accept their judgment in other matters. They also publish many American authors."

He pointed out that although *Rush to Judgment* was successful in the United States and Western Europe, it was never published in the Soviet Union. The reason, he said, is that I had not demonstrated sufficient respect for them, and I was repeating that mistake at the film festival. I thanked him for his candor. I suspect, but I do not know, that he likely reported back that his mission had been accomplished.

The next day the judges met again to award prizes in other categories. My favorite then was a very low-budget film made by film students in a class in East Germany. It was about a statue of Kathe Kollwitz in East Berlin. She was a German artist who expressed her concern for the victims of hunger, war and poverty through her drawings, woodcuts, etchings and lithographs. During World War I, when an appeal for children and elderly men to join the armed forces of Germany was made, she courageously opposed her government and said, "There has been enough of dying. Let not another man fall."

I had long admired her work and her perspective. The film began with a statue of Kollwitz seated in a chair. Citizens sitting on park benches or strolling through the park noticed that some children had climbed up onto her lap and were touching the statue's face. Other kids were sitting on the arm of the statue.

The pedestrians and those reposing on benches were asked about the scene. On camera they proclaimed that it was insulting to allow children to climb all over the sculpture. Each had a suggestion to keep the children away. *A sign should be posted. An officer should be on duty. A fence, over which the children cannot climb, should be erected.*

The film ended with a brief interview of the artist who had created the statue. He was asked what he had in mind. He simply stated that Kathe so loved children that he sculpted a seated figure with flat planes so that children could climb up onto it and sit in her lap and touch her face.

The controlling official said that the film I had nominated was not "political," followed by the dreaded and dismissive proclamation that it "lacked socialist reality." I observed that it was quite political, but I conceded that it was not as political as his disparagement of it. There was a period of embarrassed silence. No other judge expressed an agreement with me although several had previously given the film high marks on the posted scorecards.

I was never invited back to be the American judge at the Leipzig International Documentary Film Festival.

No book written by me has ever been published in the Soviet Union. The Soviet bureaucrats were apparently no more enamored of an independent voice than were their counterparts in Washington.

As is the case with most authors, I have not been concerned with the politics of the publishing house that agrees to publish my work. In 1967, Taurus Ediciones, S.A., with offices in Madrid, Spain, published *Juicio Precipitado [Rush to Judgment]*.

Francisco Franco had seized control of Spain with the help of Nazi Germany and Fascist Italy in 1939. He was still the dictator when Taurus published *Juicio Precipitado,* and he continued on for almost another decade until his death.

An editor with the Spanish publisher, no doubt closely associated with the government, met with me. He advised me that he and his government were aware of the threats I had received in the United States and of my own government's expressed hostility to my efforts to uncover the facts. He concluded that if at anytime I had the need to seek sanctuary, Spain would be willing to welcome me. He reminded me that even the great Zola was forced to flee France for looking into and publishing information about the Dreyfus case. I thanked him for the offer and assured him that I was quite certain that I would not ever feel compelled to leave my country. I added, however, that if the circumstances required it, I would gratefully accept his offer.

I was bemused by the fact that while Falangist Spain published my work, the Soviet Union refused to do so and all of the countries allied with it during the Cold War, including Poland, Czechoslovakia, Hungary, East Germany, Bulgaria, Romania and others outside of Europe, also refused. During the period after the assassination until the agreement with the British publisher Bodley Head, I was without funds and an offer from any country to accept my work and pay even a nominal fee would have been greatly appreciated—but no such offer came.

I had asked my British publishers to attempt to have the book published in every country. They tried, but the Soviet bloc was adamant. The questions that lingered—did the Soviets oppose my inquiry? And if so, why?—may have been answered later in one of the top secret documents I received from the government in 1975.

The minutes of a Warren Commission secret session revealed that the CIA had told Chief Justice Earl Warren a legend. It stated that Lee Oswald, who was the assassin, had met with the leader of the KGB in charge of assassinations in the United States while they were in Mexico City. Oswald, according to the story, then went back to the United States and killed the president. The CIA also told Warren that the Soviet Union was not involved in the assassination but that if the facts were revealed Americans would believe that the USSR was complicit and World War III might result. Warren then decided to state that Oswald was the lone assassin in order to prevent that catastrophe. The fact that Oswald was not involved in the assassination and that he had not been in Mexico City was not known to Warren; he relied upon the CIA and enlisted in the crusade to save civilization.

The theory, concededly unsupported by documents, that the CIA had also advised the Soviet Union of its precarious position, and cautioned them against asserting that there had been a conspiracy to assassinate the president, might account for that country's reluctance to publish books challenging the commission, including *Rush to Judgment*.

A Bodyguard of Lies

*"Truth is so precious that she should always
be attended by a bodyguard of lies."*
—Winston Churchill

Churchill was speaking of conditions in wartime. Unfortunately, the spy organizations consider themselves to always be at war, and too often against the rights of their own citizens. Since World War II the United States has been involved in a series of wars, some never ending. Yet even during the pacific periods, when our country was at peace, the CIA was at war. To understand that is to comprehend the CIA's mindset.

As was the case with *Rush to Judgment,* the intelligence agencies in the United States during the early 1990s were concerned about my manuscript *Plausible Denial.* Since the book demonstrated that the Central Intelligence Agency was complicit in the arrangements to assassinate President Kennedy, that Agency opposed its publication through its numerous assets. Their reach did not extend to a very small publisher, Thunder's Mouth Press, but they no doubt felt confident that it was not likely to reach a wide audience.

That prediction was incorrect and the reviews were far more favorable than I could have predicted given the evidence cited in the book and the inescapable conclusion of the CIA's guilt. The *Los Angeles Times* wrote that the "evidence for Hunt's complicity is quite persuasive." The *San Francisco Chronicle* asserted that *Plausible Denial* was "a convincing indictment of the Central Intelligence Agency as the primary conspirator behind the murder of John Fitzgerald Kennedy on November 22, 1963." *TIME* magazine said that the book "targets high-level CIA figures as the plotters behind the assassination" and added its own comment that "20 years of investigations have shown that the CIA was no stranger to complicity in assassinations." *Kirkus Reviews* concluded that the book "sounds like the last word on the assassination."

Of course that suggestion or hope could not be fulfilled. The CIA, with its unsupervised multi-million-dollar budget and with its bought assets in the media, was certain to respond. That agency had been engaged in efforts to destroy me just for raising a question about the Warren Commission's magic bullet theory. *Plausible Denial* went far beyond that simple analysis and led to the doorstep in Langley. An awful and mighty fabricated response was inevitable. It was predictable that it would come from a person on the CIA payroll, unwilling to admit who his masters were.

The CIA, in a now fully exposed cover story, stated that E. Howard Hunt, the Watergate felon and a CIA operative who made no secret of his hatred for President Kennedy, was not in Dallas on November 22, 1963. Only Hunt and the CIA made that claim. However, Hunt had told several contradictory stories under oath about his whereabouts that day. Eyewitnesses, including those who had been employed by the CIA, later stated that they saw Hunt in Dallas on the day Kennedy was assassinated. There is testimony that Hunt was the paymaster for the assassination and that he was seen in Dallas paying the participants.

Hunt had stated that he was home with his children watching the tragic events on television for seventy-two hours starting just after the assassination. Hunt's own adult children refused to testify at his trial in support of that false story. Not one was willing to come forward to support that alibi. A jury sitting in the United States District Court found against Hunt and his alibi. I wrote about the trial and cited the relevant evidence in *Plausible Denial*.[43]

After the trial, Hunt constructively admitted his role in the assassination. In an interview with a reporter for the *Financial Times* of Canada, Hunt stated that he would reveal the entire story of his complicity if paid several million dollars so that he could leave the country and move to a nation without extradition agreements with the

---

43. Mark Lane, *Plausible Denial* (Thunder's Mouth Press, 1991).

United States. And finally in a deathbed confession to his son St. John Hunt, he admitted his role in the assassination of the president.

Christopher Andrew has offered himself as an objective historian, author, and host of television programs.[44] He has neglected to state that he is a much-prized asset of the CIA. Andrew lectures for the CIA, and makes a living writing books for the CIA that are favorable to the CIA and are featured and promoted on the CIA's official website, cia.gov. He also is paid to write reviews denouncing books that are critical of the CIA.

While he proclaims that he is a historian, he appears primarily to be a CIA transmission belt; he obtains information from his associates in the intelligence communities and passes it along to an unsuspecting public as the result of his own research. He is British and the only non-American to have been trusted by the CIA to have served on the Twentieth Century Fund Task Force on the Future of the U.S. Intelligence Community. An English history professor who has access to top secret information that most Americans don't even suspect exists, and is helping to determine the future of the CIA and other spy organizations, raises questions about his independence and objectivity that he is unwilling to answer.

Andrew admits that he read *Plausible Denial*. Nevertheless, Andrew wrote that Hunt "had been wrongly accused of being in Dallas on the day of the assassination."[45] In a book filled with citations and footnotes, many of them misleading or inaccurate, Andrew offered no citation to the record, no fact and no basis for that statement. The only truthful citation could have been "the CIA told me to write that." Since Hunt was in Dallas there could be no evidence to the contrary.

Andrew also states that I had been a successful writer, but during "the late 1960s and early 1970s" I was less successful due to the fact that the "most popular books were now those that exposed some of the excesses of the conspiracy theorists."[46] Those assertions are false. Andrew cites only *Case Closed,* a book that received national attention when it was published in 1993 and that Andrew apparently believed had a

---

44. For example, *The Sword and the Shield,* by Christopher Andrew and Vasili Mitrokhin, Basic Books, 1999.
45. Christopher Andrew and Vasili Mitrokhin, *The Sword and the Shield,* (Basic Books, 1999.)
46. Ibid.

retroactive impact upon me during the 1960s and 1970s. Subsequently when the author of *Case Closed* was charged with misstatements, he retained me to represent him, publicly explaining that he believed that had Oswald lived and if I served as his counsel he would have been acquitted.

Andrew neglects to mention that in 1991 *Plausible Denial* was a *New York Times* best seller. While facts are not determinative for this historian, for those who prefer fabrications created in Langley when presented through the filter of an academic English accent, Andrew is your man.

Vasili Mitrokhin, coauthor of *The Sword and the Shield* with Andrew, was born in Central Russia in 1922, and joined the MGB during 1948. In 1953 the name of the Soviet secret police organization was changed to the KGB. Mitrokhin was particularly inept and was reprimanded by his superiors in 1956; he was then re-graded for his unsatisfactory performance and designated as unfit for operational tasks. He was sent to the archives as a librarian.

In 1992 he met with CIA officers in Riga, Latvia, showed them some handwritten notes and asked for payment and a safe and luxurious asylum in the United States. He told a story so fanciful that even the imaginative and eager CIA officers considered it to be an entirely fraudulent effort. His documents were examined and the CIA rejected them.

He said that his pages were documents that he had created, at first by looking at KGB files starting in 1972, remembering what he had seen and then, when he returned home, working from his memory, he wrote down all of the specifics including names, code names, dates and all important facts. Wilhelm and Jacob Grimm might have been impressed, but unlike the desperate Mitrokhin, they honestly entitled their work *Fairy Tales*. Although in an office surrounded by copy machines, he had not copied one single page of any Soviet document, preferring to rely upon his memory.

Later he claimed that he had spent almost all day, every day, copying the files onto pieces of paper in his own handwriting. He then, he said, smuggled them out of the building, knowing that if he was caught he might be executed. Apparently he never thought of using a copy machine to print one page to substantiate his claims.

The rules of the records room that the KGB called the Archives required that no one person could alone have access to any files; that employee was required to have another person accompany him while examining records.

How Mitrokhin managed to spend so many hours alone with the records for a very long time, complete no other task that had been assigned to him and escape notice is not explained, perhaps because it is inexplicable.

When the CIA reviewed Mitrokhin's claims, they were struck by the absence of one page of proof that real documents existed. The CIA rejected his notes, his proposed deal and his story. Scholars and experts in the field asked pertinent questions that received no answer. How could Mitrokhin devote almost all of his time to memorizing documents and later hand-copying documents? Had he no other duties? Didn't his supervisors note the absence of the work that he was being paid for?

Mitrokhin kept shopping around for a lucrative asylum opportunity. He approached British intelligence, MI6, a group both less meticulous and apparently more imaginative than the CIA, and an organization that had particular experience in exploiting a similar opportunity to its own advantage. He neglected to tell that spy organization that the CIA had rejected his offer.

The CIA and Andrew assert that Mitrokhin "re-copied" his entire "archive" during seven years of silence after he met with the CIA and British intelligence officers, during which time he revised his notes apparently to order. It also provided time for the agency to find an author both loyal and avaricious enough to publish blatantly false allegations.

Questions about Andrew arose as well. How did it come about that he had entered into an exclusive and lucrative deal with Rupert Murdoch to publish the material that made serious, and again unproven, charges against Murdoch's enemies in the British Labour Party. Murdoch and his associates were less careful in demeaning Michael Foot, the leader of the Labour Party from 1980 to 1983, claiming he knowingly accepted cash from KGB agents. Foot immediately filed an action for libel against Murdoch and his newspapers. He was successful and won an award for very substantial damages.

His own literary agent describes Christopher Andrew as the "in-house historian for MI5." Andrew's enrollment in the Security Service drew criticism from authentic historians and other commentators who questioned his impartiality.

One victim wrote sardonically that Andrew was the "loyal servant" of the "Ministry of Truth." A member of the House of Lords questioned the handling of the Mitrokhin material. Another member of the Parliament asked why the files remained secret and noted the "propensity to exaggerate, especially when there was the possibility of a financial return on the publications of their books."

Andrew published false information about me in *The Sword and the Shield*. Andrew apparently claims that a payment, $500, was made to me by a Canadian lawyer for airfare to a conference of the International Association of Democratic Lawyers in Budapest and that the sum had in some mysterious way been provided by the KGB.[47]

Secondly, according to Andrew and his lawyers, a Russian journalist was based in New York City starting in 1966. Apparently, Andrew claims that during that period some unnamed close friend working with me gave me $1,500 to encourage me to write a book that I had already written, obtained a publisher for, and was editing in London. When Andrew published the false information, I contacted a leading London law firm, Reynolds Porter Chamberlain, solicitors, who demanded that the publisher withdraw its false allegations. Counsel for the publishers responded that they never thought I had done anything wrong and that Andrew had stated quite clearly that, "Lane had not been told the source of the money" and that if it was given to me it came from "a close friend" of mine. The statement was an outright lie, but it was carefully structured so that it could not be the basis for a lawsuit since it accused me of no wrong–doing. I suspect that someone at the CIA had clued Andrew in on how to make false, but protected, statements. For example, Andrew claimed that Harry Hopkins, one of President Franklin Delano Roosevelt's closest advisors and the man largely responsible for the creation of the New Deal, the cornerstone of the domestic recovery plan for America, knowingly passed secret

---

47. I did correspond with a Canadian lawyer who asked me to raise with the Soviets the false imprisonment of a political prisoner. The CIA was aware of the fact that I persisted in that request and added that the prisoner was being held in solitary confinement and should be afforded the right to see local counsel. The request was met with a hostile and somewhat public response informing me that I was rude to persist, almost to the point of saying that I was no longer welcome in that Soviet bloc country. The Canadian lawyer's politics were well-known; he was decidedly anti-Soviet.

information to the Soviets and money to the Communist Party of the United States. Those absurd charges were clearly defamatory, but again Andrew was insulated. He made those allegations only after Hopkins had died and there could be no legal action taken.

The Russian journalist may have been in New York, but at that time I was not. I also was meeting with editors of the Bodley Head, an established, conservative British publishing firm that had agreed to publish *Rush to Judgment*. With me were Deirdre Griswold and Michael Lester; both helped with additional research and Lester served as the typist for some edits.

I was living in a flat on Kings Road, near World's End, owned by Lord Russell's peace foundation while I completed editing my book. Many folks visited me there including officers of Russell's foundation, Paul McCartney, documentary filmmaker Emile de Antonio and representatives of numerous publishers and newspapers. It was only after I completed my work and the publisher had signed a contract for world rights to my book that I returned to New York. That trip was arranged because the English publishers had negotiated a deal with Holt, Rinehart and Winston for American rights to the book. Both the American and British editions were published in 1966.

I was very encouraged with the success of the book, and I was not in need of any encouragement from the KGB. I also had been given a couple of advances and was not in need of $1,500, and no friend or associate would have thought it appropriate to offer me any money and none did. It was at that time, as we have seen, that the CIA sought to subvert my work. I also maintained records of all funds that were donated. One sum was large enough to permit me to buy an airplane ticket to Dallas from New York. It was given to me directly by Corliss Lamont, a well-known and politically active philanthropist and leader of the American Humanist Association. He also made major financial contributions to Harvard and Columbia. The second-largest contribution was from Woody Allen. It was fifty dollars.

Mitrokhin had told the CIA of his files during 1992. *Plausible Denial,* demonstrating the CIA's complicity in the assassination, was published in 1991. Yet it was not until 1999 that the allegation that the KGB had encouraged my efforts was published for the first time. The CIA was uncharacteristically patient for a very long time, if that agency is to be believed. It had, in the past, organized intricate assassination plans against dissenters, including heads of state, in far less time.

The normal channel regularly observed by the Soviet Union to "encourage" authors was to publish their works in the Soviet Union and in its numerous dependent states, as I have observed. No book that I have ever written was ever published in any of the Soviet bloc countries.

Andrew and Mitrokhin stated that the KGB gave the money to a person who was a friend of mine who then may have given it to me. There was no such transaction and Mitrokhin and Andrew did not identify the name of the "friend." They could not have fabricated the "friend" without my being able to deal directly with that falsity. When I demonstrated that I had kept records of all contributions, Max Holland, another CIA media asset who spread the story, then added that the money could have been given to me in very small amounts. Perhaps when I was discussing the case each night for months from the stage of a small theatre in New York, a couple of hundred Russian agents, wearing long leather coats, slipped in unnoticed and each paid a dollar for admission. It would have been easier for the Soviet Union to publish my book, as they had done for so many other American authors they supported. In an effort to put the story to rest, I wrote to Andrew shortly after the book was published and asked for a response:

Dear Mr. Andrew:

I am in the process of completing a book which makes an analysis of your claim that the KGB maintained a "regular contact" with me and that that organization sent some funds to me through an intermediary who was a close friend of mine. Those assertions as well as numerous other assertions in your book, *The Sword and the Shield*, are untrue.

Although you had neither the courtesy nor the curiosity to contact me before publishing your false statements about me in spite of the fact that you claim to be an historian, I am interested in securing and publishing your version of the story. Therefore I would appreciate it if you would answer the following questions.

How many pages of the Mitrokhin Archive have you seen?

Is each page dated?

What is the name of the close friend of mine who was used by the KGB?

On what dates were funds allegedly given to me?

Since several witnesses have stated that they saw and talked with E. Howard Hunt in Dallas on November 22, 1963, since all of Hunt's various and contradictory alibis have been proven to be false, since his own children refuse to support his first alibi that he was with them that day, since a jury sitting in a United States District Court has rejected his story, and finally since Hunt stated that he would tell the entire story of his role in the assassination if paid adequately, what is your basis that he was wrongly accused of being in Dallas on that day? I note that you offer no citation for that false allegation in your book.

Have you received funds from the Central Intelligence Agency for any services that you have rendered to them, including appearing at lectures for them, writing books for them which present the Agency's views, and writing hostile criticism of books which do not?

I note that in an interview you spoke disparagingly of a committee of the United States Senate, chaired by Senator Frank Church. Most contemporary historians consider Senator Church's work to have been a most worthwhile effort. On what basis do you disparage the work of Senator Church and the other members of the United States Senate who served with him in reviewing American intelligence agencies?

You state that I had limited success during the late 1960's and early 1970's because my work had been exposed by Gerald Posner in a book called *Case Closed*. Since *Case Closed* was published in 1993, can you explain how it impacted what you refer to as my limited success during the 1960's and 1970's?

As you know, *Plausible Denial* was published in 1991 in hardback, and the following year in paperback. That book was a New York Times bestseller in 1992 for months, and sold approximately as many books as did *Rush to Judgment* which was *New York Times* number one bestselling book in 1966. As you know, I am likely the only author to have written two books about the assassination of President Kennedy, approximately a quarter of a century apart, both of which were *New York Times* bestselling books.

Since you falsely assert that the KGB wanted to assist me, can you explain why *Rush to Judgment* was published widely and successfully in Great Britain, France, Italy, Germany and Spain, as well as throughout Asia and Latin America, while the book was not published to my knowledge in the Soviet Union or any nation allied with it and no publisher from any of those countries under the control of the Soviet Union ever sent me a single penny for my work on the Kennedy assassination investigation.

If the Soviets so approved of my work, why did they not publish it? This is an area in which you have some expertise; the CIA approves of your work, places you on high level committees about the future of American intelligence and, in all probability, compensates you for your services rendered to the CIA.

I know you have been represented by counsel, but this letter is not related to a lawsuit and I represent to you that none of your responses, should you respond, will be utilized in any legal action against you. As you probably are aware the statute of limitations has long since expired regarding your defamatory actions.

Very truly yours,
MARK LANE

Andrew has never replied.

But wait, there is more. Andrew and Mitrokhin tar with the same brush some other Americans as well. It seems that, according to them, "a Democratic activist in California" was "recruited as a KGB agent during a visit to Russia" and may have influenced his "wide circle of influential contacts."[48] Andrew lists them. They are Governor Jerry Brown, Senator Alan Cranston, Senator Eugene McCarthy, Senator Edward Kennedy, Senator Abraham Ribicoff, Senator J. William Fulbright and Congressman John Conyers.[49] He also had "prolonged conversations" with Senator Jacob Javits. And he infiltrated the campaigns of Jimmy Carter, Governor Brown and Senators Cranston,

---

48. Andrew and Mitrokhin, *The Sword and the Shield*. 291.
49. Ibid.

Kennedy and Rubicoff.[50] To make the list you must be a Democrat, Jewish or a very distinguished patriot. Being all three makes you a certain target.

Allow me to save you some effort and the cost of a postage stamp. There is no need to write a letter to Andrew asking for the name of the super KGB spy, the one likely without peer in history. Andrew states that the name of the KGB agent is not known. Perhaps Mitrokhin, with a mind so phenomenal that he could memorize thousands of documents and recite them verbatim, may have forgotten it or perhaps the KGB official who wrote the story forgot to mention his name. Something like my "friend" who never gave me any money.

---

50. Ibid.

The Government and the Media Respond

The CIA had refused to release thousands of documents describing its role in matters relating to the assassination. Together with the ACLU, I brought an action in the United States District Court under the Freedom of Information Act to obtain the records. In spite of claims of national security concerns made by the agency, the court ordered that it produce the documents. The CIA instructed its "assets" in the national news media in detail to criticize me and my work because, it said, the agency had been involved in the assassination. One CIA memorandum specifically stated the methods that journalists who were their "assets" should employ in that effort, even suggesting the language that should be used to destroy me. Remarkably, *New York Times* journalist Anthony Lewis, referred to as "a prominent liberal intellectual," used in his stories the numerous and specific arguments suggested by the CIA; echoes of that campaign to falsify the record still persist.

When the Warren Commission Report was published in 1964, Lewis embraced its conclusions at once, although the report was allegedly based upon evidence, including testimony and exhibits, that was classified top secret and not available to the news media or the public. Lewis did not hesitate to make a profit from his work by writing introductions to commercial editions of the Warren Report, and I suspect he was paid more for that short and simplistic panegyrical endorsement than the sum offered to me as an advance for world rights to *Rush to Judgment*.

Later, when the commission released twenty-six volumes of thousands of pages of testimony and exhibits,[51] Lewis, that very day, wrote that all of the evidence demonstrated that the Warren Commission conclusions were accurate. I studied the material for the better part of a year, working almost eighteen hours each day. It was only after I completed that enormous task that I wrote to Lewis and asked him how he had been able to get through the material in just a few hours. He has not replied. In criticizing his work I never characterized his motives, often did not even mention him, but rather referred to him generically and never engaged in name calling. But a recitation of the facts demonstrated that in this matter he was a stranger to the truth. Lewis was furious.

On November 29, 1978, Lewis wrote an unprecedented *ad hominem* attack devoted entirely to me that he published in *The New York Times.* He named it "The Mark of Zorro." The title is interesting since "Zorro" was the vicious code name devised by the Federal Bureau of Investigation to designate Dr. Martin Luther King, Jr., in its efforts to destroy him. It was chosen as a sexual innuendo to demean Dr. King by implying that he was a "swordsman."

I had just returned from Jonestown, Guyana, and a number of publishers had contacted me, each seeking to publish a book to be written by me about the massacre. I had not solicited those contacts. I had not decided to write a book about the matter, and had not stated that I was interested in writing one. I had no literary agent, and no one had stated on my behalf that I might write about the subject. Many television and news organizations sought interviews; network crews literally camped at my doorstep even after I asked them to leave and said I had no statement to make. Many people I had met in Guyana, some of them friends and many others children, had died there, and while it was obviously far less traumatic for me than for their families, I knew that I needed time to absorb the impact of the events before deciding if I was capable of understanding what had occurred and who was ultimately responsible. Among those offering book contracts were

---

51. Volumes 1 through 15 contained the transcripts of the testimony of hundreds of witnesses; Volumes 16 through 26, many of them comprised of between 900 and 1,000 pages, included thousands of documents.

numerous major publishers, including the book publishing company for *The New York Times*. I declined to meet with any of them.

I remained in my home and office with my loyal collie, my law partner April Ferguson and her young daughter. Since the telephone rang incessantly (this was before the advent of e-mail), I severed communication with the insistent media by leaving it off the hook. However, my partner's daughter wanted to make calls to her friends. I said that she could as long as she remembered to disconnect the line after each call. She forgot once; it rang immediately and she answered it. It was Barbara Walters asking to speak to me. It was one thing not to answer the phone but quite another to refuse to talk to Barbara when she knew where I was and since I knew her and respected her as an honest journalist. We talked and I agreed to an interview with her. It was the only media request that I accepted.

And then Lewis struck. His two-column article was featured on the op-ed page of the *Times*.[52] He referred to me as a "ghoul," a "pitchman," one who had been "preying on the gullible" and a "creature." He was outraged that I had questioned the findings of the Warren Commission. He falsely accused me of misconduct in Jonestown and said that there would be civil suits for damages against me and that there would be proceedings against me by the bar associations. He said, in reference to my work in writing *Rush to Judgment,* that I made a profit by selling "assassination bumper stickers" and charged "high lecture fees" for profit. Everything that Lewis said was untruthful and none of his fanciful predictions were realized. No bar association even looked into the matter since there was nothing for them to consider. No one filed a law suit since there was no basis for one. I never sold a bumper sticker or even displayed one nor have I seen one about an assassination. Often I spoke about the assassination of President Kennedy without asking for an honorarium, and when a modest fee was offered, the funds went directly to the Citizens' Commission of Inquiry, a group with a distinguished board of directors, in order to send investigators and researchers to Dallas to interview witnesses.

Lewis had questioned my ethics, but presented no facts. Of course, I was not the only person Lewis defamed. When the great American filmmaker Oliver Stone made *JFK*, he was subject to unprecedented attacks. Lewis played a major role in the character assassination of

52. *The New York Times,* November 30, 1978. A23.

Stone. He condemned Oliver's "character," stating that to suggest that Warren engaged in a "cover-up" was "contemptible." Yet years before, the lawyers for the Warren Commission had conceded that Warren had engaged in a cover-up and sought to justify those actions by stating that they were required for national security reasons.

However the sting of Lewis's diatribe was not its falsity and name calling, but rather its direction to the news media and the publishing industry. Lewis, demonstrating his contempt for the First Amendment, directed "talk show hosts and editors" to refuse to permit me to be heard. He directed publishers to refuse to publish any book I might write. He said that "it is time for the decent people of the United States to tune out Mark Lane." Immediately, *The New York Times* withdrew its offer to publish a book by me as an eyewitness to the Jonestown massacre. When I decided to write *The Strongest Poison,* every publisher in the United States that I contacted refused to consider it, citing the Lewis manifesto. One small publishing house, Hawthorn Books, a division of Elsevier-Dutton, a company based in Holland, offered a contract. I celebrated with the representative of the publishing company at a restaurant in New York after the contract was signed, and I asked her if she was familiar with the Lewis direction. She said the company had read the op-ed piece and decided that "This is America. You can't do that here."

Lewis has taught at Columbia University's School of Journalism, has held the James Madison chair in First Amendment Issues since 1982, and has been honored by a coalition against censorship for his "commitment" to First Amendment rights. No, this is not an attempt at humor.

Apparently the Lewis concept of the First Amendment is that he will defend with all the honor he may muster the right of any American to exercise free speech so long as the content is consistent with the Lewis agenda. Failing that test he may attempt to deny the right to free speech and freedom of the press. Our founders, among them Tom Paine, Thomas Jefferson and John Peter Zenger, and yes, James Madison, had a different view.

Later, a false biography of me was published in *The New York Times* as a feature story under a four-column headline.[53] It was written by Pranay Gupte. It said that "Representing the American Indians, he faced riot, arson and conspiracy charges after an incident at Wounded Knee

---

53. *The New York Times*, November 21, 1978.

South Dakota, he [Lane] declared that the trial would be a 'major civil rights case for the American Indians.' But the Indians were convicted, and legal experts do not view the case as a major civil rights test." The "incident" Gupte referred to was a seventy-one day occupation of Wounded Knee by the American Indian Movement which became the most publicized story of 1973. The "Indians" who were defendants at the trial were Dennis Banks and Russell Means. We won the case. It was fully reported in *The New York Times*. The case was dismissed by United States District Court Judge Fred Nichol, based upon a motion I had filed, due to the ongoing misconduct of the government prosecutors. The government appealed to the United States Court of Appeals for the Eighth Circuit; that appeal was unanimously rejected by the Court. The government declined to ask for a United States Supreme Court review, thereby finalizing the case and certifying the victory of the defendants.

Since all of that had been published in *The New York Times*, one would think that Mr. Gupte, who was at *The New York Times*, might have noticed it. Gupte also said that while I was a member of the New York State legislature from "Manhattan's West Side," I "questioned the ethics of a former Speaker." He reported that several persons had characterized my conduct in that matter as "irresponsible." I represented the East Side of Manhattan, including Yorkville, which is entirely on the East Side, and East Harlem, which, as its name implies, is also entirely on the East Side. Joseph Carlino was not the former Speaker when I raised the question; he was the Speaker of the Assembly. *The New York Times* supported and endorsed my work in that effort as did many thousands of people who journeyed to Albany to support the inquiry and to urge that Rockefeller's $100 million fallout shelter program be abandoned. Due to the support of newspapers in New York City and the public, the program was never implemented and together we had saved the state a huge sum. All of that too was reported in *The New York Times* at the time.

I called Mr. Gupte at the *Times* in an attempt to secure the basis for his entirely false information. He never returned my calls. However, many of the reporters there and other staff members were friends or acquaintances of mine and I was able to obtain Mr. Gupte's home telephone number, which I believe was in Brooklyn. I called him at home and after he admitted that he was Pranay Gupte, and that took several minutes, I asked him to name the "legal experts" who told him that the Wounded Knee case was not a major civil rights test. He said he did not remember a single name. Of course, I knew there was no expert because anyone familiar with the facts would have known that we had prevailed, the Indians were not convicted, and the case was dismissed. I asked Gupte how he had heard that we had lost the case. He said he could not remember. Of course, the Gupte piece began by stating that my opposition to the Warren Report "has proven remunerative," thus echoing the CIA direction that my "financial interest" in the Kennedy assassination should be stressed whenever the subject of the murder was relevant.

I do not know if Gupte was paid by the CIA for his work on their behalf, but if he sought my counsel I would advise he might take that matter up with his shop steward and agent and remind them, in the words of Othello, *he has done the state some service and they know't.*

Gupte publishes on his website his ethical standard for journalists that he has named, "The Pranay Principles." I insist that I am not making this up. It is reassuring to know that he who defames you in *The New York Times* by publishing false allegations has created a code of ethics, albeit self-named and alliterative. His Second Commandment begins, "Never forget who signs your check." He has demonstrated that he has not.

I have singled out *The New York Times* for this discussion, although its reportage was rather typical of major newspapers, primarily because it is the most august daily newspaper and the only one I read every day and generally feel comfortable relying upon. I have noticed similar coverage in many other publications. The exceptions of which I am aware are few, but do include the *St. Louis Post-Dispatch*, primarily due to the work of Richard Dudman, and the *San Francisco Chronicle*, due to the work of its book review editor.

I still begin each morning with a cup of coffee and *The New York Times*, and I assure you it is not due to some latent charitable instinct on my part. When I think of that newspaper, of course I still remember its past villains, including reporter John Crewdson, Lewis and Gupte, but I also recall with affection and respect the finest journalist I ever met, Peter Khiss, and during the early days of my law practice, Jack Roth, who covered the Criminal Courts Building in Manhattan, and the many friends of mine who worked for that institution. When we talked about the Warren Report, most seemed ashamed of the position taken by the newspaper. I know also that institutions do not have an irrevocable persona, but tend to reconsider positions with a new generation of reporters and editors. I believe the *Times* owes, if not an apology, an explanation to its readers.

The intelligence agencies and their assets in the media had made it clear that anyone who pursued the truth about the death of the president did so at some personal cost and risk. The fact that these forces made it difficult for many of the researchers, investigators and authors to obtain and publish information that did not conform to the orthodox perception, however, should be noted.

The CIA and the Media

A fter the CIA had widely distributed its then-secret memorandum instructing its assets to destroy critics of the Warren Report, including me, and offered specific language for book reviewers, columnists and interviewers to employ in those efforts, it developed a method for making the false charges appear to originate elsewhere. A survey of the language that the assets used reveals how many of them utilized the methods and even precise and identical language that had been provided to them.

This is the method now employed. An independent publication is chosen to mask the source. A CIA puppet is placed there and given an impressive title. The CIA then provides the propaganda. It appears as an independent concept when published. The CIA, employing its official website, cia.gov, then cites the "independent" writer and the "independent" publication as the source as it spreads its false allegations throughout the world. In the intelligence world some refer to this as sheep-dipping. Their wolf had been dipped into a sheep's bath and came up smelling quite neutral.

In 2002 Max Holland, describing himself as a "*Nation* contributing editor" with that publication's consent and approval, published disinformation in *Studies in Intelligence*, either because *The Nation* declined to publish it or because it was not offered to it. Since then the modus operandi of the CIA's mole has been refined and is a bit more sophisticated, and, therefore, more obscure.

During 2006, Max Holland struck yet again. This time his article was published first in the *Nation*, apparently at the behest of the Central

Intelligence Agency, and then widely publicized through the use of the official website of the CIA, describing the article as one written by a "contributing editor" of *The Nation*. At the outset, Holland informs the readers of *The Nation* that Norman Redlich, "a *Nation* contributor since 1951," was a member of the Warren Commission "staff." Holland also states that there were "twenty-seven people" on the commission staff. Redlich was not a staff member; he was one of the fourteen lawyers listed as "Assistant Counsel."[54] There were twelve people listed as "staff members;" Redlich was not one of them. In addition, there was a General Counsel, who also was not a staff member.

The article was entitled "The JFK Lawyers' Conspiracy." It claimed that four attorneys had entered into a conspiracy to place "the Warren Report into undeserved disrepute." The four lawyers referred to were New Orleans District Attorney Jim Garrison, Senator Gary Hart, G. Robert Blakey, "who was a professor at Cornell Law School when he became chief counsel and staff director of the House Select Committee on Assassinations (HSCA)," and me. The word conspiracy has a precise meaning and definition. According to the standard, *Black's Law Dictionary* (8th ed.), a conspiracy is "An agreement by two or more persons to commit an unlawful act, coupled with an intent to achieve the agreement's objective, and (in most states) action or conduct that furthers the agreement; a combination for an unlawful purpose. 18 USCA § 371." If Holland is neither an attorney, nor has access to a copy of the dictionary, it would have been a good idea for him to have consulted one or the other. He might also ask a lawyer the meaning of the word "defamation."

The first count in Holland's fanciful "conspiracy" was my suggesting that there be a thorough investigation into the assassination, which Holland states began in 1964. He falsely claims that I was involved in spreading "innuendo" about an ostensibly sinister delay in the Warren Commission's investigation and that I wrote *Rush to Judgment* two years later, changing my position. I did not criticize the time spent by the commission in its inquiry; I criticized its inaccurate conclusions. The title, *Rush to Judgment*, rests upon my observation that on the very day of the assassination, J. Edgar Hoover, Director of the FBI, stated that Oswald was the assassin and that he had acted alone. Those statements

---

54. Warren Commission Report, p. v.

made by Hoover were made before any investigation had begun. When the Warren Report was published in 1964, it adopted the conclusions that Hoover had proclaimed as fact almost two years before. It is very difficult to find a single truthful assertion in Holland's article, although one exists.

I called for an inquiry, conducted my own investigation, and subsequently published *Rush to Judgment,* all done before I ever met Senator Hart, Jim Garrison or Blakey. In fact, I have not yet met Senator Hart. The only time I met Blakey was after he had been appointed counsel for the HSCA thirteen years after my work had begun. It was a formal meeting that lasted a very short period of time in which Blakey made clear that he preferred to ignore evidence of a conspiracy and to utilize the CIA's second line of defense that if Oswald didn't act alone, organized crime did it. I clearly pointed out my opposition to Blakey's concepts and left the hearing room. I met Jim Garrison some time after I completed writing *Rush to Judgment*. The facts do not exactly add up to the "conspiracy" of four lawyers meeting and agreeing to discredit the Warren Report.

And now for an accurate statement by Holland. He complained that "Lane's basic allegation (was) that the government was indifferent to the truth." All along, I had been led to believe that shibboleth was the motto of *The Nation* and a concept that defines the role of the people and the press in a democratic society.

Holland also makes false statements and draws false conclusions about the role of Jim Garrison in the prosecution of Clay Shaw. It was, he claims, a "legal farce." He also asserts that "if Shaw hadn't died prematurely in 1974," he would likely have brought legal action against Garrison. In Louisiana, as in all of the states, the statute of limitations determines when a lawsuit may be brought. The Shaw trial ended in 1969. A visit to the possibly applicable law discloses that a lawsuit for defamation is time-barred after one year, a lawsuit for fraud is time-barred after one year, and a lawsuit for professional malpractice is time-barred after one year. Shaw had access to numerous attorneys and did not bring an action against Garrison for five years. His death, premature or otherwise, had no impact upon any right that he knowingly allowed to expire.

After Clay Shaw was acquitted, with the permission of the court, I interviewed many of the trial jurors. I saw them each individually and asked them their views of the evidence. Of course, they all knew that

Jim Garrison had repeatedly stated that the CIA had killed President Kennedy. They also listened attentively to the evidence and many considered that Shaw's conduct had been suspicious, and that witnesses who testified against him were, in some instances, credible. Most of the jurors told me that they were troubled by the prosecution's failure to present evidence demonstrating that Shaw had been related to the Central Intelligence Agency. Since Shaw, his attorneys, and the CIA all claimed that there had been no such relationship, they concluded that Shaw's guilt had not been established beyond a reasonable doubt. That trial was concluded in 1969.

After the publication of the Holland article, I contacted *The Nation* and stated that I would bring legal action against it for defamation unless *The Nation* published my letter disputing the article. I was informed that there was an enforceable word limit upon letters to the editor and that the editors of the publication reserved the right to edit it, delete portions and modify it in any way they wished for purposes of "clarity." I thought my letter was quite clear.

I was a member of an organization in Charlottesville, Virginia, comprised of readers of *The Nation*. A number of those readers drafted and signed a petition requesting that my letter be published in full. It was signed by most of the members, including two professors at the University of Virginia. The response nationally was similar, with some scholars using the Internet to call for a boycott against *The Nation*. I did not support that call because I believe in the extension of the First Amendment, which provides publications with the right to print dubious statements. Many readers were outraged that *The Nation* had betrayed its traditions.[55]

---

55. I knew then, as I know now, that publications have a history, but that they do not have an immutable tradition. Publications speak with the voice of the present owner.

   The New York Post, for example, was founded in 1801 by Alexander Hamilton; its most famous editor was William Cullen Bryant, the poet and abolitionist. When Dorothy Schiff bought the *Post* in 1939, it became the home for James Wechsler, its editor, and featured many popular columnists, including Eleanor Roosevelt, Murray Kempton, Eric Sevareid, and Max Lerner. It was at that time a bastion of liberal thought. Since then, it has been purchased by Rupert Murdoch and represents a very different view.

   The Nation was founded in 1865 by abolitionists. Its mission, according to its founding prospectus, stated that *The Nation* will "make an earnest effort to bring

On February 10, 2006, I sent to *The Nation* a letter for publication. I suggested that they publish it as it was written or that they notify me of the name of their litigation counsel. The letter follows; it was published as it was written.

Ms. Katrina vanden Heuvel
Editor and Publisher
The Nation
33 Irving Place
New York, NY 10003

Ms. Katrina vanden Heuvel:

It began with a CIA document classified "Top Secret." How do I know that? A decade after the assassination of President Kennedy, with the assistance of the ACLU, I won a precedent-setting lawsuit in the United States District Court in Washington, D.C. brought pursuant to the Freedom of Information Act. The court ordered the police and spy organizations to provide to me many long-suppressed documents.

The CIA document stated that it was deeply troubled by my work in questioning the conclusions of the Warren Commission. The CIA had concluded that my book, *Rush to Judgment,* was difficult to answer; indeed, after a careful and thorough analysis of that work by CIA experts, the CIA was unable to find and cite a single error in the book. The CIA complained that almost half of the American people agreed with me and that "Doubtless polls abroad would show similar, or possibly more adverse, results." This, "trend of opinion," the CIA stated, "is a matter of concern" to "our organization." Therefore, the CIA concluded, steps must be taken.

The CIA directed that methods of attacking me should be discussed with "liaison and friendly elite contacts (especially politicians and editors)," instructing them that "further speculative discussion only plays into the hands of the opposition." The CIA

---

to the discussion of political and social questions a really critical spirit, and to wage war" upon various vices "by which so much of the political writing of the day is marred." It listed those vices as "exaggeration and misrepresentation." Today, it speaks in the voice of Katrina vanden Heuvel.

stressed that their assets in the media should "Point out also that parts of the conspiracy talk appear to be deliberately generated by Communist propagandists." Further, their media contacts should "use their influence to discourage" what the CIA referred to as "unfounded and irresponsible speculation." *Rush to Judgment*, then the New York Times number one best selling book, contained no speculation.

The CIA in its report instructed book reviewers and magazines that contained feature articles how to deal with me and others who raised doubts about the validity of the Warren Report. Magazines should, the CIA stated, "employ propaganda assets to answer and refute the attacks of the critics," adding that "feature articles are particularly appropriate for this purpose." The CIA instructed its media assets that "because of the standing of the members of the Warren Commission, efforts to impugn their rectitude and wisdom tend to cast doubt on the whole leadership of American society." The CIA was referring to such distinguished gentlemen as Allen Dulles, the former director of the CIA; President Kennedy had fired Dulles from that position for having lied to him about the Bay of Pigs tragedy. Dulles was then appointed by Lyndon Johnson to the Warren Commission to tell the American people the truth about the assassination.

The purpose of the CIA was not in doubt. The CIA stated: "The aim of this dispatch is to provide material for countering and discrediting the claims" of those who doubted the Warren Report. The CIA stated that "background information" about me and others "is supplied in a classified section and in a number of unclassified attachments."

With this background we now turn to the article by Max Holland published by *The Nation* in its February 20, 2006 issue. It states that there was a "JFK Lawyers' Conspiracy" among four lawyers, Sen. Gary Hart, Professor Robert Blakey, Jim Garrison the former District Attorney of New Orleans and later a state judge in Louisiana, and me.

Before I wrote *Rush to Judgment* I had never met any of the other three "co-conspirators." I still have not had the pleasure of meeting Sen. Hart and I know of no work that he has done in this area. I met Prof. Blakey only once; he had been appointed chief counsel for the House Select Committee on Assassinations and at that meeting I told him that I was disappointed in his approach and methods. Not much of a lawyer's conspiracy.

Each of the other statements as to alleged fact are false and defamatory. Mr. Holland states that I am not scrupulous, that I am dishonest and that I spread innuendo about the sinister delay in the Warren Commission investigation, an assertion not made by me but fabricated in its entirety by Mr. Holland. As a silent echo of his CIA associates, Mr. Holland does not point to one assertion as to fact, of the thousands I have made about the facts surrounding the death of our president that he claims is inaccurate.

Finally, Mr. Holland strikes pay dirt. He uncovers, are you ready for this, the fact that I had asserted that "the government was indifferent to the truth." I confess. Is that now a crime under the Patriot Act? Isn't that what *The Nation* is supposed to be asserting and proving?

Mr. Holland states that the KGB was secretly funding my work with a payment of "$12,500 (in 2005 dollars)." It was a secret all right. It never happened. Mr. Holland's statement is an outright lie. Neither the KGB nor any person or organization associated with it ever made any contribution to my work. No one ever made a sizable contribution with the exception of Corliss Lamont who contributed enough for me to fly one time from New York to Dallas to interview eye-witnesses. The second largest contribution was $50.00 given to me by Woody Allen. Have Corliss and Woody now joined Mr. Holland's fanciful conspiracy?

Funds for the work of the Citizens Committee of Inquiry were raised by me. I lectured each night for more than a year in a Manhattan theatre. The New York Times referred to the very well-attended talks as one of the longest running performances off Broadway. That was not a secret. I am surprised that Mr. Holland never came across that information, especially since he refers to what he calls "The Speech" in his diatribe.

Apparently, Mr. Holland did not fabricate the KGB story; his associates at the CIA did. There is proof available for that assertion, but I fear that I have taken too much space already.

Am I being unfair when I suggest a connection between Mr. Holland and the CIA? Here is the "CIA game plan:" Fabricate a disinformation story. Hand it to a reporter with some liberal credentials; for example, a contributing editor to *The Nation*. If the reporter cannot find a publication then have the CIA carry it on its own website under the byline of the reporter. Then the CIA can quote the reporter and state, " according to . . . . ."

Mr. Holland writes regularly for the official CIA website. He publishes information there that he has been given by the CIA. The CIA, on its official website, then states "According to Holland . . . " If you would like to look into this matter of disinformation laundering enter into your computer—"CIA.gov + Max Holland". You will find on the first page alone numerous articles by Mr. Holland supporting and defending the CIA and attacking those who dare to disagree as well as CIA statements attributing the information to Mr. Holland.

A question for *The Nation*. When Mr. Holland writes an article for you defending the CIA and attacking its critics, why do you describe him only as "a Nation contributing editor" and author. Is it not relevant to inform your readers that he also is a contributor to the official CIA website and then is quoted by the CIA regarding information that the agency gave to him?

An old associate of mine, Adlai Stevenson, once stated to his political opponent, a man known as a stranger to the truth,—if you stop telling lies about me I will stop telling the truth about you. I was prepared to adopt that attitude here. But I cannot. Your publication has defamed a good friend, Jim Garrison, after he had died and could not defend himself against demonstrably false charges.

You have not served your readers by refusing to disclose Mr. Holland's CIA association. *The Nation* and Mr. Holland have engaged in the type of attack journalism that recalls the bad old days. If I fought McCarthyism in the 1950s as a young lawyer, how can I avoid it now when it appears in a magazine that has sullied its own history. The article is filled with ad hominem attacks, name calling, fabrications and it has done much mischief. I will hold you and Mr. Holland accountable for your misconduct. I can honorably adopt no other course.

To mitigate damages I require that you repudiate the article and apologize for publishing it. That you publish this letter as an unedited article in your next issue. That you do not publish a reply by Mr. Holland in which he adds to the defamation and the damage he has done, a method you have employed in the past. That you provide to me the mailing addresses of your contributing editors and members of your editorial board so that I may send this letter to them. I am confident that Gore Vidal and Bob Borosage, Tom Hayden and Marcus Raskin, all of whom I know, and many others such as Molly Ivins, John Leonard and Lani Guinier who I do not know but who I respect and admire, would be interested in the practices of *The Nation*. In addition, I suggest that ethical journalism requires that in the future you fully identify your writers so that your readers may make an informed judgment about their potential bias.

If you have a genuine interest in the facts regarding the assassination you should know that the House Select Committee on Assassinations (the United States Congress) concluded that probably a conspiracy was responsible for the murder and that, therefore, the Warren Report that Mr. Holland defends so aggressively, is probably wrong. In addition, the only jury to consider this question decided in a trial held in the United States District Court in a defamation case that the newspaper did not defame E. Howard Hunt when it suggested that Hunt and the CIA had killed the president. The forewoman of the jury stated that the evidence proved that the CIA had been responsible for the assassination.

I have earned many friends in this long effort. Those who have supported my work include Lord Bertrand Russell, Arnold Toynbee, Prof. Hugh Trevor-Roper, Dr. Linus Pauling, Sen. Richard Schweicker, Paul McCartney, Norman Mailer, Richard Sprague, Robert Tannenbaum; also Members of the House of Representatives, including Don Edwards, Henry B. Gonzales, Andrew Young, Bella Abzug, Richardson Preyer, Christopher Dodd, Herman Badillo, Mervyn Dymally, Mario Biaggi and, above all, according to every national poll, the overwhelming majority of the American people. I have apparently earned a few adversaries along the way. Too bad that they operate from the shadows; that tends to remove the possibility of an open debate.

Very truly,
MARK LANE

I informed *The Nation* that there were CIA documents that should be troubling to any publication in a free society. I referred to a publication of the CIA dated January 4, 1967, about various authors, including me, who disagreed with the Warren Commission's conclusions. A CIA document dated April 21, 1967, describing a plan to refute the authors and a CIA document dated August 2, 1966, before *Rush to Judgment* was published, which was entitled "SUBJECT: Review of Book—Rush to Judgment by Mark Lane." Those documents are published below verbatim. The CIA memorandum states that "our organization is directly involved: among other facts, we contributed information to the investigation." The CIA asserted that the aim of its dispatch was "to provide material for countering and discrediting" the authors they disagreed with and that they should do so by employing "propaganda assets" to respond to the critics.

DOCUMENT I:
Chiefs, Certain Stations and Bases
Document Number 1035-950
For FOIA Review on Sept 1975
Countering Criticism of the Warren Report
Dated 4/1/67
PSYCH

1. Our Concern. From the day of President Kennedy's assassination on, there has been speculation about the responsibility for his murder. Although this was stemmed for a time by the Warren Commission report (which appeared at the end of September 1964), various writers have now had time to scan the Commission's published report and documents for new pretexts for questioning, and there has been a new wave of books and articles criticizing the Commission's findings. In most cases the critics have speculated as to the existence of some kind of conspiracy, and often they have implied that the Commission itself was involved. Presumably as a result of the increasing challenge to the Warren Commission's Report, a public opinion poll recently indicated that 46% of the American public did not think that Oswald acted alone, while more than half of the those polled thought that the Commission had left some questions unresolved. Doubtless polls abroad would show similar, or possibly more adverse, results.

2. This trend of opinion is a matter of concern to the U.S. government, including our organization. The members of the Warren Commission were naturally chosen for their integrity, experience, and prominence. They represented both major parties, and they and their staff were deliberately drawn from all sections of the country. Just because of the standing of the Commissioners, efforts to impugn their rectitude and wisdom tend to cast doubt on the whole leadership of American society. Moreover, there seems to be an increasing tendency to hint that President Johnson himself, as the one person who might be said to have benefited, was in some way responsible for the assassination. Innuendo of such seriousness affects not only the individual concerned, but also the whole reputation of the American government. Our organization itself is directly involved: among other facts, we contributed information to the investigation. Conspiracy theories have frequently thrown suspicion on our organization, for example by falsely alleging that Lee Harvey Oswald worked for us. The aim of this dispatch is to provide material for countering and discrediting the claims of the conspiracy theorists, so as to inhibit the circulation of such claims in other countries. Background information is supplied in a classified section and in a number of unclassified attachments.

3. Action. We do not recommend that discussion of the assassination question be initiated where it is not already taking place. Where discussion is active, however, addresses are requested:

    a. To discuss the publicity problem with liaison and friendly elite contacts (especially politicians and editors), pointing out that the Warren Commission made as thorough an investigation as humanly possible, that the charges of the critics are without serious foundation, and that further speculative discussion only plays into the hands of the opposition. Point out also that parts of the conspiracy talk appear to be deliberately generated by Communist propagandists. Urge them to use their influence to discourage unfounded and irresponsible speculation.

    b. To employ propaganda assets to answer and refute the attacks of the critics. Book reviews and feature articles are particularly appropriate for this purpose. The unclassified attachments to this guidance should provide useful background material for passage to assets. Our play should point out, as applicable, that the critics are (i) wedded to theories adopted before the evidence was in, (ii) politically interested, (iii) financially interested, (iv) hasty and inaccurate in their research, or (v) infatuated with their own theories. In the course of discussions of the whole phenomenon of criticism, a useful strategy may be to single out Epstein's theory for attack, using the attached Fletcher Knebel article and Spectator piece for background. (Although Mark Lane's book is much less convincing than Epstein's and comes off badly where contested by knowledgeable critics, it is also much more difficult to answer as a whole, as one becomes lost in a morass of unrelated details.)

4. In private or media discussion not directed at any particular writer, or in attacking publications which may be yet forthcoming, the following arguments should be useful:

   a. No significant new evidence has emerged which the Commission did not consider. The assassination is sometimes compared (e.g. by Joachim Joesten and Bertrand Russell) with the Dreyfus case; however, unlike that case, the attacks on the Warren Commission have produced no new evidence, no new culprits have been convincingly identified, and there is no agreement among the critics. (A better parallel, though an imperfect one, might be with the Reichstag fire of 1933, which some competent historians (Fritz Tobias, A.J.P. Taylor, D.C. Watt) now believe was set by Van der Lubbe on his own initiative, without acting for either Nazis or Communists; the Nazis tried to pin the blame on the Communists, but the latter have been much more successful in convincing the world that the Nazis were to blame.)

   b. Critics usually overvalue particular items and ignore others. They tend to place more emphasis on the recollections of individual eyewitnesses (which are less reliable and more divergent—and hence offer more hand-holds for criticism) and less on ballistic, autopsy, and photographic evidence. A close examination of the Commission's records will usually show that the conflicting eyewitness accounts are quoted out of context, or were discarded by the Commission for good and sufficient reason.

c. Conspiracy on the large scale often suggested would be impossible to conceal in the United States, esp. since informants could expect to receive large royalties, etc. Note that Robert Kennedy, Attorney General at the time and John F. Kennedy's brother, would be the last man to overlook or conceal any conspiracy. And as one reviewer pointed out, Congressman Gerald R. Ford would hardly have held his tongue for the sake of the Democratic administration, and Senator Russell would have had every political interest in exposing any misdeeds on the part of Chief Justice Warren. A conspirator moreover would hardly choose a location for a shooting where so much depended on conditions beyond his control: the route, the speed of the cars, the moving target, the risk that the assassin would be discovered. A group of wealthy conspirators could have arranged much more secure conditions.

d. Critics have often been enticed by a form of intellectual pride: they light on some theory and fall in love with it; they also scoff at the Commission because it did not always answer every question with a flat decision one way or the other. Actually, the make-up of the Commission and its staff was an excellent safeguard against over-commitment to any one theory, or against the illicit transformation of probabilities into certainties.

e. Oswald would not have been any sensible person's choice for a co-conspirator. He was a "loner," mixed-up of questionable reliability and an unknown quantity to any professional intelligence service.

f. As to charges that the Commission's report was a rush job, it emerged three months after the deadline originally set. But to the degree that the Commission tried to speed up its reporting, this was largely due to the pressure of irresponsible speculation already appearing, in some cases coming from the same critics who, refusing to admit their errors, are now putting out new criticisms.

g. Such vague accusations as that "more than ten people have died mysteriously" can always be explained in some more natural way: e.g., the individuals concerned have for the most part died of natural causes; the Commission staff questioned 418 witnesses (the FBI interviewed far more people, conducting 25,000 interviews and reinterviews), and in such a large group, a certain number of deaths are to be expected. (When Penn Jones, one of the originators of the "ten mysterious deaths" line, appeared on television, it emerged that two of the deaths on his list were from heart attacks, one from cancer, one was from a head-on collision on a bridge, and one occurred when a driver drifted into a bridge abutment.)

5.   Where possible, counter speculation by encouraging reference to the Commission's Report itself. Opoen-minded foreign readers should still be impressed by the care, thoroughness, objectivity and speed with which the Commission worked. Reviewers of other books might be encouraged to add to their account the idea that, checking back with the Report itself, they found it far superior to the work of its critics.

[At the bottom of the first page of this document are the words:]

DESTROY WHEN NO LONGER NEEDED

CIA DOCUMENT II:
Background Survey of Books Concerning
the Assassination of President Kennedy
Dated 4 Jan 67

1.   (Except where otherwise indicated, the factual data given in paragraphs 1-9 is unclassified.) Some of the authors of recent books on the assassination of President Kennedy (e.g., Joachim Joesten, Oswald: Assassin or Fall Guy; Mark Lane, Rush to Judment [sic]; Leo Sauvage, The Oswald Affair: An Examination of the Contradictions and Omissions of the Warren Report) had publicly asserted that a conspiracy existed before the Warren Commission finished its investigation. Not surprisingly, they immediately bestirred themselves to show that they were right and that the Commission was wrong. Thanks to the mountain of material published by the Commission, some of it conflicting or misleading when read out of context, they have had little difficulty in uncovering items to substantiate their own theories. They have also in some cases obtained new and divergent testimony from witnesses. And they have usually failed to discuss the refutations

of their early claims in the Commission's Report, Appendix XII ("Speculations and Rumors"). This Appendix is still a good place to look for material countering the theorists.

2. Some writers appear to have been predisposed to criticism by anti-American, far left, or Communist sympathies. The British "Who Killed Kennedy Committee" includes some of the most persistent and vocal English critics of the United States, e.g., Michael Foot, Kingsley Martin, Kenneth Tynan, and Bertrand Russell. Joachim Joesten has been publicly revealed as a onetime member of the German Communist Party (KPD); a Gestapo document of 8 November 1937 among the German Foreign Ministry files microfilmed in England and now returned to West German custody shows that his party book was numbered 532315 and dated 12 May 1932. (The originals of these files are now available at the West German Foreign Ministry in Bonn; the copy in the U.S. National Archives may be found under the reference T-120, Serial 4918, frames E256482-4. The British Public Records Office should also have a copy.) Joesten's American publisher, Carl Marzani, was once sentenced to jail by a federal jury for concealing his Communist Party (CPUSA) membership in order to hold a government job. Available information indicates that Mark Lane was elected Vice Chairman of the New York Council to Abolish the House Un-American Activities Committee on 28 May 1963; he also attended the 8th Congress of the International Association of Democratic Lawyers (an international Communist front organization) in Budapest from 31 March to 5 April 1964, where he expounded his (pre-Report) views on the Kennedy assassination. In his acknowledgments in his book, Lane expresses special thanks to Ralph Schoenman of London "who participated in and supported the work"; Schoenman is of course the expatriate American who has been influencing the aged Bertrand Russell in recent years. (See also para. 10 below on Communist efforts to replay speculation on the assassination.)

3. Another factor has been the financial reward obtainable for sensational books. Mark Lane's Rush to Judgment, published on 13 August 1966, had sold 85,000 copies by early November and the publishers had printed 140,000 copies by that date, in anticipation of sales to come. The 1 January 1967 New York Times Book Review reported that book as at the top of the General category

of the best seller list, having been in top position for seven weeks and on the list for 17 weeks. Lane has reportedly appeared on about 175 television and radio programs, and has also given numerous public lectures, all of which serves for advertisement. He has also put together a TV film, and is peddling it to European telecasters; the BBC has purchased rights for a record $45,000. While neither Abraham Zapruder nor William Manchester should be classed with the critics of the Commission we are discussing here, sums paid for the Zapruder film of the assassination ($25,000) and for magazine rights to Manchester's *Death of a President* ($665,000) indicate the money available for material related to the assassination. Some newspapermen (e.g. Sylvan Fox, The Unanswered Questions About President Kennedy's Assassination; Leo Sauvage, The Oswald Affair) have published accounts cashing in on their journalistic expertise.

4.   Aside from political and financial motives, some people have apparently published accounts simply because they were burning to give the world their theory, e.g., Harold Weisberg, in his *Whitewash II*, Penn Jones, Jr., in *Forgive My Grief*, and George C. Thomson in *The Quest for Truth*. Weisberg's book was first published privately, though it is now finally attaining the dignity of commercial publication. Jones' volume was published by the small-town Texas newspaper of which he is the editor, and Thomson's booklet by his own engineering firm. The impact of these books will probably be relatively slight, since their writers will appear to readers to be hysterical or paranoid.

5.   A common technique among many of the writers is to raise as many questions as possible, while not bothering to work out all the consequences. Herbert Mitgang has written a parody of this approach (his questions actually refer to Lincoln's assassination) in "A New Inquiry is Needed," New York Times Magazine, 25 December 1966. Mark Lane in particular (who represent himself as Oswald's lawyer) adopts the classic defense attorney's approach of throwing in unrelated details so as to create in the jury's mind a sum of "reasonable doubt." His tendency to wander off into minor details led one observer to comment that whereas a good trial lawyer should have a sure instinct for the jugular vein, Lane's instinct was for the capillaries. His tactics and also his nerve were typified on the occasion when, after getting the Commission to pay his travel expenses back from England, he recounted to that

body a sensational (and incredible) story of a Ruby plot, while refusing to name his source. Chief Justice Warren told Lane, "We have every reason to doubt the truthfulness of what you have heretofore told us"—by the standards of legal etiquette, a very stiff rebuke for an attorney.

6.   It should be recognized, however, that another kind of criticism has recently emerged, represented by Edward Jay Epstein's Inquest. Epstein adopts a scholarly tone, and to the casual reader, he presents what appears to be a more coherent, reasoned case than the writers described above. Epstein has caused people like Richard Rovere and Lord Devlin, previously backers of the Commission's Report, to change their minds. The New York Times' daily book reviewer has said that Epstein's work is a "watershed book" which has made it respectable to doubt the Commission's finding. This respectability effect has been enhanced by Life magazine's 25 November issue, which contains an assertion that there is a "reasonable doubt,)" as well as a republication of frames from the Zapruder film (owned by Life), and an interview with Governor Connally, who repeats his belief that he was not struck by the same bullet that struck President Kennedy. (Connally does not, however, agree that there should be another investigation.) Epstein himself has published a new article in the December 1966 issue of Esquire, in which he explains away objections to his book. A copy of an early critique of Epstein's views by Fletcher Knebel, published in Look, 12 July 1966, and an unclassified, unofficial analysis (by "Spectator") are attached to this dispatch, dealing with specific questions raised by Epstein.

7.   Here it should be pointed out that Epstein's competence in research has been greatly exaggerated. Some illustrations are given in the Fletcher Knebel article. As a further specimen, Epstein's book refers (pp. 93-5) to a cropped-down picture of a heavy-set man taken in Mexico City, saying that the Central Intelligence Agency gave it to the Federal Bureau of Investigation on 18 November 1963, and that the Bureau in turn forwarded it to its Dallas office. Actually, affidavits I the published Warren material (vol. XI, pp. 468-70) show that CIA turned the picture over to the FBI on 22 November 1963. (As a matter of interest, Mark Lane's Rush to Judgment claims that the photo was furnished by CIA on the morning of 22 November; the fact is that the FBI flew the photo directly from Mexico City to Dallas immediately after Oswald's

arrest, before Oswald's picture had been published, on the chance it might be Oswald. The reason the photo was cropped was that the background revealed the place where it was taken.) Another example: where Epstein reports (p. 41) that a Secret Service interview report was even withheld from the National Archives, this is untrue; an Archives staff member told one of our officers that Epstein came there and asked for the memorandum. He was told that it was there, but was classified. Indeed, the Archives then notified the Secret Service that there had been a request for the document, and the Secret Service declassified it. But by that time, Epstein (whose preface gives the impression of prolonged archival research) had chosen to finish his searches in the Archives, which had only lasted two days, and had left town. Yet Epstein charges that the Commission was over-hasty in its work.

8. Aside from such failures in research, Epstein and other intellectual critics show symptoms of some of the love of theorizing and lack of common sense and experience displayed by Richard H. Popkin, the author of The Second Oswald. Because Oswald was reported to have been seen in different places at the same time, a phenomenon not surprising in a sensational case where thousands of real or alleged witnesses were interviewed, Popkin, a professor of philosophy, theorizes that there actually were two Oswalds. At this point, theorizing becomes sort of logico-mathematical game; an exercise in permutations and combinations; as Commission attorney Arlen Specter re marked; "Why not make it three Oswalds? Why stop at two?" Nevertheless, aside from his book, Popkin has been able to publish a summary of his views in The New York Review of Books, and there has been replay in the French Nouvel Observateur, in Moscow's New Times, and in Baku's Vyshka. Popkin makes a sensational accusation indirectly, saying that "Western European critics" see Kennedy's assassination as part of a subtle conspiracy attributable to "perhaps even (in rumors I have heard) Kennedy's successor." One Barbara Garson has made the same point in another way by her parody of Shakespeare's "Macbeth" entitled "MacBird," with what is obviously President Kennedy (Ken O Dunc) in the role of Duncan, and President Johnson (MacBird) in the role of Macbeth. Miss Garson makes no effort to prove her point; she merely insinuates it. Probable the indirect form of accusation is due to fear of a libel suit.

9. Other books are yet to appear. William Manchester's not-yet-published The Death of a President is at this writing being purged of material personally objectionable to Mrs. Kennedy. There are hopeful signs: Jacob Cohen is writing a book which will appear in 1967 under the title Honest Verdict, defending the Commission report, and one of the Commission attorneys, Wesley J. Liebeler, is also reportedly writing a book, setting forth both sides. Bur further criticism will no doubt appear; as the Washington Post has pointed out editorially, the recent death of Jack Ruby will probably lead to speculation that he was "silenced" by a conspiracy.

10. The likelihood of further criticism is enhanced by the circumstance that Communist propagandists seem recently to have stepped up their own campaign to discredit the Warren Commission. As already noted, Moscow's New Times reprinted parts of an article by Richard Popkin (21 and 28 September 1966 issues), and it also gave the Swiss edition of Joesten's latest work an extended, laudatory review in its number for 26 October. (In view of this publicity and the Communist background of Joesten and his American publisher, together with Joesten's insistence on pinning the blame on such favorite Communist targets as H.L. Hunt, the FBI and CIA, there seems reason to suspect that Joesten's book and its exploitation are part of a planned Soviet propaganda operation.) Tass, reporting on 5 November on the deposit of autopsy photographs in the National Archives, said that the refusal to give wide public access to them, the disappearance of a number of documents, and the mysterious death of more than 10 people, all make many Americans believe Kennedy was killed as the result of a conspiracy. The radio transmitters of Prague and Warsaw used the anniversary of the assassination to attack the Warren report. The Bulgarian press conducted a campaign on the subject in the second half of October; a Greek Communist newspaper, Avgi, placed the blame on CIA on 20 November. Significantly, the start of this stepped-up campaign coincided with a Soviet demand that the U.S. Embassy in Moscow stop distributing the Russian-language edition of the Warren report; Newsweek commented (12 September) that the Soviets apparently "did not want mere facts to get in their way."

CIA DOCUMENT III
MEMORANDUM FOR:
SUBJECT: Review of Book—Rush to Judgment by Mark Lane

1. I reviewed the attached proof copy of the above book per your request. It represents a recapitulation of Lane's theories regarding the assassination of President Kennedy, and alleged shortcomings of the Warren Commission, which he has expressed publicly over the past few years. Like J. Epstein, author of Inquest, Lane is guilty of the same fault he charges to the Warren Commission—a rush to judgment.

2. CIA first comes into focus on page 302. Lane imputes something sinister in the fact that this Agency received a copious requirement regarding Jack Ruby from the Commission on 24 February 1964 and seemingly never got around to answering it until 15 September 1964 (the Commission's 13 page memorandum, a follow-up query by J. Lee Rankin and this Agency's reply, appear in volume XXVI of the Commission Report, pages 466-467). Lane conveniently ignores paragraph two of the CIA reply which specifically directs the Commission's attention to an "earlier" answer. In addition, almost the entire memorandum was clearly outside our jurisdiction. I discussed this matter with (name redacted) who was involved intimately in making the necessary name checks and providing an answer. I also remember the situation quite will. Within two weeks of the original request, Mr. Rankin's office was advised telephonically that the major tracing had been completed and that we had no "information on Jack Ruby or his activities"; furthermore, that the CIA had "no indication that Ruby and Lee Harvey Oswald ever knew each other, were associated, or might have been connected in any manner." According to (redacted) this is the exact wording used during the telephone conversation and later reported in paragraph two of our formal reply. The Commission also was advised at that time that the remaining names appearing in the Commission's memorandum were being checked, and that an answer would be submitted upon completion of the task. This was a large undertaking, particularly since this Staff was being pressed for other types of assistance by the Commission. Mr. Rankin's

follow-up letter also was answered by phone. We reiterated the above conclusions and added that we had just completed the rest of the name tracing in depth and were in the process of preparing an answer. Because of the complexity of the task, several drafts were attempted and rejected before the final version was sent to the Commission.

3. On pages 351 and 352, Lane discusses the photograph of the unknown individual which was taken by the CIA in Mexico City. The photograph was furnished by this Agency to the FBI after the assassination of President Kennedy. The FBI then showed it to Mrs. Marguerite Oswald who later claimed the photograph to be that of Jack Ruby. A discussion of the incident, the photograph itself, and related affidavits, all appear in the Commission's Report (VOL. XI, p. 469; VOL XVI, p. 638.) Lane asserts that the photograph was evidently taken in front of the Cuban Embassy in Mexico City on 27 September 1963, and that it was furnished to the FBI on the morning of 22 November. As in the case of Epstein, Lane is incorrect regarding the date and place the photograph was taken, and the date it was furnished to the FBI (Epstein says we gave it to the FBI on 18 November). Lane acknowledges that the picture is not that of Jack Ruby or Lee Harvey Oswald. He says that the CIA originally thought the man was Oswald, but was mistaken. He then twits the Commission, the FBI, and the CIA for being unable to locate the unknown individual, asserting that "it is unfortunate that the full resources of the United States intelligence agencies were unable to locate the man whose picture had been taken by the CIA."

4. On page 373, Lane takes exception to the Commission's statement that "it had access to the full CIA file on Oswald." Lane states, that at least on one occasion, the CIA refused to permit one of its photographs to be displayed to the Commission unless the background had been removed. Lane was referring to the aforementioned photograph of the unknown individual which was cropped to protect the source and to delete the background.

Now we have Holland's response. In a letter to *The Nation,* he stated that I "make much of a CIA document that sounds very sinister— until you actually read it and put it into context. The document was written in April 1967, the height of the bout of madness otherwise known as the Garrison investigation." He added that "the CIA was very concerned about having such allegations gain widespread acceptance."

In the January 4, 1967, CIA background survey of books concerning the assassination of President Kennedy, the names of several authors are listed, including Joachim Joesten, Leo Sauvage, Harold Weisberg, Penn Jones, Jr., Richard H. Popkin and me. There is no reference to Jim Garrison or Clay Shaw in that dispatch.

The April 1967 document makes no mention of Jim Garrison or his investigation into the facts surrounding the assassination and does not even mention the name Clay Shaw. It is devoted entirely to authors who independently wrote books, including those who wrote books before Jim Garrison even began his investigation, and it gives specific instructions to its assets about how those books should be reviewed. It mentions Joachim Joesten, who was published even before *Rush to Judgment* was, and suggests the specific language that should be used by book reviewers.

The August 2, 1966, memorandum is a review of *Rush to Judgment* with the names of the recipients deleted. It neither mentions Jim Garrison nor his investigation.

Subsequently, *The New York Times* published an op-ed column by Holland about the assassination of President Kennedy. The *Times* also failed to inform its readers that Holland was a CIA asset. The article by Holland presented allegations that were entirely false. I sent a letter to *The New York Times* that it did not publish. It follows:

To the Editor:
Either I have grown too mellow in my later years or *The New York Times* has improved in significant ways. I subscribe and daily rush to the editorial page and the Op-Ed page for views about the war, our justice system and to read Frank Rich, among others. Perhaps that is why I was so disappointed to see that on the anniversary of President Kennedy's assassination you published an article by Max Holland and a television photographer, stating that Oswald was the lone assassin. You should have identified Mr. Holland for your readers. He is the official writer for the CIA on the question of the assassination and his articles, almost exclusively, comprise the CIA position. To see Mr. Holland and the JFK assassination, his specific defense of the CIA and his defamation of those who

do not share the views of the CIA, click on to the official CIA website as follows—cia.gov + Max Holland.

Of course, just because Mr. Holland is the voice for the CIA on this question, an agency, according to traditional national polls, which more American believe to have been involved in the assassination than believe that Oswald acted alone, is no reason to reject his odd views. The fact that he is demonstrably wrong is the reason.

In the article ("J.F.K.'s Death, Re-Framed," Op-Ed, Nov. 22), only the title appears to be accurate. Holland cites only one eyewitness and states of him that Amos L. Euins, "a ninth grader," spoke to the Dallas County sheriff and that, according to Holland, "No one's recollection about the first shot was more precise [than Euins']."

Here are some facts Mr. Holland failed to report to your readers:

Amos L. Euins, a 15-year-old boy, said on November 22 that he saw a man in the window of the Book Depository with a rifle. James Underwood, assistant news director at KRLD-TV in Dallas testified that he heard Euins tell a motorcycle officer he "had seen a colored man lean out of the window upstairs and he had a rifle. Underwood said that he interviewed Euins on the spot, asking the boy if the man he saw had been "white or black." Euins replied, "It was a colored man." "Are you sure it was a colored man?" Underwood asked. Euins answered, "Yes, sir."

After Euins had described the man in the building as a Negro to both a motorcycle policeman and a newsman, he was taken to the Dallas Sheriff's office, where an affidavit was prepared for him. That affidavit stated that the man he saw was a "white man."

Before Euins testified, according to his mother, the family received threatening telephone calls. When he appeared before the Warren Commission, Euins said that he had not told the Sheriff's office that the man in the window was white: They must have made a mistake, because I told them I could see a white spot on his head." However, he was willing to alter his original statement, and he told the Commission, that he no longer knew whether the man was white or black."

Of course, Mr. Holland knew the facts set forth above. They were published in 1966 in *Rush to Judgment,* at page 281. In the book each assertion was cited to documents published by the Warren Commission or testimony before the Commission. For those few words quoted above there were thirteen citations to the official government record, citations 147 through 159. That book was not a well kept secret. It was *The New York Times* best selling book. And of course, the CIA, and agency that had reviewed *Rush to Judgment,* even before its publication date (and could cite no errors but offered many suggestions to the news media about how to discredit me and suppress the book) was familiar with the text. Euins' testimony has been available in Volume II, pages 201-210 of the 26 volumes published by the Warren Commission more than four decades ago.

It is now relevant to review the testimony of the young man Holland claims to have had a "precise" recollection of the events. He was interrogated by Arlen Specter, an innovative creator of the Magic Bullet Theory which was adopted by the Warren Commission, is central to its findings. It asserts that only three shots were fired. If another shot was fired there could have been no lone assassin. Earl Warren was present during the sworn interview. Specter asked Euins: "The question I have for you is where were you when the fourth shot was fired." Euins told Specter where he had been. Specter (not yet the father of the *only three shots were fired* theory), continued: "You were still at point B when he fired the fourth time?" and later "Did you see him pull the gun (sick) back in the window after the fourth shot?"

Specter asked Euins to describe the man who had fired four shots. "I wouldn't know how to describe him, because all I could see was the spot (on his head) and his hand." When Specter asked if the man was "slender or fat," Euins replied, "I didn't get to see him."

Euins is the only eye-witness referred to by Holland in his op-ed piece. If Euins was the "precise" witness Holland said he was then perhaps four shots had been fired. If so the Commission, Specter and the CIA and Holland (if I am not being redundant) were again proven to be inaccurate.

The first officer to talk to Euins was Sergeant D.V. Harkness of the Dallas Police Department. The Warren Commission conceded that Sgt. Harkness "radioed to headquarters at 12:36 PM that I have a witness that says it came from the fifth floor of the Texas School Depository" (Warren Commission Report, page 64). The CIA, Holland and the Warren Commission contend that all shots were fired from the sixth floor. Efforts by the defenders of the official view to explain away discrepancy after discrepancy do not enhance their credibility and tend to encourage the serious doubts of almost all of the American people.

MARK LANE
Former member of the New York State Legislature
Practicing attorney for 56 years
and author of several books on contemporary legal issues

I believe that Holland's writing has betrayed two characteristics. He is close to the CIA, and he writes recklessly without adequate concern for the facts. The relatively recent statement by Holland that Clay Shaw died "prematurely" struck me as being odd. Premature is defined as "occurring before the assigned time." I decided to look into the premature death of Clay Shaw.

When Clay Shaw died on August 15, 1974, there were unsubstantiated rumors about the cause, as there have been about so many matters related to the assassination of the president. I had written almost half a century ago that when reasonable people understand that their government has not told them the truth about a serious matter affecting their lives, it provides a fertile field for imagination. For that reason when I wrote *Rush to Judgment,* each assertion was warranted by a reference to the unquestioned source and I engaged in no speculation. Yet I also know that a rumor without a substantial basis in fact may be true although it certainly may not be relied upon.

Shaw, it was said, had undergone radiation treatment for brain cancer, had become delirious and had refused to take medication. His lawyer, Edward F. Wegman, had arranged for a "sitter" to be with him and had given strict instructions to the sitter to contact him at once if Shaw died. This information and all that follows is based upon the official ten-page New Orleans Police Department Report dated August 28, 1974. It is now available on the Internet.

Shaw died at 12:40 AM at his home. Wegman was notified, immediately dressed and arrived at Shaw's residence approximately one hour later. Although Wegman knew that the sitter had been engaged in cleaning "the victim's face and while doing so, the victim gasped and apparently expired,"[56] he did not contact the police department or the Orleans Parish Coroner's Office. Instead he called a funeral home, the House of Bultman, run by friends, at 1:30 AM. The funeral parlor representatives arrived in less than half an hour and removed the body and the "procedure of arterial injection and aspirating of the body cavities took place." Those efforts prevented an autopsy from taking place.

Clearly, the two detectives assigned to the case and their supervisor, a lieutenant, were suspicious, as was the chief of detectives who "instructed" them to "initiate an investigation into the death." One day had elapsed after the death before they learned of it. Then, an unusually extensive local police investigation into the cause of death was initiated. Shaw's attorney, identified in the police report as "E. Wegman," told the police officers that he had not notified the New Orleans Police Department and the New Orleans Coroner's Office of the death "because it was his understanding that that it was not necessary." That was not the law and Wegman was an experienced lawyer.

Thirteen days after the death, the police completed their inquiry and issued a report. The report states that Shaw's condition was terminal; however, it added that the "exact cause of Mr. Shaw's death could never be determined without the results of an autopsy." Shaw's trial lawyer did not request an autopsy and had taken action that prevented it from becoming a possibility.

While Holland wrote that the prosecution of Shaw was a farce and without basis, the House Select Committee on Assassinations found that evidence developed by Jim Garrison and his office had "established an association of an undetermined nature between David Ferrie, a suspect in the assassination of President Kennedy, and Clay Shaw and Lee Harvey Oswald."

During June 1984, I was present at the deposition of Richard Helms, the former Director of the CIA. The attorney for E. Howard Hunt, a party in the case, sought to foreclose the issue by asking Helms if the CIA had anything to do with the assassination of the president. I expected no confession; I did anticipate an outraged and ringing denial. Neither occurred. The tepid response was, "to the best of my knowledge," the CIA had not murdered the president. Counsel

---

56. All of the quoted citations regarding this episode are from the New Orleans Police Department Report.

persisted, hoping for a more definitive assurance. He asked if the CIA had covered up the facts surrounding the assassination. Helms paused, perhaps remembering that he was a convicted criminal who had committed perjury in his testimony before a committee of the United States Senate. Then he stated that, "to the best of my knowledge," the CIA had not done that.

When it was my turn I asked Helms if he had ever heard of Clay Shaw. At once the CIA's lawyers, two were present, and Hunt's lawyers, two more, huddled with Helms. When the time-out ended Helms asked me, "Clay Shaw?" Then he added, "Can you help me a little as to who Clay Shaw was." The past tense indicated that Helms was aware of more facts than he pretended to know.

Helms had been called as a witness in a previous case involving Hunt. I had obtained a copy of his testimony in that matter. I told Helms that Shaw was the person whom he, Helms, had previously identified, while under oath, as being a contact of the CIA's Domestic Contact Division, and that Shaw was the person Helms had sworn had carried out missions for the CIA. I read his previous testimony to him and asked if he had made it. Helms replied that it did not refresh his recollection, but if it said in the transcript that he had made those statements, "I guess I did."

During the colloquy between counsel, Helms took out a single sheet of paper and looked at it. When I asked him if Shaw worked for the CIA he studied that document. I asked him if that sheet was a copy of the transcript of his earlier testimony in which he admitted the CIA–Shaw relationship. He said that it was. I asked how he obtained that page and one of his CIA attorneys stated, "His counsel provided it" for Helms's "perusal."

That additional assertion indicated that Helms, Hunt's lawyers and the CIA lawyers had all agreed to dissemble and to agree that Helms should deny facts under oath that they knew to be true. Their conduct was unethical and bordered on criminal. I was not concerned about their duplicity; I was satisfied that we had established the link between Shaw and the CIA. I called Jim Garrison at once and reported the exchanges. He said that if he had had that information at the time of the trial Shaw would have been convicted. Possibly he was correct. I could never prophesize what twelve men and women, good and true, might decide in the jury room, but I knew that the case against Shaw would have been immeasurably stronger if Shaw had not committed perjury at his trial and if the CIA had not been the constant source of disinformation.

Had Shaw survived until after June 5, 1984, when Garrison discovered that Shaw had been associated with the CIA, he might have faced legal difficulties. There is no statute of limitations for murder in Louisiana; even if there were a time-limiting statute it would have been tolled in the event of deliberate concealment of material facts. Shaw had died almost ten years before the date Garrison learned that the CIA admitted that the connection had existed. His death prevented him from facing the possibility of a motion to reopen the murder case against him.

Vincent Bugliosi and
Rewriting History

Actually he named it *Reclaiming History*. After reviewing the facts you choose which title is more appropriate. When it first appeared I declined to review it for magazines and newspapers for several reasons. I saw little reason to publicize a book that no one was reading. Also I had a personal interest in the matter since Bugliosi, who had never interviewed me, stated that I was a "fraud" for denying the conclusions of the Warren Report. He wrote, it is a "fact" that "virtually all intelligent people who are knowledgeable of the facts (both of which Lane is) know that Oswald killed Kennedy and almost assuredly acted alone." He continued that, therefore, "one is compelled to conclude that from the very beginning, Lane was a fraud in his preachments about the Kennedy assassination." Off with my head. As for you, dear reader, who may agree with me that the Warren Commission Report was flawed, are you also a fraud or merely ignorant or unintelligent?

I also declined to bring legal action against him at that time for the same reasons. The book had been heralded with much publicity, Hollywood fanfare and purportedly serious and certainly favorable reviews in the established press. When *Rush to Judgment* was published the CIA directed its assets to review it most unfavorably. Some of the same people are still at it, now marching in lockstep with Bugliosi. Rupert Murdoch's *Wall Street Journal,* for example, gave it a rave review written by Max Holland. The *WSJ* neglected to inform its readers that Holland is published on the CIA official website (cia.gov) as the

CIA expert employed in defending that agency from any charge of implication in the assassination of President Kennedy.

The *WSJ* also failed to inform its readers that Holland had repeatedly published defamatory articles on the CIA official website against critics of the Warren Commission. Holland, for his part, refrained from telling readers of the *WSJ* that Bugliosi had praised him in the very book that he was reviewing. Bugliosi in his book had very kind words for his future reviewer, Max Holland, calling him "a serious student of the assassination whose primary agenda is to ferret out the truth." That weasel-like reference was, I am sure, inadvertent, since Bugliosi did not reveal Holland's mole-like work for the CIA.

Nevertheless, almost no one seemed interested in it. Years ago, while visiting the Barnes and Noble bookstore in Charlottesville, Virginia, I asked a clerk if the Bugliosi book was there. She replied, "You mean the cinder block; yes we have it; no one is buying it." I did not inquire further, never to know if no one was purchasing the book or no one was buying its concept.

I confess, for I am a man who admits it when he makes a mistake, I purchased a copy. I knew that it was not on *The New York Times* best-seller list for either books of fiction or fact, but anxious to see how it was doing I checked with Amazon and discovered that it was the 802nd most popular book at that time. Only 801 books at Amazon were selling at a faster clip. Until then I had not realized that there were so many different books for sale at any given time or that I had ever been a member of so small a minority. A little more than one month after publication date is the crucial time for a book's sales. While the first week's sales primarily result from media exposure and reviews, as the book matures subsequent sales figures are based primarily on word of mouth—the opinions of those who have actually read it. I can recall no other book so well promoted that fell into oblivion so quickly.

Of course, Bugliosi will have an explanation for so telling a rejection by the American people; he always does. Bugliosi had stated that there "are two reasons" why a book he had written previously was a failure, that is why so few people bought it. "One reason, I think, is because the book had not been available the way it should be [sic]. And the second reason is for the first time in my literary career I have not gotten on the main talk shows in the morning, the morning network shows."[57]

---

57. Brainy Quote.com

You may be asking what has changed my mind about reviewing Bugliosi. Tom Hanks has. He announced that he was going to produce, with HBO, a thirteen-part mini-series to prove the accuracy of the Warren Commission Report. Ten of the programs, each one hour long, would deal with Bugliosi's view of the events, and three hours would be given to Bugliosi to attack those who disagree with him. He expects to air these programs in November 2013, during the fiftieth anniversary of the assassination. Hanks expects the program to be very successful, stating that "a lot of conspiracy types are going to be upset." And then he adds, "If we do it right, it'll be perhaps one of the most controversial things that has ever been on TV." Hanks is entitled to his position; here is mine. If the program repeats the defamatory and entirely false statements that Bugliosi included in his book, I assure you I will file a lawsuit against all those associated with the project, since I have already put them on notice and sent them the documents demonstrating Bugliosi's errors. A high point of that proceeding would be Hanks trying to answer questions about what is in Bugliosi's book, a work that I am quite confident he has never read. In Hollywood, generally some clerical employee reads a work and then drafts a two-page essay about the substance. That document is then given to someone closer to the star who realizes that it is far too long, and then reduces it to a paragraph or two.

Do you think it is likely that Tom Hanks knows anything about the sources utilized for the book? Among those Bugliosi relies upon are Max Holland and Christopher Andrew. Holland appears several times throughout the work and Bugliosi identifies him as a "Warren Commission chronicler and assassination researcher" (p. 77). He refers to him as an "assassination researcher, Max Holland" (p. 456). He also makes this reference, "as writer Max Holland says" (p. 940). He also refers to him as "the very literate Max Holland" (p. 999). And in summation, he asserts that "no one has put" it "any better than writer and assassination researcher Max Holland" (p. 1346). Then, when Holland personally attacked Oliver Stone, Bugliosi wrote, "Max Holland said it well" (pp. 1434–5).

In addition, he lists Holland as a source for information in footnotes 129–30, 133, 780, 812 and 813. Bugliosi fails to inform his readers that Max Holland is a CIA media asset.

Holland also relies upon statements made by Andrew, but fails to identify that source as an asset of the Central Intelligence Agency. I doubt that that information found its way into the summary that Hanks might have read, but I am providing him adequate time to do some research before the cross-examination begins.

For the last several years, when asked to speak at a conference about the assassination of John Kennedy or comment upon a new scientific finding again refuting the coincidence theory of history, I have respectfully declined with these words: *it is round*. For the world is not flat and further proof of that theory is not required by most of us and of little interest to almost all of us.

Bugliosi's version of the long since thoroughly discredited Warren Commission Report requires a body strong enough to pick it up [the publisher boasts that it weighs five and one half pounds] and a great deal of determination if one contemplates actually trying to read it.

Publishers Weekly, almost always the author's sympathetic friend, refers in its review to Bugliosi's "obsession" and states that "Bugliosi is not always temperate in his language, for example, twice he makes the nonsensical claim that Warren Commission 'critics were screaming the word conspiracy before the fatal bullet had come to rest.'"

I was, I believe, the first to publicly raise concern about the conclusions of the FBI; I raised questions, did not offer any conclusions, and I did so quietly, in an article I had written and in an interview conducted by a *New York Times* veteran and exemplary journalist. It was J. Edgar Hoover, director of the FBI, who had first raised the issue of conspiracy by stating that Oswald had acted alone, and remarkably he did so very soon after the arrest of Oswald. Later I wondered how that statement could be made so prematurely, even before the FBI had conducted a reasonable inquiry. No screaming, no unrested bullet and no allegations of conspiracy.

Bugliosi's obsession took some considerable time to evolve. Decades had passed since the assassination while Bugliosi remained silent. A special committee of the United States Congress had conducted an investigation and concluded that in all likelihood there had been a conspiracy. Of course the committee's chief counsel, its experienced former assistant district attorneys, its studious investigators, and all the member of Congress who endorsed that view, being neither ignorant nor stupid, were according to Bugliosi's definition, "frauds."

It may be instructive to examine the then-developing evidence prior to Bugliosi's tardy interest in a matter that had passionately concerned millions of Americans. The leading CIA official in charge of defamation directed against those who did not accept the Warren Commission view of the events, and who helped to prevent the publication of *Rush to Judgment,* was David Atlee Phillips, who bragged that he ran the Western Hemisphere for the CIA. Phillips was based in Mexico City when Oswald was alleged to have been there. Oswald was not there but William F. Buckley was. He was employed by the CIA as a secret agent as he later admitted to me under oath. Buckley played an active role in defending the CIA by insisting that Oswald had been the lone assassin.

On February 6, 1985, a jury in a United States District Court found that my client, a newspaper defendant that had alleged that E. Howard Hunt and the CIA had been involved in the assassination of President Kennedy, was not guilty of libel.

The jury verdict in the case preceded Bugliosi's interest in the assassination. His present book proclaims that he has been at work on the subject for twenty years. That means that his work began not long after the jury had spoken, and just as the CIA was utilizing all of its assets to deny its involvement and to support efforts that would conclude that Oswald had acted alone. I know of no evidence that demonstrates that Bugliosi acted for the agency, either knowingly or inadvertently. It would be interesting, however, to learn where the funding for a massive book that few would read and for twenty years of work had originated.

One fact is obvious. In Bugliosi's huge volume there is an enormous list of names in the index, including Elvis Presley, Paul Newman, Ann Landers, Frank Sinatra, "Blaze Starr, a stripper," "Sunshine (dog), 51" [although there is no reference to Sunshine on page 51, a distressing, oft-repeated feature of Bugliosi's book where citations, even for a scholarly researcher, become bridges to nowhere], Sterling Hayden, and of course that nostalgic favorite, Charles Manson. In Bugliosi's jaunt through Hollywood, on page 1353, we learn that Oliver Stone, whom Bugliosi detests, is the "only child of a Jewish father and French Catholic mother."

The name of Arthur Krock is absent. Mr. Krock's credibility is relevant, particularly since he did not offer documentary support for his prophetic words published during October 1963. Here, however, we are not considering a supermarket tabloid or the warnings of Chicken Little. The publication is *The New York Times* and the journalist is a recipient of three Pulitzer Prizes and generally considered to be the most responsible and respected writer of his time. He knew the Kennedy family well.

Krock was a conservative who chided Kennedy through the editorial page of the *Times* regarding what he considered to be the president's too liberal position on the question of civil rights.

On October 3, 1963, Krock published an historic column in *The New York Times*. Entitled "The Intra-Administration War in Vietnam," Krock revealed that the White House had declared war on the CIA and that the CIA was responding. Krock wrote, "the CIA had flatly refused to carry out instructions from Ambassador Henry Cabot Lodge" and that in one instance the CIA had "frustrated a plan of action Mr. Lodge brought from Washington." The reason was that the CIA "disagreed with it." The issue that caused the CIA such concern was the efforts to end the war in Vietnam.

Krock wrote that "the CIA's growth" was "likened to a malignancy" that his source, "a very high official," was "not even sure the White House could control . . . any longer."

Krock wrote that by releasing this information the "executive branches have expanded their war against the CIA from inner government councils to the American people via the press." Did we listen then? Are we listening now?

Here are Arthur Krock's frightening and prophetic words. Relying upon the "high official," certainly with the president's approval, Krock wrote, and *The New York Times* published these words:

"If the United States ever experiences an attempt at a coup to overthrow the government it will come from the CIA."

The next month President Kennedy was assassinated.

And today, more than four decades later, Bugliosi, in his attempt to blame one man and thus exonerate the CIA, could not find room in more than 1,600 pages of rhetoric, alleged "end notes and source notes," to mention the president's eminent friend and advisor who had predicted his demise based upon information coming from the White House just before the assassination.

While deciding not to publish Krock's words, Bugliosi thought far more relevant the allegation that Oswald had seen a couple of movies. Hence the entrance of Sinatra, Jennifer Jones and Sterling Hayden among others. Bugliosi relied upon the discredited words of a CIA employee, hearsay at best and a deliberate false statement at worst, to present a fictionalized version of Oswald's alleged response to a fictional film that demonstrates, according to Bugliosi, that we cannot know what impact the non–event had upon Oswald. Those fiction works included scenes of attempted murders. For proof of their relevancy, Bugliosi wrote: "The impact of those films on Lee's fantasy life cannot be known. He never discussed them with anyone beyond a comment made to Marina . . . . "[58]

That comment was a hearsay allegation published by Priscilla Johnson, an old CIA hand who had interviewed Marina Oswald for a book.[59] Years before, Johnson had interviewed Lee Harvey Oswald in Moscow for the CIA. Just after Oswald was murdered, the CIA arranged for Johnson to make false statements about Oswald as part of its disinformation campaign.

Bugliosi had been published before with a book called *Helter Skelter;* which Bugliosi wrote with another person, Curt Gentry. Gentry was an award-winning author who had published numerous successful books before *Helter Skelter;* Bugliosi had earned neither of those distinctions. Bugliosi included no page of acknowledgements in *Helter Skelter,* no doubt, because there was, as a reader of the book will learn, no one worthy in Bugliosi's view of being cited. Neither the police officers who investigated the murder scene, nor the police officers who had solved the crime, nor the police officers who had made the arrests, nor the other lawyers at the district attorney's office who had drafted the indictment, nor the investigators at that office who carefully prepared the case, and not even Mr. Gentry who probably wrote the book.

Bugliosi makes it clear in page after page that the Los Angeles Police Department and the District Attorney's Office, which employed him, made numerous errors and serious mistakes in judgment; and when he entered the case his brilliance and knowledge won the day and saved the City of Los Angeles a humiliating defeat in court. He brings a bit of that approach to his present work proclaiming over and over that any rational person who reads it must, without exception, agree with all of his seminal conclusions.

Does the fact that few bought Bugliosi's book demonstrate that he is wrong? Of course not. It does reveal that an informed American public, in overwhelming numbers, simply cannot accept his conclusions, as he makes statements that even the Warren Commission would not seriously entertain. It reflects upon his methodology of proclaiming

---

58. *Reclaiming History,* p. 765.
59. Regarding the book about her, Mrs. Oswald later stated that much of the book that Johnson had written was false and known to be false by Johnson.

false and entirely unsupported charges and offering, instead of facts, wild accusations.

A few years ago the United States Supreme Court made a decision. I publicly analyzed that finding, disagreed with it, and found it to be a disturbing precedent. Later Bugliosi wrote a book about the decision[60] and referred to the five justices of the United States Supreme Court as "justices who committed one of the biggest crimes in American History."[61] Not content with that absurd and defamatory allegation, Bugliosi added the justices were "the felonious five."[62] A felon, as all lawyers, including former prosecutors, must know, is a person who has been charged with the commission of a felony through a grand jury indictment, then tried by a jury and found guilty (unless he had pleaded guilty) and then sentenced by a judge. Of course, none of the justices had even been charged with a crime in court, only in a book by Bugliosi.

Still not content with his personal attack, Bugliosi stated that the majority of the Supreme Court justices had committed treason, a capital offense, and that they were "criminals in the very truest sense of the word." When Bugliosi is on an emotional rampage, even rules about redundancy suffer. Bugliosi then added that the five United States Supreme Court Justices had "the morals of an alley cat." In a somewhat intemperate remark he wrote that the Chief Justice of the United States "should be making license plates, not sitting as Chief Justice."[63]

Again Bugliosi demonstrated his lack of concern for language and the obligations imposed by a precise understanding of the law.

Bugliosi brought that same understanding of the law and language to his current work, stating that Lee Harvey Oswald confessed his guilt by *denying* that he owned the rifle in question. With that standard the former prosecutor must have obtained many confessions in his career.

Bugliosi came to this subject late, after many witnesses had died or quite reasonably remembered less than they had a quarter of a century earlier when their memories were fresh. He claims to have devoted the last twenty years of his life to examining the facts. In large measure he relied upon discredited FBI reports and CIA reports that had set

---

60. Vincent Bugliosi, *The Betrayal of America: How the Supreme Court Undermined the Constitution and Chose Our President* (New York, Thunder's Mouth Press, 2001).
61. BrainyQuotes.com.
62. Ibid.
63. Bugliosi, *The Betrayal of America*, p. 86.

forth the intelligence organizations' view of the record. He apparently rejected the judgment of those lawyers for the Warren Commission who later stated that they had been misled by the intelligence agencies that they had so heavily relied upon.

Bugliosi does not claim to have first-hand knowledge about the most relevant facts. He also claims that he debated with me three times.

When did the most recent debate take place? Bugliosi could not pin the exact date down, but he believes that it was in the "late 1980s or early 1990s." It is not just that he can't recall the date; he can't recall the decade. But he remembers quite accurately, he claims, what transpired. In reality, Bugliosi betrayed to the audience that he knew nothing about the facts surrounding the assassination. His ignorance was so blatantly apparent that audience members criticized me for debating someone who had no knowledge but who nevertheless insisted that the Warren Commission Report was accurate based upon his faith in our leaders.

Bugliosi admits that he agreed to act in a foreign television program as the "prosecutor" for Oswald *before* he knew anything of substance about the case; only then, he states in his book, did his research begin. The Warren Commission merely concluded that it found no credible evidence of a conspiracy. Bugliosi states that if you do not agree with his conclusion that it is absolutely certain that Oswald was the lone assassin then you are ignorant, stupid, or a fraud.

Many Americans viewed the assassination as one of the most tragic national events in their lifetime. They were offended that the Warren Commission took statements from the witnesses and sealed them so that the American people could neither know what the commission was doing nor what the witnesses had said and marked them "top secret" while no major newspaper or radio or television station called for public hearings. The American people then watched the murder of the suspect on television, an event that took place while Oswald was in the basement of the Dallas Police building surrounded by Dallas police officers. Most Americans longed for the truth. For decades Bugliosi, an attorney and a prosecutor, remained silent. Only when offered a role on a fake mock trial television program did he demonstrate any interest in the case, as he states in his book. He began his work to marshal the record in order to make his presentation for a television audience.

There were many Americans motivated for love of their country, not for reasons of personal profit, separately for the most part and later together in large measure, who looked into the case and the surrounding facts. They interviewed witnesses, conducted forensic experiments, read the one-volume Warren Commission Report and the twenty-six volumes comprised of that evidence that the Commission was willing to make available. Others, at their own expense, made frequent trips to the National Archives to examine recently declassified documents.

There were doctors and lawyers, journalists, housewives, teachers, forensic pathologists, retired women and men, and students—hundreds, then thousands of students. When some day we build a wall not just to honor those who have died in foreign wars but to celebrate those who worked tirelessly for the truth, their names should be engraved in a place of honor.

Bugliosi is wrong again as he awards me with too much credit. No one person through lectures and books swayed millions of Americans.

The FBI and J. Edgar Hoover had declared Oswald to be the lone assassin almost immediately after Oswald's arrest and before any investigation had been initiated. The Warren Commission endorsed that conclusion and relied primarily upon the FBI and its agents to conduct its investigation. Bugliosi adopted that same approach. For example, in his book Bugliosi writes, "Every night for several months he (Lane) gave a rousing speech on the assassination at a small Manhattan theater he had rented, Theater Four on West Fifth Street."[64]

It was not "rousing," it was a presentation of the facts, and I doubt Bugliosi was ever present when I spoke. In addition, Theater Four was never located on West Fifth Street. The first clue might be that it was not named Theatre Five. It was located on West Fourth Street. One citizen reviewer in correspondence with Amazon.com pointed out an anomaly: "while there is an East Fifth Street in Greenwich Village in Manhattan, there is no West Fifth Street there." Bugliosi saw no need to consult a primary source before publishing his inaccurate statement with absolute certainty. *The New York Times* would have been a source, still is, and other newspapers that reviewed the speech and any number of Manhattan telephone books could have helped. Or Bugliosi might have called me. He did not. Since he devoted an entire chapter to me that would have been the accepted routine to follow.

Bugliosi, never one to look for the facts once the FBI had instructed him as to what they were, relied upon an inaccurate FBI report initiated

---

64. *Reclaiming History,* p. 1001.

in Dallas, Texas, on July 31, 1964, which claimed that I had "spoken at Theatre Four, 424 West Fifth Street, NYC." The FBI reported an address that did not exist on a street that did not exist. Good enough for Bugliosi, who accepted the inaccurate information and then adopted it as his own in his book.

Clearly, the error in publishing the wrong address is not of significance except for disclosing, once again, that in small and large matters, Bugliosi relied upon flawed FBI documents while primary documents and witnesses to the contrary were readily available. Which brings us to another question. Did the publisher never hear of the term shared by the entire industry: *fact checker?* I have been published by small and large firms, and I am indebted to the many fact checkers that my publishers have consulted with, and I have never heard of a serious nonfiction work that was published without such a support system. They could have been busy here. Bugliosi's book, page after page, swarms with hundreds of demonstrably inaccurate assurances.

Bugliosi states that I never even mentioned in *Rush to Judgment* that Lee Harvey was arrested. He writes of me, "he doesn't even mention Oswald's arrest."[65] That statement, as is the case of hundreds of others, is false. In *Rush to Judgment* I not only stated that that Oswald was arrested, I provided the place of the arrest and the time of the arrest. I wrote that "Oswald was arrested in the Texas Theatre at approximately 1:50 PM that day" having previously referenced November 22, 1963, and explicitly citing the three pages of the Warren Commission Report where that information was set forth.[66] That information was easily retrievable since it began Chapter 5, entitled "Why Oswald Was Wanted." [67]

The evidence here indicates that this was not merely one of the numerous careless errors that abound; it provides a look into Bugliosi's methodology. Years ago one of the defenders of the Warren Commission made the same false claim in a magazine article. At a debate later held at Stanford University, when shown the relevant page from *Rush to Judgment* he admitted that he was wrong and that, in fact, I had discussed that matter in my book on page 81. I set forth the details of that entire exchange in *A Citizen's Dissent,* published in 1968.

---

65. *Reclaiming History,* page 1003.
66. *Rush to Judgment,* page 81.
67. Ibid.

The evidence seems to suggest that Bugliosi directed his research-ers to find any derogatory statement ever published about me, as well as others who disagreed with him, so that he could include it in his continuing diatribe. He clearly either failed to check the apparent sources for the facts or, having found them, decided not to allow the facts to stand in the way of his false conclusion. Bugliosi again demon-strated his standard; any accusation, even if patently false and demon-strably so, even if withdrawn by the original source, should be offered as fact, so long as it is aimed against one of his targets.

Bugliosi has difficulty, and apparently no interest in, separating fact from fiction. He regularly refers to the staged television presentation he appeared in as the "trial of Lee Harvey Oswald." There was no trial. Of course, generally one of the prerequisites for a trial is a live defendant. Often the defendant is an irreplaceable witness who can tell his lawyer what the facts are, or at least his version of them. In addition, the defendant is often the most important witness for the defense at trial as he testifies before the jury.

Bugliosi swears that it was pretty damn close to a real trial since the witnesses who "testified" on television had taken "an oath" to tell the truth. Fear of a perjury indictment is the fuel that drives the energy of a real trial. No indictment could follow the television program. All Bugliosi could say to the untruthful witness was, "OK that's it. You will never work in television again."

Bugliosi states that "the historical importance of the trial"[68] made it more reliable than the Warren Commission Report and the investigation by the House Select Committee on Assassinations. It was a staged television program.

Bugliosi looked the jurors in the eye. He spoke in an outraged and deadly serious tone, offering these thoughts: *You jurors at this trial are about to serve as jurors at one of the most important trials in the history of this country.* Except that they were not jurors, they were actors; there was going to be no trial, just a fictional television work, and "this country" was actually Great Britain as the television program was being taped, photographed and directed in London.

While it is difficult to take Bugliosi's work seriously, the subject matter, the death of the president, requires that we do so. Let us then examine just one area: the numerous allegations that Bugliosi has made

---

68. *Reclaiming History,* p. xvii.

regarding Acquilla Clemons and Helen Louise Markham, two witnesses to the murder of a police officer.

First, the facts. In seeking to determine the circumstances surrounding the death of Officer J. D. Tippit, the Warren Commission reached only one conclusion that was a logical consequence of the evidence: that Tippit was shot to death near the intersection of East 10th Street and Patton Avenue in the Oak Cliff section of Dallas early in the afternoon of November 22. The FBI purportedly "conducted approximately 25,000 interviews and reinterviews" of persons having information of possible relevance to the investigation, but it inexplicably omitted to question an eyewitness to the Tippit shooting. Her name is Acquilla Clemons. The Warren Commission said that she did not exist. However, after the film *Rush to Judgment,* in which I was seen interviewing her, was released, that official position became, in intelligence doublespeak jargon, inoperable. Bugliosi defends the commission by stating rather clumsily that I had implied in *Rush to Judgment* "that the commission knew of her existence and didn't want to know the truth she had to tell." Bugliosi continued, "But Lane presents no evidence that the FBI or Warren Commission knew of Mrs. Clemons' existence." Every statement made by Bugliosi in this regard is false.

I had *implied* nothing. I had stated, as a fact, that the FBI and the Warren Commission knew of the existence of Mrs. Clemons. I then presented not only the evidence for that assertion, but absolute proof of its accuracy. On August 21, 1964, before the Warren Commission Report was published, J. Edgar Hoover, the director of the FBI, sent a letter to J. Lee Rankin, the general counsel of the Warren Commission, stating that I had discussed "the existence" of Mrs. Clemons during a radio program. Hoover sent to the Warren Commission "two copies of a verbatim transcription" of that program. Bugliosi knew that to be a fact since it was reported, with citations to the Warren Commission documents, in *Rush to Judgment,* published in 1966. I had made the same point in numerous public lectures; the record reveals that the FBI was always present and often reported my remarks to the commission.

Mrs. Clemons, a heroic African American woman living in the racist environment of Dallas in 1963, was warned by white Dallas police officers that if she told anyone what she had witnessed (that Oswald was not involved in the murder of Tippit and that two other men had been), she could be killed. She told me that she was afraid but said that since she was a religious woman she believed that she must tell the truth about the death of a police officer. Bugliosi referred to her as "another of the endless and countless kooks in the Kennedy assassination."

In this fashion Bugliosi disposed of the statement of this witness and many others who did not support his conclusions. The witness with inconvenient testimony was a liar, a fool, a nut or a kook. Only Bugliosi, who had not been there, had never talked to most of the witnesses, and was not concerned about the matter for almost a quarter of a century, knew the truth.

Thank you for your patience as we have examined the Bugliosi methodology. Now let us go to the heart of the matter, Bugliosi's reliance upon Helen Markham as a witness to the murder of Officer Tippit. Bugliosi states and restates that she is a reliable witness, and that he has relied upon her and her identification of Lee Harvey Oswald in a Dallas Police lineup. Markham is more than a reliable witness to the Tippit killing in Bugliosi's mind. Perhaps recognizing that there is no credible evidence that implicates Oswald in the assassination of the president, Bugliosi makes a remarkable statement. He asserts that even without the "evidence proving that Oswald killed Kennedy, it was obvious that Oswald's murder of Tippit *alone* proved it was he who murdered Kennedy"[69] (italics added). As proof for this claim, he cites a Dallas police officer who, when he arrested Oswald in the Texas Theatre, without any evidence that Oswald had committed a crime, allegedly said, "I think we have got our man on *both* accounts."[70]

As we have seen, Bugliosi tends to characterize those he disagrees with by the use of unpleasant names. Five members of the United States Supreme Court are "traitors"; an important, sincere and honest witness, Clemons, is "a kook"; Bolden is apparently "a liar"; and I am, of course, "a fraud." Clemons and Bolden, two crucially important witnesses, both African Americans, are not even mentioned in his book except in the index, which refers the reader to a note in a CD.

I have chosen a different method to present the facts. First we have Bugliosi's view, then my statement of the facts, and now we will go to the record. The actual statements of the witness made under oath,

---

69. *Reclaiming History*, p. 961.
70. Ibid.

observations by counsel for the Warren Commission and the Warren Commission Report follow so that you can reach your own conclusions.

While Bugliosi relies upon Markham, a lawyer for the Warren Commission, who had observed her unusual conduct and testimony, described her unkindly as a "screwball." That description was uncharitable and no doubt resulted from the frustration of counsel trying to get one straight and consistent answer from the witness. Yet, when a witness to any event, certainly including a murder, testifies, that witness places his, or in this case, her, credibility before the triers of the facts. Mrs. Markham may have been a somewhat confused person before November 22, or perhaps the trauma of seeing a police officer murdered was so unsettling that her subsequent testimony was of little or no value. Whatever the cause of the almost unprecedented confusion, the testimony must be critically examined before stating as Bugliosi does that she was a reliable witness.

Bugliosi offers his own fictionalized description of what had transpired. He writes that Tippit had:

his right hand, like a western sheriff, on his gun butt . . . And then, "BANG! BANG! BANG! BANG! Bullets fly across the hood of the car.

Bugliosi, in continuing his own account, offered as fact additional and undocumented speculation:

Tippit had a bad habit . . . of never looking anyone straight in the eye . . . This may have accounted for how Oswald got the jump on him.

Bugliosi then solemnly recounts what he told the "jury" at the trial of Lee Harvey Oswald about these events. He is, of course, referring to the actors in the fictionalized television presentation.

These are Bugliosi's conclusions in his book about the testimony of Ms. Markham:

* I misidentified myself to Ms. Markham as "Captain Fritz of the Dallas Police Department" when I interviewed her.
* I refused to give a tape recording of my discussion with Markham to the Warren Commission but was ultimately forced to do so.
* I invented the description of the man Markham had seen as being "short, stocky and with bushy hair" and sought to put those words into her mouth.

★ Markham was a reliable and truthful witness against Oswald.

★ She picked Oswald out of a police lineup as the person she saw shooting Tippit.

★ She testified before the Warren Commission positively identifying Oswald as the person she had seen.

Every statement made by Bugliosi referred to above is untrue.

Here I will present a brief summary of the responses to Bugliosi's accusations as I invite you to read the documents and, if you wish, to check them against the documents published by the Warren Commission.[71]

While it is true that Markham finally did say that Oswald was the man she had seen, to call it a "positive identification" one must, as both the commission and Bugliosi were eager to do, ignore the circumstances of that identification. Markham had repeatedly under oath told the commission that she had not identified anyone at the police lineup. Oswald was in that lineup. For an extended time the only thing Markham was "positive" about was that she did not recognize anyone in the lineup.

The statement that Markham picked Oswald out of the lineup is also false as we have seen.

The statement that I tried to put words into Markham's mouth, an original Bugliosi fabrication, is belied by a review of the facts. Since Markham had told reporters, long before I had spoken with her, that the man she had seen shoot Tippit was "short" (*Oswald was not short)* that he was "stocky" (*Oswald was thin*) and that he had "bushy hair" (*Oswald had thinning hair and a receding hairline),* I called her to discuss her original description. She in part conceded the accuracy of her original assessment of the shooter and in part rejected it. The original words were hers, not mine, as Bugliosi knew but declined to reveal.

I did not refuse to give a tape recording of the interview with Markham to the Warren Commission until I was forced to do so. Bugliosi knows that his assertion is not true.

---

71. Portions of Helen Markham's testimony are reproduced in *Rush to Judgment,* in the chapter entitled "The Murder of Officer Tippit: The Eyewitnesses," pp. 178–89.

Subsequently, after the commission received the tape recording, it submitted it to the FBI laboratory for examination. While I had made a copy of the recording, I had sent the original to the commission. The FBI confirmed that the recording was accurate, that it had been made from the start of the conversation to the end and had not been edited, altered, or deleted in any fashion.

Bugliosi wrote that I had introduced myself to Markham by stating that I was "Captain Fritz of the Dallas Police Department."[72] That statement is false, and Bugliosi knew it was false when he made it. The tape recording relied upon by the Warren Commission, a transcript that Bugliosi read, proved that I introduced myself as follows:

"My name is Mr. Lane. I'm an attorney investigating the Oswald case."

The entire recording demonstrated that I never stated that I was from the Dallas or any other police department. Bugliosi knew those facts when he published his entirely fabricated accusation, an accusation that even the Warren Commission had rejected.

Was Markham a reliable and truthful witness as Bugliosi asserts? She had committed perjury before the Warren Commission, and she was aware that she had done so. She asked counsel for the commission if she would get into trouble for having lied under oath.

You now have read Bugliosi's position and mine. Now let us read the testimony of Helen Louise Markham when she appeared before the Warren Commission. She was asked by commission counsel about the police lineup that she viewed. There were four men in the lineup including Lee Harvey Oswald.

Q: Now when you went into the room you looked these people over, these four men?
Markham: Yes, sir.
Q: Did you recognize anyone in the lineup?
Markham: No, sir.
Q: You did not? Did you see anybody—I have asked you that question before—did you recognize anybody from their face?
Markham: From their face, no.
Q: Did you identify anybody in these four people?

---

72. *Reclaiming History,* p. 1006.

Markham: I didn't know nobody.
Q: I know you didn't know anybody, but did anybody in that
          lineup look like anybody you had seen before?
Markham: No. I had never seen none of them, none of these men.
Q: No one of the four?
Markham: No one of them.
Q: No one of all four?
Markham: No, sir.

At that point, counsel decided that it was important to lead the witness.

Q: Was there a number two man in there?

Mrs. Markham replied, "Number two is the one I picked."
Counsel began another question: "I thought you just told me that you hadn't," but Mrs. Markham interrupted to answer inexplicably, "I thought you wanted me to describe their clothing."
Counsel then inquired:

Q: You recognized him from his appearance?
Markham: I asked—I looked at him. When I saw this man I wasn't
          sure, but I had cold chills just run all over me.

From stating on several occasions that she recognized nobody in the lineup, she ended up saying that she "wasn't sure." Apparently good enough for Bugliosi and the Warren Commission to state that she had made a positive identification of Oswald, which seems to have been based upon the chill factor.

Approximately three weeks before Markham testified, she and I had a telephone conversation. When the commission asked me to testify I told them about it. At that point the Warren Commission invited Markham to Washington, D.C., where she testified that she had never spoken with me. Based upon her statement, Warren said that he doubted that my statement about the telephone call was accurate. I then informed the commission that I had tape-recorded the conversation, hoping that they would then direct me to make it available to them. At the time, it was not a crime to record the conversation, but it would have been a crime to make and divulge the tape. I thought that if the Chief Justice ordered me to divulge it, I would probably be safe from prosecution. He did not. Nevertheless, I subsequently sent the

recording to the Warren Commission. I had made a copy for myself
and sent the original to the commission. The recording was examined
by experts at the Federal Bureau of Investigation who asserted, as we
have seen, that it was a complete and unedited document. On July
23, 1964, the commission recalled Markham and played the tape for
her. Counsel for the commission said, "We have a tape recording of a
conversation that purports to be a conversation between you and Mark
Lane on the telephone." Markham stated, "I never talked to that man."
The exchange before the commission follows:

Q: Is that not your voice on the tape?
Markham: I can't tell about my voice, but that man—I never talked
            to no woman or no man like that . . . I'll tell the truth
            (raising right hand) and those words that he's saying—
            that's nothing like the telephone call I got—nothing.

As Markham listened to the tape, she heard herself agree that the
man she saw was short, a little on the heavy side, with somewhat bushy
hair. At that point, she said, "This man—I have never talked with. This
lady was never on the telephone. This man that called me like I told
you, he told me he was from the city hall, the police department, the
police department of the city hall."

Q: Well, now, do you remember having this conversation
            with somebody?
Markham: Yes, I do. But he told me he was from the police department
            of city hall and he had to get some information.

Counsel was aware of the fact, as was Markham, that the unedited
tape began as follows:

Lane: Mrs. Markham?
Markham: Yes.
Lane: My name is Mr. Lane. I'm an attorney investigating the
            Oswald case.
Markham: Yes.

Nowhere on the tape was there any mention that I said I was
from the Dallas Police Department or in any way associated with the
police. While Markham seemed even more confused, it was quite clear

to counsel for the Warren Commission that I had never said that I was from the Police Department.

Q: Now, did he tell you he was from the police department?
Markham: Yes, sir.
Q: Now, on this tape recording right here, this man is asking you what the police did.
Markham: I know it.
Q: And he said they—the police took you and took your affidavit.
Markham: That man—I have never talked to that man. I talked to a man that was supposed to have been from the police department of the city hall.
Q: Do you recognize this as the voice of the man you talked to?
Markham: No, it is not.
Q: This is not the same voice?
Markham: No.
Q: How do you explain the fact that the woman's voice on this tape recording is your voice?
Markham: I never heard that.
Q: You never heard the man's voice before?
Markham: And I never heard this lady's voice before—this the first time.
Q: Do you have any doubt in your mind at all that the lady's voice on the tape now is your voice?
Markham: It is my voice, but this man told me he was from the city police.

The tape recording reveals that Markham gave a description of the events that was different from the statements made by every other witness who arrived on the scene. She said that she had talked with Officer Tippit as he was stretched out in the street and that he was talking to her, but he could not "get it plain enough" for her to hear or understand what he was saying. She said she was present when he was placed in an ambulance and was still alive at that point. The Warren Commission concluded that several shots were fired, "hitting Tippit four times and killing him instantly." Although she had stated that she had spent some time alone with him when no one else was present, every other witness stated that immediately after the shooting a large group of spectators appeared.

One is constrained to feel sorry for Mrs. Markham and whatever problems she was experiencing. What is unacceptable is to rely upon her "positive identification" of Oswald and her description of anything relating to the Tippit killing, including my conversation with her, especially if one is going to, as Bugliosi does, also rely upon her as proof that Oswald killed President Kennedy. She knew she had committed perjury, and she asked counsel for the commission if she was going to be prosecuted. She was assured that she would not be prosecuted.

While Bugliosi declined to talk with me, although he devoted an entire chapter to making statements about my work that were untrue, he did talk with Dr. Cyril H. Wecht, a distinguished forensic pathologist and attorney who had devoted a great deal of time to examining the medical evidence. Dr. Wecht had concluded, and had consistently stated over the years, that he was convinced by the evidence that two bullets struck JFK in the head, fired in synchronized fashion. One bullet had been fired from the grassy knoll area, in front and to the right of President Kennedy, and one bullet had been fired from the rear. Bugliosi's chapter entitled "A Conversation with Dr. Cyril Wecht" tends to demonstrate that had Bugliosi interviewed me before writing about me it probably would have made little or no impact upon his determination to distort the record.

On July 11, 2007, I asked Cyril if he had read Bugliosi's chapter about him and if it was true. He replied, "What is true is that I talked to him." As to the content of the chapter, Dr. Wecht said, "He took bits and pieces out of context and presented my views and opinions in a much distorted and unrecognizable fashion."

I told Dr. Wecht that Bugliosi concluded that chapter by stating that Dr. Wecht's words demonstrated "that there is no credible evidence whatsoever that any shots were fired from the president's right side or right front (grassy knoll)" and that "the conspiracy theorists' leading medical forensic expert cannot even *hypothesize* a shooting from the right side or right front that is intellectually feasible."

Dr. Wecht stated that Bugliosi's words were inexplicable since he, Dr. Wecht, had stated to Bugliosi and continues to believe that all of the relevant evidence, including the medical evidence, the x-rays of the president that he had examined, and the statements of the physicians, had long ago convinced him that a shot had been fired from the grassy knoll area. He added that his view had been reinforced by all of the most recent tests and forensic examinations that demonstrate that a shot had been fired from the grassy knoll.

I have pointed out numerous distortions of the record present in just the few pages that I read of Bugliosi's book and have offered proof that his assertions are inaccurate. I have read the reviews by informed citizens published on the Mary Ferrell Foundation website and even on the website of Amazon.com, an attempted purveyor of the book, and I have been impressed by the scholarship of those critics who have exposed the numerous other flaws in Bugliosi's work including his lack of understanding of the forensic evidence and his reckless disregard for the truth regarding the testimony of witnesses.

The members of the Warren Commission offered an untruthful version of the facts during a time of national crisis. They acted politically, and whatever their motives had been (we cannot preclude a distorted view of patriotism and a genuine search for a falsely based national tranquility), they deliberately produced a document that sought to mislead our nation. For such conduct, traducing the law and violating their sacred obligation to report the truth, there can be neither an acceptable explanation nor excuse.

Bugliosi, four decades later, published a volume far more extreme in language and in conclusions. Likely, rarely before have so many forests been sacrificed in so reckless a project.

BOOK THREE

THE SECRET
SERVICE

Abraham Bolden

He was called the Jackie Robinson of the United States Secret Service. Since I knew Jackie, I knew that it was not a simple accolade and that it encompassed an onslaught of racism and unearned suffering. It has been said that such pain is redemptive. That may be so, but not necessarily in this world.

Abraham Bolden was the first African American to be assigned to the White House detail to protect the president as a member of the United States Secret Service. John Kennedy had personally invited him. Many of his new colleagues were former hard-drinking police officers, born and raised in Southern states, who referred to President Kennedy as a "nigger lover" who was "screwing up the country" with his civil rights initiatives. Some Secret Service agents assigned to the White House detail said that if shots were fired at the president, they would take no action to protect him. A few of the agents said that they would resign from the Secret Service rather than give up their lives to shield him. Abe Bolden heard those and similar assertions many times.

Unlike some other national leaders who ignored their Secret Service agents who were always present, Kennedy made sure that they were comfortable, and he engaged them in conversations about matters unrelated to their work assignments. When the president passed by, he often stopped to chat with Bolden, asking about his family and sending his regards to them. This seemed to outrage Agent Harvey Henderson, Bolden's immediate supervisor.

Bolden vividly recalled the scene when Henderson was seated on a couch drinking beer and staring at him in a room with other agents. Henderson said, "Bolden." Abe acknowledged the greeting, "Yeah,

Harvey." Then, staring at Bolden and speaking slowly to emphasize each word, Henderson said, "I'm going to tell you something and I don't want you ever to forget it. You're a nigger. You were born a nigger, and when you die you'll still be a nigger. You will always be nothing but a nigger. So act like one!" The other agents present were silent.

At that point Bolden thought it might be better to return to his less glamorous work in Chicago rather than continue with the prestigious assignment to the White House detail. He was depressed by the poor level of protection provided to the president by agents, some of whom were addicted to drinking, some of whom "were cocky senior agents" who showed little respect for Kennedy, and some of whom were "inexperienced probationary agents and trainees." Bolden left the White House detail to work in Chicago. He was not discreet about his observations. He said that "every agent in the Chicago office knew my feelings about the White House detail and that I believed that its 'protection' of President Kennedy was a complete sham."

Sometime after the assassination Bolden, then in Washington, attempted to contact the Warren Commission so that he could offer to testify. He called the White House switchboard to obtain the number of Rankin, the commission's general counsel. That call was overheard by another agent. The Secret Service invited him to return at once to Chicago, falsely stating that there was a case that required his immediate presence there. There was no case, and when he arrived the threats and the interrogation began. "You called the White House didn't you, Abe? We have the records and we know that you tried to call someone there." He was told that he was in trouble and warned that "loose lips sink ships." A Secret Service inspector said, "Listen, Abe, Kennedy is dead. We did our best to protect him and it didn't work out. We are not going to stand by and let you bury our careers and destroy the Secret Service."

Bolden was indicted for attempting to sell information to a suspect. My own research into the matter, including interviews with Bolden while his appeal was pending, constrained me to believe that he was framed and that no crime was ever anticipated or committed. An examination of the court records, the criminal records of the accusers, the almost unprecedented actions of the judge and the appellate court, and the character of the judge and prosecutor, convinces me beyond any doubt that Bolden was denied a fair trial.

At Bolden's first trial the jurors were unable to reach a verdict, and a mistrial was declared. At that trial the judge informed the jury that the evidence demonstrated that Bolden was guilty. Later the judge defended himself by saying that he did not say that *he believed* Bolden was guilty, merely that the evidence showed that he was. That bizarre assertion relies upon a distinction without a difference. The judge violated the judicial canon of ethics and committed the most meaningful misconduct possible as a judicial officer. He then insisted upon presiding at the second trial as well, where his biased view was evident. The judge and the prosecutor systematically removed every black and Hispanic prospective juror. In Chicago, Bolden was tried by an all-white jury at a trial controlled by a biased judge who had said he was guilty and prosecuted by a lawyer who had apparently suborned perjury. He was convicted.

I have tried many hundreds of cases during the last sixty years. Judges, being human, often have fixed opinions about a case. Many of the judges both in state and federal courts have been fair. I have known judges who I was quite certain believed that my client was guilty and that his defense was meritless. Yet that private opinion was never communicated to the jury. That is my standard for determining whether a judge meets the strict discipline of his profession.

The conviction was followed by another unrelated trial at which the testimony of a crucial government witness at Bolden's trial testified that he had committed perjury to secure Bolden's conviction and had been instructed to do so by the prosecutor. The prosecutor did not deny that he had suborned perjury. Yet the conviction was permitted to stand, and no action was taken against the prosecuting attorney. The hysteria surrounding the assassination of President Kennedy was the foundation for the creation of scoundrel time in America from which the judiciary was not immune.[73]

---

73. The judge who tried the Bolden case, Joseph S. Perry, was born in Alabama in 1896. After the prosecution of Bolden, Edward V. Hanrahan, a "law-and-order prosecutor" known as "Fast Eddy," organized a Chicago Police Department raid on the headquarters of the Black Panther Party. They killed Fred Hampton and Mark Clark while they were sleeping. The FBI had provided an informant with a powerful barbiturate, secobarbital, to place in Hampton's dinner several hours before the police break-in. Later Hanrahan was indicted for conspiracy to present false evidence and obstruction of justice regarding that illegal raid. A wrongful death civil suit was brought by the families of those who had been murdered. It was dismissed by Judge Perry. Perry's biased ruling was reversed

After Bolden was convicted he was sentenced to six years in prison. When I learned that he was being held in the Springfield Medical Center for Federal Prisoners, I was concerned. In his book, *The Echo from Dealey Plaza,*[74] Bolden wrote:

> Lane was no novice, and knowing what Springfield might mean for me, he called a press conference in which he announced where I was being held, and described his fear that the government might try to silence me further by declaring me insane. Mark Lane's statements were broadcast widely.[75]

Not long after Bolden was incarcerated in the prison area at Springfield, he was placed in solitary confinement in the hospital section of the facility and forced to take mind-altering drugs. After his lawyer learned that he had not been before a classification committee and that his official status had not been changed, rendering the transfer and involuntary use of medication both in violation of the regulations and illegal, he was transferred to the prison facility and the medication was discontinued.

The indictment and subsequent trial of Abraham Bolden had their anticipated effect. He was not permitted to testify before the Warren Commission, and that decision was made not just by corrupt prosecutors and biased judges but by Earl Warren himself. Since one of the responsibilities of the commission was to evaluate the role of the Secret Service, James Rowley, the director of the agency, was called as a witness.[76] Warren presided, and as always, Dulles was at his side. Two lawyers and three other Commission members were also present.

---

by the United States Court of Appeals for the Seventh Circuit. Before the case was retried the defendants settled the action for $1.85 million. Hanrahan, after much political maneuvering, was never convicted. He ran for various offices but was defeated in every election. Fred Hampton had been a highly respected and beloved community organizer. The Chicago City Council unanimously passed a resolution establishing December 4, 2004, as "Fred Hampton Day." A street in Maywood, Illinois, Hampton's hometown, was named to honor him.

74. Abraham Bolden, *The Echo from Dealey Plaza: The True Story of the First African American on the White House Secret Service Detail and His Quest for Justice After the Assassination of JFK,* (Harmony Books, 2008).
75. Ibid, p. 252.
76. All references to Rowley's testimony are to Vol. V, pages 449–455.

Rowley admitted that agents were drinking when they were on duty, which he conceded was a violation calling for termination from the agency. However, when asked if the men had been reprimanded, he answered that each man had been told that what they did was wrong and "I am quite sure that they all understand it at this time."

When asked if he had "any other complaints similar to this," Rowley testified, "we had one last month" and quickly added that the agent "is currently under indictment."[77]

He asked to go off the record to discuss the matter; but Warren responded, "There is no reason to discuss that case here, Chief." There followed some banter about when Bolden, the unnamed agent, made his "complaints" about the misconduct of members of the White House detail; but neither Warren, nor Dulles, nor the general counsel to the commission ever inquired or learned about the nature of the "complaints." Bolden was never interviewed by the commission. He had been indicted in May 1964 just in time for Rowley, who testified in June, to make that claim to Warren. Warren, Dulles and Rankin were on a mission to reassure America that all was well and sat there side by side, simian-like, with their eyes, ears and mouths covered. In that blissful state of ignorance they determined that they had met their obligation to evaluate the Secret Service protection. If it had inquired about Bolden's "complaints;" the commission would have obtained a great deal of information to properly evaluate the efforts and planning of the Secret Service to protect the president.

In its report the commission concluded, after stating that there were "many standard operating procedures of the Secret Service in addition to its preventive intelligence operations," that "examination of these procedures shows that in most respects they were well conceived and ably executed by personnel of the Service."[78]

The Warren Commission made this summary statement:

> The Commission finds that the Secret Service agents in the motorcade who were immediately responsible for the President's safety reacted promptly at the time the shots were fired. Their actions demonstrate that the President and the

77. An indictment, Warren acting as a judge had often observed, has no probative value; it proves nothing; it is merely a mechanism by which a prosecutor brings a case toward trial against a person presumed to be innocent.
78. Warren Commission Report, pages 444–5.

Nation can expect courage and devotion to duty from the agents of the Secret Service.[79]

It was almost as if Kennedy had survived. After the politicians had concluded that Rowley was doing a heck of a job, a more serious investigation took place; and the result was quite different. In 1978, the House Select Committee on Assassinations (HSCA), with the participation of experienced lawyers not burdened with preconceptions, was in this instance willing to listen to eyewitnesses, not just the head of the bureaucracy. After a careful review its conclusions were startling to those who had relied upon the Warren Commission. Under the heading "THE SECRET SERVICE WAS DEFICIENT IN THE PERFORMANCE OF ITS DUTIES,"[80] the HSCA concluded that:

> The Secret Service possessed information that was not properly analyzed, investigated, or used by the Secret Service in connection with the President's trip to Dallas; in addition, Secret Service agents in the motorcade were inadequately prepared to protect the President from a sniper.[81]

The HSCA was specifically concerned about the refusal of an agent to protect the president when the firing began:

> No actions were taken by the agent in the right front seat of the Presidential limousine to cover the President with his body, although it would have been consistent with Secret Service procedure for him to have done so.[82]

The committee stated that incorrect instructions were given to the agent by the Secret Service and that those instructions were responsible for the failure of the Secret Service agent to act appropriately.[83]

Unlike the Warren Commission, the HCSA had obtained the testimony of Abraham Bolden.[84] They knew that members of the Secret Service assigned to protect the president disliked him and had vowed never to take a bullet to save his life.

---

79. Warren Commission Report, p. 454.
80. *The Final Assassinations Report*, Bantam Books, page 289.
81. Ibid, p. 290.
82. Ibid, p. 300.
83. Ibid.
84. Ibid, p. 295–6.

The only responsibility for Secret Service members assigned to the White House detail is to protect the president. It is for that sole commitment that they received specialized training. The Secret Service driver is obligated to drive at a maximum speed if shots are fired and the Secret Service agent in the passenger seat is required to cover the president's body with his own.

The first bullet struck President Kennedy in the back. It caused a painful but not a fatal wound. Five and six tenths of a second later, a bullet fired from the front struck his head and killed him. That brief period is an eternity for Secret Service agents to accomplish their mission. The driver is required to speed up immediately and the other agent required to rush to the back seat and throw the president down and cover his body with his own.

When the first shot was fired, the driver slowed down the limousine. The agent in the passenger seat sat still in frozen indifference, not moving to the rear of the vehicle, not even attempting to reach the man he was sworn to protect. At that defining moment in history, the agents in the limousine violated their oaths and cowered instead of acting appropriately. The agents violated their sworn duty but were true to the commitment they had previously made to each other when they stated that they despised the president's civil rights initiatives and would never take a bullet to save his life.

Bolden was also prepared to tell the Warren Commission about the assassination that had been planned to take place on November 2, 1963, almost three weeks before Dallas. President Kennedy was scheduled to arrive in Chicago that morning in order to ride in a motorcade and attend the Army–Air Force football game at Soldier Field. The Secret Service was warned about a death threat. The manager of a Chicago motel was suspicious about two guests. She had seen several automatic rifles equipped with telescopic sights lying on a bed in the room they had rented. On the bed also was the outline of the route that President Kennedy would travel in Chicago. It would have taken the president past the building with the weapons and the two male occupants. The Secret Service placed the two men under surveillance. It should not have been much of a challenge; the suspects had carelessly left incriminating evidence in a room protected only by a "Do Not Disturb" sign. Yet it proved to be a task the Secret Service was not able to handle or had decided to bungle.

The agents lost track of the men and at some level it was decided not to pursue the matter. Bolden said that "no one was sent to the room to fingerprint it or get an I.D.The case was lost and that was the end of it." When Kennedy was informed that two heavily armed, possible hit men were loose in the city, he cancelled plans for the visit. The White House reported that the president had a cold.

About three weeks later, when the president was killed by a shot fired from behind a wooden fence on a grassy knoll, officers, weapons drawn, ran up the hill to search the area behind the fence. They found men there who produced valid Secret Service credentials.[85] Those credentials were apparently created by a top secret group within the CIA operating illegally as the Technical Services Division (TSD).

A memorandum written by Sidney Gottlieb of the CIA's secret TSD revealed that the CIA had provided to the Secret Service all important forms of identification to be used by Secret Service agents, focusing upon documents to be used by those agents during presidential campaigns. During 1963, Gottlieb, at the request of the CIA, had also devised a method for killing Castro just as rapprochement between Cuba and the United States seemed possible.

Bolden was not aware of all of the secret plans devised by the CIA. However, had his request to testify before the Warren Commission been accommodated, he would have revealed that during January 1964, less then two months after the assassination, the Secret Service withdrew the CIA-prepared identification documents and issued new credentials prepared by its own agency.[86] To an inquiring group of investigators, that information might well have served as the Rosetta stone.

Later, representatives of the Dallas Police Department, the FBI, the Secret Service, the CIA and the Warren Commission said it was a joint effort, referring of course, to their investigation. There did seem to be evidence of inter-agency cooperation even before the shots were fired.

---

85. Vol VII, page 535. A commission attorney, Wesley J. Liebeler, who must have known that there were no Secret Service agents behind the fence, as the Secret Service had made that clear months earlier, declined to ask any questions about the men with those credentials.
86. James W. Douglass, *JFK and the Unspeakable* (Maryknoll, NY: Orbis Books 2008), pages 266 and 449.

The Actions of the Secret Service Agents in the Presidential Limousine

Secret Service Agent William R. Greer was driving the presidential limousine. Sitting to his right was another Secret Service agent, Roy H. Kellerman. Kellerman was in charge of the White House detail for the two days that President Kennedy was scheduled to be in Dallas. Kellerman testified, "I was in charge of the detail for this trip for President Kennedy for this trip to Texas for those two days."[87] However, Kellerman was an emergency fill-in for the Secret Service agent who had made the plans for the visit to Dallas and was in charge of the detail. Agent Gerald A. Behn, apparently at the last minute, decided to take a vacation and directed the ill-prepared Kellerman to take his place. Behn was not the only absentee that day.

Eleven of the most experienced members of the White House detail had been transferred at their own request to other assignments within sixty days before the assassination, requiring less experienced agents to take their places. Each request for a transfer had been granted. The Warren Commission never explained those anomalous events leading up to November 22, 1963. There are only two references to Behn in the Warren Commission Report. The first is the assertion that he was in charge of the White House detail and had inquired

---

87. Vol. 2, p. 63.

about "potential sites for the luncheon that was planned for President Kennedy on November 22."[88] The second reference is that after the assassination, Kellerman and Hill "telephoned the head of the White House detail, Gerald A. Behn, to advise him of the assassination."[89] The commission never discussed what precluded Behn from being present when there had been so many threats to the president regarding that visit or why the most experienced members of the White House detail had been permitted to abandon their posts at the crucial time.

After the first shot was fired, according to the commission, "Agent Greer immediately accelerated the presidential car."[90] That statement was false and was known to be false by the commission as demonstrated by all of the available evidence, including eyewitness testimony of spectators and of Secret Service agents and documents, including the Zapruder film. It is true that the presidential limousine had the capacity to accelerate quickly. Kellerman testified, "I have driven that car many times, and I never ceased to be amazed, even to this day, with the weight of the automobile plus the power that is under the hood; we just literally jumped out of the God-damned road."[91] However, the acceleration began only after President Kennedy had been assassinated. Many of the witnesses stated that after the first shot was fired, Greer had brought the limousine to a stop and that he took no evasive action by swerving the vehicle and that he was not told to leave the scene quickly by Kellerman until after the president had been killed. Here is the relevant testimony of Greer and Kellerman.

Greer, the driver, testified, "So I heard this noise . . . and then I heard it again. And I glanced over my shoulder and saw Governor Connally like he was starting to fall. Then I realized there was something wrong. I tramped on the accelerator."[92] Kellerman testified that when he spoke to Greer about leaving the area, "the car leaped forward from an acceleration."[93] Kellerman explained the delay by stating that when he first heard the rifle shot he thought that the "report (was) like a

---

88. WCR, p. 31.
89. WCR, p. 57.
90. Ibid, page 4.
91. Vol. 2, page 74.
92. Vol. 2, p. 117.
93. Vol. 2, p. 77.

firecracker, pop."[94] He also said that "I heard a voice from the back seat and I firmly believe it was the president's, 'My God, I am hit.' " [95] A bullet had previously entered the president's throat and Kellerman's testimony, supported by no credible evidence, was a fabrication.

Greer testified that when he heard the shot fired, he did not believe it was a firecracker; he explained, "I heard a noise that I thought was a backfire of one of the motorcycle policemen, and I didn't—it did not affect me like anything else. I just thought that is what it was." By the time he even considered accelerating, a final shot had killed President Kennedy.

Secret Service agents are trained to distinguish the sound of a rifle shot from a backfire or firecracker. Anyone who has ever fired or heard the sound of a high-powered rifle shot can usually distinguish it from the sound created by a firecracker or a backfire. Even I, who have not fired a rifle since I was eighteen years old while taking basic training during World War II, can tell the difference.

Secret Service agents assigned to the White House detail who may be assigned to drive the presidential limousine are trained at the first sound of what might be gunfire to immediately accelerate and to take evasive action by swerving. They are repeatedly instructed that slowing the vehicle is not an option and is counterproductive.

Secret Service Agents riding in, but not driving, the presidential limousine are instructed that at the first indication of a noise that might be a shot to immediately cover the body of the president in an effort to prevent him from being assassinated. We need no testimony from eyewitnesses to support Kellerman's own testimony and the Zapruder film, which demonstrates without question that Kellerman never moved from his seat after the first shot was fired until he arrived at the hospital with the dead president in the backseat of the limousine.

One Secret Service agent in the follow-up car, Clint Hill, testified that he left the running board and caught up with the limousine after the president had been killed. Hill testified that "I jumped from the car, realizing that something was wrong, ran to the Presidential limousine."[96]

---

94. Vol 2, p. 73.
95. Ibid.
96. Vol. 2, p. 138.

Hill testified that by the time he "jumped on the car . . . the president at that time had been shot in the head."[97]

The fastest runner in the world, in a one-mile race, wearing running shoes and a track suit, cannot attain a speed in excess of fifteen miles an hour. The limousine was specifically designed to accelerate to more than one hundred miles per hour in a very short time. After President Kennedy had been struck in the head, Hill was able to catch the limousine while wearing street shoes and dressed in a suit. The limousine was at that time moving very slowly.

The only Secret Service agent near the president's limousine who met his obligation that day was Clint Hill. However, he had not been assigned to protect the president; his assignment had been for some time to protect Mrs. Kennedy. No Secret Service agent assigned to provide protection for the president acted responsibly; not one. Some Dallas police officers who were either off duty or assigned to traffic control, none of whom had been trained by the Secret Service, responded to the shots appropriately.

The testimony of two uniformed Dallas Police Department officers is relevant. Bobby W. Hargis was one of the most important witnesses to testify. He was questioned for just a few minutes.[98] He was questioned by an assistant counsel, no member of the Warren Commission was present. His name was never mentioned in the Warren Commission Report.[99]

He testified that he was to the left rear of the presidential limousine while riding a motorcycle.[100] He testified that when the fatal bullet struck the president, "the bullet hit him in the head, the one that killed him and it seemed like his head exploded, and I was splattered with blood and brain."[101] He testified that after the president was killed the limousine accelerated.[102]

The testimony of Hargis indicates that the fatal shot was fired from the area of the grassy knoll, that is from the right front of the limousine, and not from the Book Depository Building to the rear. It

---

97. Vol. 2, p. 139.
98. Hargis testimony, Vol. VI, p. 293-6.
99. WCR, index, p. 883.
100. Vol. 6, p. 294.
101. Ibid.
102. Ibid.

also demonstrates that the limousine did not accelerate until after all of the shots, including the fatal one, had been fired, which may explain why the Warren Commission neither mentioned his name nor his testimony in its report. Another factor that may have influenced the commission to retroactively remove Hargis from the scene was his immediate response to find the assassin. He testified that he "got off my motorcycle and ran to the right hand side of the street behind the light pole,"[103] thereby running toward the grassy knoll near the railroad overpass.[104]

Another Dallas Police Department officer offered startling information when he testified. Joe Marshall Smith was questioned by Wesley J. Liebeler, an assistant counsel who became the most persistent supporter of the official line. No member of the commission was present. Smith testified that he was in Dealey Plaza when the shots were fired.[105] He told Liebeler that "this woman came up to me and she was just in hysterics. She told me, 'They are shooting the president from the bushes.' So I immediately proceeded up there."[106] He ran up the grassy knoll. It was there that he very likely encountered the assassin. The Warren Commission Report does not mention his name.

There is a body of evidence that demonstrates that in fact Secret Service agent Greer had brought the limousine to a complete stop. Vincent M. Palamara has conducted interviews with Secret Service agents and others regarding the assassination and has compiled statements from others. His meticulous and accurately reported interviews provide proof regarding the actions of Greer on November 22nd. In his work, *Survivor's Guilt*, he reports that a sampling of sixty witnesses reveals Greer's misconduct. His interviews and his research provide the basis for the following summary.

Texas Senator Ralph Yarborough said, "When the noise of the shot was heard, the motorcade slowed to what seemed to me a complete stop (though it could have been a near stop) . . . After the third shot was fired, but only after the third shot was fired, the cavalcade speeded up, gained speed rapidly, and roared away to the Parkland Hospital." Yarborough also said, "The cars all stopped. I put in there [his affidavit],

---

103. Ibid.
104. Ibid, pp. 294–295.
105. Vol 7, p. 534.
106. Ibid, p. 535.

'I don't want to hurt anyone's feelings but for the protection of future Presidents, they [the Secret Service] should be trained to take off when a shot is fired.' "

Presidential aide Kenneth O'Donnell, who was in the motorcade, said, "If the Secret Service men in the front had reacted quicker to the first two shots at the president's car, if the driver had stepped on the gas before instead of after the fatal third shot was fired, would President Kennedy be alive today?"

Presidential aide Dave Powers, who was also in the motorcade, said, "At that time we were traveling very slowly . . . At about the time of the third shot, the president's car accelerated sharply." On November 22, 1988, Powers was interviewed by CBS reporter Charles Kuralt. Powers spoke about not speeding up in time to save JFK's life and agreed with Kuralt that if Greer had sped up *before* the fatal head shot instead of afterwards, JFK might still be alive today.

Jean Hill, the woman who gave the area the name "the grassy knoll," said, "The motorcade came to almost a halt at the time the shots rang out and I would say it [Kennedy's limousine] was just approximately, if not—it couldn't have been in the same position, I'm sure it wasn't, but just a very, very short distance from where it had been. It [JFK's limo] was just almost stopped." Hill had told ABC's Bill Lord on November 22, 1963, that the car "momentarily halted."

Mrs. Kennedy said, "We could see a tunnel in front of us. Everything was really slow then. . . . And just being down in the car with his head in my lap. And it just seemed an eternity . . . And finally I remember a voice behind me, or something, and then I remember the people in the front seat, or somebody, finally knew something was wrong, and a voice yelling, which must have been Mr. Hill, 'Get to the hospital,' or maybe it was Mr. Kellerman, in the front seat . . . We were really slowing turning the corner [Houston and Elm] . . . I remember a sensation of enormous speed, which must have been when we took off . . . those poor men in the front. . . ."

Mary Gallagher reported in her book that Mrs. Kennedy "mentioned one Secret Service man (Greer) who had not acted during the crucial moment, and said bitterly to me, 'He might just as well have been Miss Shaw![107*]'" Jackie also told Gallagher, "You should

---

107. * John and Caroline's British nanny.

get yourself a good driver so that nothing ever happens to you." Mrs. Kennedy stated, "If the agent had hit the gas before the third shot, Jack might still be alive."

A *Houston Chronicle* reporter, Bo Byers, who was in the White House press bus, twice stated that the presidential limousine "almost came to a stop, a dead stop"; in fact, he has had nightmares about this.

Dallas Police Department (DPD) officer Earle Brown said, "The first I noticed the [presidential limousine] was when it stopped . . . after it made the turn and when the shots were fired, it stopped."

Secret Service agent John Ready, in the follow-up car, said, "I heard what sounded like fire crackers going off from my post on the right front running board. The president's car slowed."

Dallas Morning News reporter Robert Baskin, who was in the National Press Pool Car, stated "The motorcade ground to a halt."

Dallas Morning News reporter Mary Woodward said, "Instead of speeding up the car, the car came to a halt." She said that the president's limousine came to a halt after the first shot. Then, after hearing two more shots, close together, the car sped up. She spoke forcefully about the car almost coming to a stop and the lack of proper reaction by the Secret Service in 1993.

Alan Smith said, "The car was ten feet from me when a bullet hit the president in the forehead . . . the car went about five feet and stopped."

According to Palamara, Ochus V. Campbell told him that after Campbell heard the shots, "he then observed the car bearing President Kennedy to slow down, a near stop, and a motorcycle policeman rushed up. Immediately following this, he observed the car rush away from the scene."

Peggy Joyce Hawkins was on the front steps of the Texas School Book Depository and "estimated that the president's car was less than fifty feet away from her when he was shot, that the car slowed down almost coming to a full stop."

Hugh Betzner said, "I looked down the street and I could see the president's car and another one and they looked like the cars were stopped . . . then the president's car sped on under the underpass."

Bill Newman recalled that after the final shot, "the car momentarily stopped and the driver seemed to have a radio or phone up to his ear and he seemed to be waiting on some word. Some Secret Service men reached into their car and came out with some sort of machine gun. Then the cars roared off." He added, "I've maintained that they stopped. I still say they did."

William E. Sale, an airman first class aircraft mechanic assigned to Carswell Air Force Base and stationed at Love Field before, during, and after the assassination, stated that, "When the agent who was driving JFK's car (Greer) came back to Air Force One he was as white as a ghost and had to be helped back to the plane."

When he testified before the commission, Kellerman was questioned, perhaps more accurately assisted, by Arlen Specter. Specter asked, "Now, in your prior testimony, you described a flurry of shells into the car. How many shots did you hear after the first noise which you described as sounding like a firecracker?" Kellerman answered, "Mr. Specter, these shells came in altogether." Both the testimony of Kellerman and the questions asked by Specter are incomprehensible. Obviously, no "shells" entered the limousine. A shell is part of a cartridge that remains with the weapon or is ejected onto the ground when the bullet is fired. Whether shots came from the Book Depository Building or from behind the fence on the grassy knoll, no "shells" entered the presidential vehicle. However, the "flurry of shots" referred to by both Specter and Kellerman, apparently after the first shot was fired, tend to refute the Warren Commission's conclusion that only three shots had been fired, an invention created by Specter, who had apparently forgotten his statement to the witness that there had been a flurry of shots.

The Secret Service Agents in the Vice President's Car

A standard approach in the medical profession to determine the efficacy of treatments or drugs is the double blind study. Rarely do we have an opportunity to employ that scientific methodology in a murder case. Here we can contrast the failure of the Secret Service agents in the presidential limousine to distinguish between a firecracker or a backfire and the sound of rifle shots with the perception of a Secret Service agent seeking to protect the vice president in a vehicle just behind the follow-up car. And of greater importance we can contrast the reaction of the agents to perform their sworn duty.

Clearly this concept was of little importance to the Warren Commission or the legion of FBI agents and CIA operatives whom they relied upon. The Warren Commission was appointed during November 1963; it issued its report during September 1964. It was not until July 1964, long after the commission had reached its final conclusion, that the commission wrote to Lyndon Johnson and Mrs. Johnson requesting from each of them a written statement about what they had witnessed that day. Not known to the commission, Lady Bird Johnson had privately dictated her recollection during a two-day period after the assassination using, as she described it, a "small tape recorder." She sent that information to the commission's counsel, pointing out that almost three-quarters of a year after the event her memory was not fresh, implying that she should have been questioned much earlier. She wrote her "recollection and impressions" had obviously faded, "at this late date," and added that "the quality of the tape recording is very poor." Nevertheless, she had arranged for a transcription to be made, which she sent to the commission.

In his statement Lyndon Johnson wrote:

> I was startled by the sharp report or explosion, but I had no time to speculate as to its origin because Agent Youngblood turned in a flash, immediately after the first explosion, hitting me on the shoulder, and shouted to all of us in the back seat to get down.
>
> I was pushed down by Agent Youngblood. Almost in the same moment in which he hit or pushed me, he vaulted over the back seat and sat on me. I was bent over under the weight of Agent Youngblood's body toward Mrs. Johnson and Senator Yarborough.
>
> I remember attempting to turn my head to make sure that Mrs. Johnson had bent down. Both she and Senator Yarborough had crouched down at Agent Youngblood's command.

Johnson said that he also "heard other explosions."

Mrs. Johnson stated that "suddenly there was a sharp loud report— a shot." She said that "our Secret Service man who was with us, Ruf Youngblood, I believe it was, vaulted over the front seat on top of Lyndon, threw him to the floor and said 'Get down.'" She added, "The car accelerated terrifically fast—faster and faster."

Evaluating how the Secret Service White House detail should have reacted, as the Warren Commission did and as critics, including myself, have done, has a somewhat limited value. A far better analysis is found in examining the conduct of another Secret Service agent, similarly trained, in a similar moment of great stress.

The two agents in the presidential limousine said in retrospect and perhaps for the purpose of excusing their own lack of response, that they thought they heard firecrackers or the sound of a motorcycle backfire. In the vice presidential car Youngblood heard a shot. Vice President Johnson heard a "report" (a term used to describe the sound of a shot) or an "explosion." Mrs. Johnson heard "a sharp loud report—a shot." All five witnesses were describing the first shot.

In the vice presidential vehicle the agent who was not driving took immediate action, vaulting over the seat, shouting at those in the back seat to "get down" and covering the vice president's body with his own. Clifton Carter, an assistant to the vice president, was in the vice presidential Secret Service follow-up car. The Warren Commission conceded that Carter stated that Youngblood was using his body to shield the vice president *before* the second shot was fired.[108] In the presidential limousine, the agent who was not driving took no action, never moved, and did not even tell the president or his wife to take cover.

The driver of the presidential limousine slowed down to almost a stop, (some witnesses said the vehicle actually stopped) after the first shot was fired and did not accelerate until the president was fatally wounded. The driver of the vice presidential car accelerated as quickly as possible.

It seems that had Youngblood been in the presidential limousine, President Kennedy might have survived. Youngblood was assigned to protect the vice president. Hill was assigned to protect Mrs. Kennedy. The driver of the vice president's car sped from the scene. Each acted correctly and promptly. The record discloses that not one Secret Service member of the elite White House detail assigned to protect President Kennedy acted appropriately, whether their assignment was to drive the limousine, ride in the limousine, or ride in the president's follow-up car.

---

108. Warren Commission Report, p. 52, italics added.

The Actions of Secret Service Agents in the Follow-Up Car

It is undisputed that the follow-up car, that is, a vehicle transporting eight Secret Service agents, was immediately behind the limousine. "Directly behind the presidential limousine was an open 'follow-up' car with eight Secret Service agents, two in the front seat, two in the rear, and two on each running board."[109]

Each agent had been specially trained to react to any possible threat to the president. That was the only purpose for their presence there. From the moment the first shot was fired until the president was killed by the last shot, not one agent in the limousine or in the follow-up car assigned to protect the president took any action.

The driver of the following car participated in yet another similar lapse or misconduct. Upon hearing the first shot, the driver was required to place his vehicle in the line of fire. He took no action. Even when it became clear to the majority of those in Dealey Plaza that a shot had come from behind the wooden fence, he made no attempt to pass the limousine on the right to afford protection to those in the presidential car.

Those in the open vehicle or on the running board remained uninvolved, except for Hill. They were all armed and automatic weapons had been assigned for the purpose of preventing rifle fire. U. E. Baughman had been the chief of the United States Secret Service

---

109. Warren Commission Report, p. 2.

from 1948 until 1961. He held that position under presidents Truman, Eisenhower and Kennedy. After the assassination he said that he could not understand why Mrs. Kennedy had to climb over the back of the vehicle, "to get help," or how it was possible that with the entire Secret Service detail on hand why the only shots that day had been fired at the president and no fire was returned. Surely, if the agents were concerned about firing into a location in the general vicinity of innocent spectators there was no reason why they could not at least level their weapons at the source of fire. That action, for which they had been trained, might have caused the person firing from the targeted location to seek cover. Baughman might have offered some valuable insight to the Warren Commission since the commission had assumed the responsibility of evaluating the actions of the White House detail on that tragic day. However, his name does not even appear in the Warren Commission Report.

Can so many failures, the voluntary loss of eleven experienced White House detail members in two months before the assassination, the sudden vacation of the chief of the White House detail, the absolute refusal of any agent assigned to protect the president to take any action to protect him, or even drive from the scene until he had been fatally shot, and bringing the limousine to an almost complete stop as soon as the first shot was fired instead of speeding from the scene, all be coincidental? If so those charged with the responsibility for examining that misconduct should have sought real answers to explain each such almost inexplicable act.

The question of CIA participation regarding the actions of men claiming that they were Secret Service agents, when they were not, is even more challenging. That matter is discussed later, in the chapter entitled "The CIA and Mind Control," for it is only after learning of the crimes committed by the CIA, many through the auspices of one of its most secret committees, the Technical Services Division, that one can begin to comprehend the mindset of those responsible for the events of November 22.

The Secret Service Speaks After Forty-Seven Years of Silence

Two years after the publication of Abraham Bolden's book in 2008, a former Secret Service agent responded, on behalf of all of them he stated, with a book entitled *The Kennedy Detail*.[110] It was promoted as a book "fifty years in coming." Actually it was at most forty-seven years, but if you are a stickler for accuracy this is not the work for you.

The author, Gerald Blaine, endorses the Warren Commission Report although there is no evidence that he has read it or the evidence it stated it relied upon. He refers to the "twenty-six volumes of the hearings." He got the number right, but only the first fifteen volumes are transcripts of the hearings. The remaining volumes, many more than 900 pages each, are made up of documents, reports, photographs and other material, most of it irrelevant.

Blaine began by stating, "While I am the author" but even that assertion is in doubt. It was purportedly written by him "with Lisa McCubbin," but Blaine is always referred to in the third person, as if someone else has written it with the exception of a six-page prologue that states that it was written by Gerald Blaine, a claim not made for the rest of the book. For example, Blaine, who was in Arlington, Virginia,

---

110. Gerald Blaine with Lisa McCubbin, *The Kennedy Detail*, (New York; Gallery Books, 2010).

when the assassination took place in Dallas, Texas, although one gets the impression that he has been holding himself out to be an eyewitness, states, or someone does, that he quit the Secret Service after a great deal of time spent with his fellow agents, having been there less than five years. "It was the hardest decision Blaine had ever had to make." Blaine "never cared much about money." Blaine "needed to do what felt right." Blaine resigned to take a much more lucrative job selling IBM products dealing with "high-level corporate security." He had used his relatively short time with the Secret Service to advance his lifestyle. He was neither the first nor the last to do so, but one of the few who offered himself as a martyr for having made that decision.

The book is a screed with a mission, in fact several missions. It attempts to prove that rumors that Secret Service agents had consumed alcoholic beverages on the very morning before the assassination took place were both malicious and false; it attempts through character assassination to demean Abraham Bolden; and it suggests that the Secret Service agents were flawless in their efforts to protect the president and that President Kennedy, in large measure, was responsible for his own death by imposing restrictions upon the agents and refusing to use the protective bubble top. Each of those efforts fails for each is based upon demonstrably false assertions made by either Gerald or Lisa.

Did the agents drink in violation of their regulations? The author writes:

> SUNDAY, DECEMBER 1, 1963: *San Francisco Chronicle* columnist Drew Pearson was a muckraking 'journalist' whose forte was digging up dirt on various government and political organizations. He knew members of the White House press corps and was well acquainted with the Kennedy Detail Secret Service agents and their stellar reputations. On December 1, 1963, Pearson wrote a scathing editorial in the *San Francisco Chronicle* demanding an investigation into the Secret Service and the role they may have played in the assassination of the president.
>
> "Six Secret Service men," he wrote, "charged with protecting the President, were in the Fort Worth Press Club the early morning of Friday, Nov. 22, some of them remaining until nearly 3 o'clock. This was earlier in the same day President Kennedy was assassinated. They were drinking. One

of them was reported to have been inebriated. When they departed, three were reported en route to an all-night beatnik rendezvous, *The Cellar.*

"Obviously men who have been drinking until nearly 3 AM are in no condition to be trigger-alert or in the best physical shape to protect anyone."

It has been stated that it was an impossibility for the Secret Service to check the occupancy of every building along the route. While this is true, it is also true that warehouse type buildings, such as that in which the assassin hid, should be searched, and the extra time spent by Secret Service men at the Fort Worth Press Club could have been spent in so doing.[111]

The allegations, we are told by Blaine/McCubbin, were false and the agents were very upset. The authors asserted:

The article sent immediate shock waves through the Secret Service, and the Kennedy Detail supervisors—Emory Roberts, Art Godfrey, and Stewart Stout—were called into Chief Rowley's office and told to have every agent write a memo giving their whereabouts during the evening of November 21 and the early morning hours of November 22. The agents were to state if they consumed alcoholic beverages and what time they retired that morning.

For the agents still crippled by a guilt that had no words, it was as if Drew Pearson had ripped out their broken hearts; any semblance of healing that might have begun was instantly shattered.

Questions were asked about who was involved and who was inebriated. Nobody could remember anybody being drunk or slightly inebriated, but questions began to arise among the agents about who the culprit might be, despite the fact that the claims seemed preposterous. If any detail agent had been drinking heavily or had been intoxicated, the other agents would have heard about it because the agent would have been immediately dismissed and removed from the detail.

111. Blaine, *The Kennedy Detail*, 306–307.

The author asserts that "the damage had been done."[112] He, or she, added, "The agents felt like they'd been stamped with guilt by an outsider, a muckraking journalist so intent on making a name for himself . . . that he never bothered to check the facts." But the author did and he concluded that the stories were false but that the claims "would haunt these already broken men for the rest of their lives."[113]

What was wrong with the effort to rewrite the history of this sordid episode? Shall we count the ways? Drew Pearson was not a *San Francisco Chronicle* columnist. He had not written an editorial for the *Chronicle*. He already had a name and was not in need of making another one. A Harris poll commissioned by *TIME* sought to discover the relative popularity of newspaper columnists. It determined that Pearson was the best-known writer in the United States at that time. That was hardly surprising since Pearson had created a column, "Washington Merry-Go-Round," which was published by The *Washington Post* beginning in 1941. He later hired a young writer named Jack Anderson to assist him. The column was syndicated with more than 650 newspapers publishing it daily, more than twice as many as the next competitor. It was determined that 60 million Americans read the Pearson column each day. It remains the longest-running column in the history of the United States.

In his investigative column Pearson expressed his political views. He supported the civil rights movement and Dr. Martin Luther King, Jr.; he opposed McCarthyism and the excesses of the House Un-American Committee.

In his early years Pearson served with the American Friends Service Committee directing post–World War I efforts at rebuilding Serbia. After World War II he was primarily responsible for the creation of the "Friendship Train," a program that raised many millions of dollars for food and medicine for war-ravaged European countries. For his humanitarian efforts Pearson was awarded the French Legion of Honour, the Medal of St. Olav by Norway, and the Star of Italian Solidarity.

Coauthor Ms. McCubbin spends a great deal of time in Saudi Arabia where her husband is employed, perhaps explaining why she was so ignorant of Mr. Pearson's remarkable accomplishments. Mr. Blaine has less excuse; surely one may assume that he actually read the

---

112. Ibid., 307.
113. Ibid., 307–8.

book before it was published. But the fact checkers at the publisher, if there were any, have much to answer for.

The author's dismissal of Pearson, while quite extraordinary, is outdone by the assertion that Pearson was incorrect about the conduct of the Secret Service agents. On June 18, 1964, James J. Rowley, the chief of the United States Secret Service, testified before the Warren Commission. That was forty-six years before *The Kennedy Detail* was published, allowing a good period of time to review the record. The transcript of that testimony appears in Volume V of the twenty-six volumes that Blaine claimed he was familiar with.[114]

J. Lee Rankin, counsel to the Warren Commission, began the questioning regarding the drinking agents:

> Mr. Rankin: Did you learn in connection with the trip when the assassination occurred that certain of the Secret Service agents had been in the press club and what is called the Cellar, at Fort Worth, the night before?
>
> Mr. Rowley: Well, that came to my attention through a broadcast that Mr. Pearson made, that the agents were inebriated the night before at the Fort Worth Press Club. I immediately dispatched Inspector McCann to Fort Worth to investigate the report, and to interview the agents.

Neither the authors nor Rowley had gotten it right. Pearson's article was syndicated, not broadcast, and he reported as fact that the agents had been drinking and added that "one of them" had been said to have been inebriated.

Rankin asked Rowley what he had discovered; Rowley replied:

> "I learned that there were nine agents involved at the Press Club. And I might say this—the agents on duty throughout that day had no opportunity to eat. When they arrived at Fort Worth, they were informed that there was a buffet to be served at the Fort Worth Club. This is what I ascertained in personal interviews. Upon going over there, they learned there was no buffet, and some of them stayed for a drink. Three, I think, had one scotch, and others had two or three beers. They were in and out—from the time they arrived, I would say roughly around 12:30, until the place closed at 2 o'clock."

---

114. Warren Commission Transcripts, Vol. V, 449–486.

They went to a bar after midnight in search of a buffet, stayed for one and one half hours at the bar drinking, and truthfully told their supervisor how little they drank, and their supervisor accepted their statements.

Rowley continued:

"Now, after that some of them went to the Cellar. This is a place that does not serve alcoholic beverages. They went there primarily, I think, out of curiosity, because this was some kind of a beatnik place where someone gets up and recites, or plays guitar."

Perhaps the agents thought it appropriate to drink in violation of the rules of their service until two o'clock in the morning, when they had crucial roles starting in a few hours to protect the president in a very charged environment. The context here is relevant. Adlai Stevenson, having recently been attacked in Dallas, had cautioned the president about visiting that city; newspaper advertisements had condemned the president and posters stating that he was "Wanted for Treason" were being circulated.

The Cellar originally opened as a speakeasy during Prohibition, is listed as a bar in directories in Fort Worth, and publishes the price of beer and well drinks on the Internet. Perhaps Rowley was correct and that no drinks were served at the Cellar that morning, and the agents, forced to leave the bar where they had been drinking until it closed, had sought to listen to folk music.

Rankin then asked if the agents had violated any Secret Service regulations.

Mr. Rowley: Yes, there was a violation. At that time there was a section in our manual in effect that said that during—

Mr. Rankin: Will you give us first the number?

Mr. Rowley: Section 10.

Mr. Rankin: Is that chapter 1, page 7?

Mr. Rowley: Chapter 1, page 7; yes, sir.

Mr. Rankin: Now, will you tell the Commission about what the regulation was?

Mr. Rowley: The use of liquor. Employees are strictly enjoined to refrain from the use of intoxicating liquor during the hours they are officially employed at their post of duty or when they may reasonably expect that they may be called upon to perform an official duty.

The one that applies here—"However, all members of the White House detail and special agents cooperating with them on presidential and similar protective assignments are considered to be subject to call for official duty at any time while in travel status. Therefore, the use of intoxicating liquor of any kind, including beer and wine, by members of the White House detail and special agents cooperating with them or by special agents on similar assignments, while they are in a travel status, is prohibited."

> Mr. Rankin: Can you tell the commission how many men were involved in these trips to the Press Club and the Cellar, where these things were done?
>
> Mr. Rowley: There were nine men involved at the Press Club, and there were ten men involved at the Cellar.

Rankin then asked Rowley the names of the men who had been drinking who were in the crucial follow-up car. Rowley stated that among them were Landis, Hill, Ready and Bennett. Hill wrote the foreword to the Blaine book; and Landis, Hill, Ready and Bennett are all listed by Blaine as sources he relied upon. Apparently none of them told Blaine that they had been drinking; or Blaine, in spite of that knowledge, had decided to falsify the record. In his prologue, which we have no reason to doubt that he actually wrote, Blaine stated, "My initial goal in writing the story of the Kennedy Detail was to set history straight, to leave a book for my grandchildren that they could read and know was truth beyond any measure of a doubt." Kids, you might want to look at some first-hand accounts, testimony and documents as well.

Rankin inquired of Rowley how he construed subparagraph (c) of Secret Service regulation 10 regarding the use of alcoholic liquors. Rowley responded:

> "Violation or slight disregard of the above paragraphs or the excessive or improper use of intoxicating liquor at any time will be cause for removal from the service. In interpreting the words "excessive" and "improper," slight evidence tending to indicate unusual or questionable conduct will be considered proof that the use of liquor has been improper or excessive. Association with others who drink to excess will be considered as an indication of using more than a moderate amount of

liquor. The excuse that liquor is used for medicinal purposes will not be accepted."

Since the regulations for violating the prohibition about drinking call for the dismissal of the agents, Rankin asked about the punishment meted out. Rowley said that "they were interviewed at the time." The seriousness of the matter was "impressed upon them." Rowley never answered Rankin's question about whether they had even been reprimanded. Rowley said the men were "dedicated" and that he was "quite sure" that the agents "all understand it." None of the agents were dismissed, apparently none of them were reprimanded, and there is no indication that their blatant disregard of the rules of the agency even found its way into any of their files.

Rowley explained to the Warren Commission why he decided not to punish the agents. He said:

> "Well, I thought that in the light of history, to place a stigma on them by punishing them at that time, from which inevitably the public would conclude that they were responsible for the assassination of the president—I didn't think this was fair, and that they did not deserve that, with their family and children."

The logical conclusion one may draw from that explanation is that the fact that the president was killed was the basis for not even reprimanding the agents who failed to protect him after drinking that same morning.

I have spent days talking with Abraham Bolden. I have closely examined the statements he has made, and read the documents that he has referred to, and I am convinced that I have never met a man of greater integrity. He knew that when he stood up to tell the truth about the Secret Service, his life might drastically change. Speaking truth to power is always a risky business, and he has suffered greatly as a result. He was motivated by his commitment to his duties as a member of the White House detail. The defamatory assertions made about him in the Blaine/McCubbin book are without foundation. They are as lacking in documentary support as the false attacks they published about Drew Pearson. Remarkably, Blaine states that "there was no corroboration of Bolden's stories." In a book where truthful statements are difficult to locate, that assertion, nevertheless, stands almost alone. Court documents, eyewitnesses, and the Secret Service file memorandum 3-11-602-111 all support the specific statement Mr. Bolden had made.

Blaine regularly repeats that there never was any hint of racism in the Secret Service and offers a few uncorroborated anecdotes in support. On February 24, 2000, ten years before the Blaine book was published, *The Washington Post* reported that a number of African American Secret Service agents had sought leave from the Equal Employment Opportunity Commission to file a class action law suit against the Secret Service for racial discrimination. Seven years later National Public Radio reported that "fifty-eight African-American U.S. Secret Service agents issued sworn statements in a class action lawsuit, claiming racial discrimination by the agency." It added that "the suit is progressing slowly. The judge has issued sanctions against the Secret Service, ordering the agency to provide evidence." The agency, by refusing to produce evidence required by the Federal Rules of Evidence and the rulings of the court, and by willing to face sanctions, knowing that fines for disobeying a court order are paid by the taxpayers, has demonstrated a lack of candor that raises additional questions about its past conduct. Blaine, in asserting that the agency was free from any form of prejudice, failed to mention the case in his book.

When President Kennedy personally chose Bolden to protect him and serve as the first African American on the White House detail, he knew that he was making history. At the time the detail was not very large, just a few more members than on a professional baseball team. Every member of the White House detail was aware of that appointment. In the book, Blaine states, "Most of the White House detail agents had never even heard of Bolden." Right, and Pee Wee Reese never heard of Jackie Robinson, his keystone partner playing second base for the Brooklyn Dodgers. That assertion, in the words of an apocryphal judge, is like the thirteenth stroke of a crazy clock that casts discredit on all that has gone before it and all that follows.

Let us now examine the Blaine doctrine that while Oswald acted alone, he was supported by President Kennedy who deliberately reduced his security and insisted that the protective plastic bubble top be removed. Those charges have all been proven to be false.

One man, Vince Palamara, has conducted more serious interviews with Secret Service agents about their conduct on November 22, 1963, than had the Warren Commission with all of its lawyers and its reliance upon FBI and CIA agents.[115] Former Secret Service Agent

115. The most accurate and persistent inquiries into the role of the Secret Service are the numerous interviews and studies complied by Vince Palamara and his blog is

Samuel A. Kinney assured Palamara on three separate occasions that he alone was responsible for the removal of the plastic bubble top from the presidential limousine. Kinney's name does not even appear in the Warren Commission Report.

Secret Service Agent Gerald A. Behn was in charge of the White House detail for the protection of President Kennedy and participated in selecting the venues for his appearances. Behn told Palamara that President Kennedy never ordered agents to stay off of the rear of the presidential limousine. Other Secret Service agents made that same statement to Palamara including Floyd M. Boring, Arthur L. Godfrey, Rufus Youngblood and Samuel A. Kinney. In addition Palamara interviewed the White House photographer, Cecil Stoughton, and Martin Underwood, the advance man for the Democratic National Committee, as well as Robert Bouck, who directed the Protective Research Section, and many others. They each stated that President Kennedy had not sought to reduce his protection and had not suggested that agents be kept off of the rear bumper of the vehicle. Those interviewed also stated that President Kennedy was not difficult to protect and that he was very cooperative with members of the Secret Service.

In most motorcades there were as many as twelve motorcycle officers riding security for President Kennedy, including his trips through Texas. The Secret Service directed that there be only four motorcycles for the trip through Dallas and that none of them be permitted to ride a flank position, which would have provided some protection. Both Agents Kinney and Godfrey denied that President Kennedy had ever made that request when Palamara interviewed them.

A good portion of *The Kennedy Detail* was devoted to the hardships suffered by the Secret Service agents assigned to the White House, and the trauma they suffered on November 22, even those who were on vacation at the time.

The eleven agents who voluntarily left the White House detail shortly before the assassination, were, according to Blaine, "the most experienced agents on the Kennedy Detail." They did not resign, they

---

by far the most complete record of their conduct. He has published on that site Abraham Bolden's analysis of *The Kennedy Detail*. A visit to that blog and other related work on the Internet by Palamara would be very rewarding for those seeking additional information.

just transferred to another assignment. Blaine states that in each case it was a "purely personal choice by the agents" that they requested and had been granted transfers to field offices. After very substantial taxpayer's funds had been invested in them for the special training required to serve on the White House detail, they decided to go somewhere else. Blaine explains the hardships they had been exposed to and was sympathetic to their plight. They had been required to stay at hotels or cottages "in either Palm Beach or Hyannis Port . . . and the occasional visit to Palm Springs."[116] They had to travel to Europe and Latin America, he explained, so "nearly one third of the agents had decided that they just couldn't do it any longer." Therefore, they left the White House Detail weeks before President Kennedy was to visit a hostile and threatening environment.

Some of the assignments for the White House detail were very time-consuming. Not long after the Kennedy's newborn baby, Patrick, died, there were concerns about the effect upon Mrs. Kennedy. John Kennedy suggested that a private cruise in the Mediterranean might provide some comfort. Mrs. Kennedy, accompanied by her sister and two friends, agreed and made the trip. Aristotle Onassis was the host of the group; Secret Service agents Clint Hill and Paul Landis joined them. It was a two-week cruise on the 325-foot yacht *Christina*.[117] Landis, according to Blaine, "was overwhelmed." He said, "Oh my gosh, Clint, it's fantastic. Unreal. It has everything, a swimming pool that turns into a dance floor, sailboats, a Chris-Craft cruiser, runabouts, anything you want to do." To spare Hill and Landis a trip to land to collect the mail, the yacht had a seaplane that handled that chore. On occasion, Hill drove a limousine to a place where the yacht would anchor so that he could pick up Mrs. Kennedy and her friends.

On November 22, 1963, Landis was standing on the running board of the follow-up car not far from President and Mrs. Kennedy. He had an excellent view of the effect of the bullets upon the occupants of the vehicle. Since the presidential vehicle had stopped, some witnesses say "almost stopped," after the first shot was fired, he had several seconds after the first shot was fired to attempt to cover President Kennedy and his wife with his body. He never moved.

---

116. Blaine, *The Kennedy Detail,* for example, 42, 97, 120–2, 122–3.
117. Ibid., 132–3.

The Assassin is Confronted

On July 23, 1964, Joe Marshall Smith appeared at the U.S. Attorney's Office in Dallas to be questioned by Wesley J. Liebeler, an assistant counsel of the Warren Commission. No member of the Warren Commission was present, and no other lawyer participated in the questioning. After a few minutes of testimony, Liebeler excused Officer Smith. Smith's first response appeared on page 532 of volume VII of the Warren Commission documents, and his last words were reported on page 539.

It is possible that Smith, a thirty-two-year-old with almost eight years of service as a Dallas police officer, was the most important witness to testify before any lawyer for the Commission. He testified that a few minutes before 9 AM on November 22, he was instructed to direct traffic for the motorcade and to be on the lookout "for anyone throwing anything from the crowd." He was not instructed to scan the buildings in the area to his best recollection. He testified that other police officers were also given traffic control duties. The members of the Dallas Police Department were not instructed to provide security for the president. There were only two other officers assigned to the entire Dealey Plaza area.

Smith testified that just after he heard the shots "this woman came up to me and she was just in hysterics. She told me, 'they are shooting the president from the bushes.' So I immediately proceeded up here (indicating the trees near the wooden fence on the grassy knoll)." He began to search the parking lot behind the wooden fence.

At that point a man emerged from the area behind the fence. Smith considered him to be the leading suspect who had fired the shot that killed President Kennedy from that location. "I pulled my pistol from my holster," he testified, as he thought he had likely confronted the assassin and approached the suspect. At that point the suspect produced Secret Service credentials. Smith said that he was not alone on that occasion, "(a) deputy sheriff (was) with me." Shortly thereafter the Secret Service released its roster revealing that there was no Secret Service agent on foot in Dealey Plaza and that all of the Secret Service agents were part of the motorcade.

Liebeler, who was among the most inexperienced of the junior lawyers, refused to conduct a serious inquiry into Smith's explosive testimony. Clearly Liebeler thought that his task was to prove that all of the shots came from the sixth floor of the book depository building and that he was commissioned to exclude all contrary evidence. At the time that Smith was questioned, eight months after the assassination, Liebeler had known for more than half a year that there was no Secret Service agent prowling behind the wooden fence at the time of the assassination. He made no effort to determine the description of the faux agent, to learn his height, weight and clothing, standard questions asked by police officers whenever seeking to discover a suspect's identity. Liebeler was a man on a mission; his mission was to support the Warren Commission's preconceived fiction even if that required he ignore the fact that a suspect, protected by falsely created and distributed Secret Service credentials, was stopped by a police officer. The officer thought that the suspect's presence behind a fence precluded him from being a spectator and he was in the location from which a weapon had been fired at the presidential limousine.

During the few minutes that Smith was permitted to testify, Liebeler asked him if, as he ran to arrest the presumed assassin, he "observed the windows on the side of the Texas School Book Depository Building from which the shots were fired." Leibeler, who had not been in Dallas on November 22, was instructing the witness who had been there as to the origin of the shots and ignoring the definitive testimony of the officer. Smith also testified that before he heard the shots, "I had my back to the Texas Book Depository Building." Following that statement, Liebeler asked Smith if he scanned the windows of the Texas Book Depository Building at all. At that time, Liebeler showed Smith an aerial photograph that he said was of the "Texas School Book Depository Building" (Commission Exhibit 354). However, the photograph showed only the roof of several buildings. Commission Exhibit 356 is a clear photograph taken from ground level of the building, but Liebeler did not show that photograph to Smith. Since Smith didn't look at the building, the entire line of questioning was absurd and made even more ridiculous by Liebeler's presentation of a useless photograph.

Before asking additional questions about the book depository building, Liebeler asked Smith if he was sure "that your back was in fact turned toward the book depository building?" Smith answered in the affirmative. Then Liebeler, persisting in his effort to abandon the subject of the arrest of the possible assassin behind the fence, asked Smith about other windows: "Could you observe those windows from the point where you were standing?" Again, Smith said that he "could not."

Liebeler continued to pursue the matter, although Smith's answers had been dispositive, asking him, "If you could have seen, it would have been with great difficulty . . . Is that correct?" Smith again said, "Correct."

Liebeler continued to pursue questions that focused on the book depository building, even asking if Smith saw "Lee Harvey Oswald come in or out of the building or in that area at all?" Running out of questions about the book depository building, and eager to avoid any questions about the suspect Smith was about to arrest, Liebeler asked for irrelevant hearsay information: "When did you first hear about Oswald's capture?"

Liebeler, who had made no effort to secure information about where the suspect went after producing false credentials, if he met any other person before he left the area, or even if he was armed, stated, "I don't think I have any more questions."

To the police officer who had already testified that he almost captured a person who lied about his law enforcement credentials, who was behind the fence at the time that the shot was fired, and who was prepared with false documents to escape arrest, Liebeler asked, "Did you find anything that you could associate in any way with the assassination?"

Liebeler had access to a report to the chief of the Dallas Police Force, Jesse E. Curry, that was written by Officer Smith. In it the officer stated, "I heard the shots and thought they were coming from the bushes of the overpass."

Ronnie Dugger was the editor of *The Texas Observer,* a well-respected publication. On December 13, 1963, Dugger reported on his interview with Officer Smith. Obviously that article, published more than half a year before Liebeler questioned Smith, was available to the junior lawyer. In it, Dugger said that Smith told him that he had gone directly to the area behind the wooden fence and saw "a man standing behind the fence, further shielded by cars in the parking lot behind him, might have had a clear shot at the president as his car began the run downhill on Elm Street toward the underpass." Liebeler, who was fixated on the depository building, never asked Smith about the "clear shot" that the suspect commanded from his location. Patrolman Smith told Dugger that as he ran into the area behind the fence, he "caught the smell of gunpowder there." Smith said, "I could tell it was in the air." Some corroboration comes from United States Senator Ralph Yarborough, who was in the motorcade and who also said "you could smell powder" from the time shots were fired. Dugger stated, "Oswald and his rifle were reportedly six stories high and perhaps seventy-five yards behind the president's car at the time of the shooting." Yarborough was in the third car of the motorcade with then vice president and Mrs. Johnson. Dugger wrote that "some officials questioned here [in Dallas] could not explain why Senator Yarborough could smell gunpowder." Yarborough was never called as a witness to testify, either before members of the commission, or even junior lawyers. Liebeler never asked Smith any question about smelling gunpowder behind the wooden fence where the suspect was lurking.

Yarborough's name appears four times in the Warren Report. On page 2 the report states that he was in a car with Lyndon Johnson and Mrs. Johnson. On page 42 it states that he had come from Fort Worth with Governor and Mrs. Connally and the president. On page 52 it cites Volume V, page 561, as the place where a specific statement by Lyndon Johnson may be found in which Yarborough is mentioned as being present in the car with him. That statement actually appears on page 562.

As was the case with other lawyers who had sacrificed their integrity in what they claimed was service to their country, Liebeler was rewarded for his work on an important case. He did not become a United States senator as Arlen Specter did, but he was given a job teaching at a university. Liebeler, according to his friends at UCLA who wrote in his defense, "came to UCLA in 1965 as a new law teacher fresh from the role of assistant counsel to the Warren Commission." They added that his "strongly held perspectives were not for everyone" and that he "could be exasperating, sometimes downright maddening." When questioned under oath about his contacts with intelligence agencies, he stated, without explaining, "I was interviewed by a CIA agent once when I was much younger."

I met Liebeler at a restaurant at the Pan Am building in New York City after he was hired as an assistant counsel by the commission. He began the conversation by stating, "I am not Jewish although some people are misled into thinking that I am Jewish because of my name." Those assertions came after I had merely said, "Hello, Mr. Liebeler, I am Mark Lane." Later when I discussed that odd exchange with friends, I was unable to comprehend why he initiated our meeting with that statement.

Sometime later I met with Edward J. Epstein at Cornell University where I had lectured on the Kennedy assassination. I asked him to try to conduct some interviews with people associated with the commission so that we might understand their modus operandi. Subsequently, Epstein called me and said that he had interviewed Liebeler. When I asked him what he had learned, he said almost nothing except that the interview began in a very strange fashion. Epstein told me that as soon as they introduced themselves to each other, Liebeler assured him that he was not Jewish, although some people thought that he might be because of his name. Epstein said that he was puzzled; I was re-bemused.

When Liebeler was a teacher at the law school at UCLA, he assigned my book, *Rush to Judgment,* as a project. Each student was directed to read the book carefully, check various citations and footnotes, approximately 5,000 of them, and write a brief, pointing out errors they had discovered. He was disappointed to learn that none of his bright young charges had discovered any.

Later, Liebeler, according to *The Nation*, stated that the Warren Commission had done a great job, except that they got "the entrance wounds in the wrong place." The Warren Commission's assertion that the president was shot from the back by Lee Harvey Oswald and not from the front from someone on the grassy knoll, rested in large measure upon the insistence that they got the entrance wounds in the right place.

BOOK FOUR

MEXICO CITY

The Scenario Begins

David Atlee Phillips was fond of his location in Mexico City. His office ran the Western Hemisphere for his organization. The climate was perfect; even now in August the temperature was never above seventy-five degrees Fahrenheit and never dropped below fifty-three because the city is located on the central plateau far above sea level.

Above all, he was gratified by the political climate. His organization could have chosen Washington, D.C.; Langley, Virginia, its national headquarters; or New York City. But there were local and state police agencies there, some of them inquisitive, and there was the ever-present *New York Times* and *The Washington Post*, and his work, especially now, required the absence of prying eyes. Phillips, one of the highest-ranking officials of the CIA, was responsible for all operations of the Central Intelligence Agency to be carried out in the Western Hemisphere.

The newspapers were not bothersome in Mexico City and the police authorities had long since been co-opted by the use of several methods. Select mid-level officers were fed secret intelligence about minor or semi-major criminal activities permitting those favored to quickly "solve" open cases through what appeared to be brilliant investigative work. They rose through the ranks knowing that they owed their careers to the CIA. Those open to bribery were easily recruited, and the few important officials who were loyal to their own country were placed in situations, filmed sexual assignations as one device, so that their cooperation and silence was extorted. For those reasons the CIA chose Mexico City, rather than a city in the United States, to make plans that directly involved the United States.

If Phillips successfully completed his complex assignment, he could expect rewards from his employer. Promotion to chief of station and finally, chief of all operations in the Western Hemisphere, not just the responsibility, were positions he coveted. Almost beyond his imagination was the Career Intelligence Medal, a secret CIA award that very few had ever earned. He won them all through his brilliant and innovative creations.

He worked assiduously and established the legend that a man, to be selected shortly, had been to Mexico City and while there visited both the Soviet and Cuban embassies. A search of intelligence files resulted in a few candidates, but one appeared most satisfactory. Lee Harvey Oswald had ties to the intelligence community and had been interviewed by a CIA asset, Priscilla Johnson, as soon as he arrived in Moscow.

Sufficient false information would be fed to J. Edgar Hoover, knowing that he would within hours of the assassination make his irrevocable response "Oswald was the assassin and he acted alone." No agent of the FBI would dare to find any evidence that could lead to a contrary conclusion. The FBI would be on board.

Priscilla Johnson, on behalf of the CIA while posing as a news reporter, would release her version of the interview she had conducted with Oswald in 1959 stating that Oswald hated his country. When I wrote *Plausible Denial* more than two decades ago, Priscilla Johnson retained counsel who informed me and my publisher that if I dared to publish the statement that she was connected to the CIA, she would file a devastating lawsuit against us both for defamation. I assured the publisher that I would take full responsibility. I published the statement then, invited her to sue, and have not heard from her since. The CIA sent Priscilla Johnson on the mission of interviewing Oswald. At the time she claimed to be a reporter for the North American Newspaper Alliance (NANA), which was owned by a former officer of the CIA's predecessor, the OSS. It published CIA-associated reporters including Virginia Prewett who, on behalf of the CIA, sought to cover up the facts surrounding the murder of Orlando Letelier. David Phillips considered Johnson to be one of his important media assets.

In 1967, the CIA scored one of its major victories by arranging for Svetlana Stalin, the only daughter of the dictator of the Soviet Union, to defect to the United States and condemn her father. The CIA obtained a safe house for her; it was the home of Priscilla Johnson's family. Johnson remained with Svetlana as her constant companion. She participated in both writing and translating the autobiography for Svetlana. Johnson also purportedly helped Marina Oswald write her book that presented the government's view of the events. When it was published Marina stated that it was false in all major respects.

It was presumed by Phillips and his associates as they began to create the Oswald Legend that after the death of President Kennedy, still many weeks ahead, there would be demands by many committees of the Congress for the facts. Allen W. Dulles, former director of the CIA, would be the appropriate person to lead the investigation; but since President Kennedy had quite publicly fired him for having repeatedly made false statements to him, some questions might be asked even by a complicit media. A titular head was required as well as members from both the Senate and the House, and both parties, and of course, the ubiquitous Allen Dulles, who still maintained important contacts with the new president. If possible, an FBI informant should also have a position.

President Johnson, after conferring with the intelligence community, appointed a presidential committee to investigate. The White House, and later the commission itself, explained why the commission was required. It was to head off and prevent an investigation by congress since several congressional committee heads had announced the intention of conducting hearings. His choice for chairman was Chief Justice of the United States Earl Warren. Warren stated that he would not serve but Johnson persisted until the justice agreed. Republican and Democratic members of both houses were appointed, as was Allen Dulles. Rep. Gerald Ford, a Republican asset of the FBI, was one of the members. Later the FBI provided Ford with a special briefcase so that he could steal Warren Commission secret documents and deliver them to FBI officials. The purpose was to brief in advance the FBI witnesses with the questions that they would be asked. Of course, Dulles provided the same service to the CIA.

In attempting to design an inescapable trap for Oswald, Phillips was troubled by what he considered to be possibly fatal obstacles to the plan. Oswald would deny that he had been to Mexico City and might be able to provide proof that he was elsewhere at that time. That will not be a problem, he was assured. Oswald will not live to defend himself or even talk to a lawyer. Two days after his arrest, Oswald was murdered in the Dallas Police and Courts Building by an FBI asset, Jack Ruby, while the prisoner was being guarded by numerous police officers. The FBI and the Dallas Police Department had not permitted Oswald to meet with a lawyer, although he had publicly made that request.

There still remained the problem of Oswald's wife and two children. The children were too young to be relied upon as witnesses, but Marina, soon to be his widow, might have some information to offer. She was to be immediately taken into custody by the Secret Service and denied access to counsel. Later the CIA arranged for Priscilla Johnson to spend time with her. Marina was told that if she did not remain silent, she would be deported to the Soviet Union and that her children would remain in the United States to be raised by the state as orphans.

With those assurances in place, Phillips went to work. A major feature of the plan was to create a scenario that would prevent any responsible body appointed to conduct the inquiry from doing so. "National Interests" and "Patriotism," the last refuges for scoundrels, always remained the basis for turning away from the facts; and those concepts were cleverly employed by Phillips. He became the architect of the advance frame–up. He was not on the grassy knoll when the fatal shot was fired. But he was in Mexico City many weeks earlier when the plan to prevent the possibility of an honest inquiry as to who was responsible was initiated.

The "lone assassin" was the story the CIA would try to sell. Yet the CIA had built in a safeguard in case their original efforts failed. They had arranged alternative scenarios. Jim Garrison, District Attorney of New Orleans, and later a state court appellate judge in Louisiana, said that as long as no one suspected that the CIA was complicit in the assassination the agency would be satisfied. He pointed out that the CIA had devised a scheme that resembled the layers of an onion. The first impression was that Oswald did it alone. If that story was rejected, there was a fallback theory to take its place. Remove that layer and you encounter the next choice, organized crime. That false lead would make for an ideal culprit. No group would respond by stating that it was organized crime and that in this matter the syndicate was innocent. Also, most people did not approve of those who controlled the sale of drugs and prostitution and regularly dealt in murder and numerous other illegal acts and, therefore, would not be surprised or dissatisfied to learn that they were also involved in assassinations. There were many layers as indicated by clues scattered about, but the concept was that before you might reach the CIA you would have to reject all others that preceded it.

In addition, if you were going to write a book or produce a film on the subject, choosing criminals as your villains would cause a lot less trouble for you than asserting that your own government killed your president.

The Legend Is Established:
The CIA's Mexico City Caper

The CIA and David Atlee Phillips developed the Legend that Lee Harvey Oswald had been to Mexico City during September 1963. That assertion was not true, yet the complicated legend that the CIA constructed about Oswald's journey to Mexico became the basis for removing Warren and his commission as independent investigators.

According to the legend, Lee Harvey Oswald was in Mexico, primarily Mexico City, from September 26, 1963, until October 3, 1963. He visited the Cuban embassy on September 27, 1963, and was observed there by Silvia Duran, a Mexican national employed by the embassy. Duran provided a written statement about her observation, which the CIA could present. The man who was identified as Oswald spent considerable time with Duran and was given to angry and memorable outbursts and "became very excited or angry" requiring Duran to call "Consul Ascue" who was engaged in "a heated discussion in English with Oswald" leading "Ascue" to state that "if it were up to him, he would not give him a visa."

The legend stated that on October 3, 1963, Oswald called the Russian embassy. He asked to speak with "comrade Kostin," codename for Valery V. Kostikov, and inquired if there were any messages for him, establishing that he had a continuing relationship with the Soviet official. According to the CIA, Kostikov, who functioned as a counsel in the embassy, was really a KGB staff officer in charge of the Thirteenth

Department, or liquid affairs department, with the responsibility of planning and carrying out assassinations in the Western Hemisphere. It was also charged with planning acts of sabotage.

Oswald allegedly was photographed entering and exiting from the Soviet embassy. The CIA possessed those photographs. Oswald's telephone calls to the Soviet embassy were furtively recorded by the CIA and those recordings, as they were prepared to state, were also in the possession of the CIA.

While the CIA would state that it was certain that Oswald was the assassin and that he had acted alone, it feared the facts of his visits to the Soviet embassy and his meeting with Kostikov taken together with his visits to the Cuban embassy to provide an escape to Cuba after having assassinated President Kennedy would cause the American people to conclude that the Soviets and the Cubans had assisted in the conspiracy. Demands for retaliation by the United States could result in a major war in which forty million Americans might die. That would be the analysis given to any organization inquiring into the facts. Subsequent to the development of the legend the Warren Commission was appointed.

It would be the recommendation of the CIA that the matter be probed no further, that the commission accept the CIA, FBI, and Dallas Police conclusions and refrain from highlighting Kostikov's job description, while focusing on other evidence that could be developed to indicate Oswald's lone guilt.

The CIA reported to Warren that it "had worked in close liaison with Mexican law enforcement authorities," and that "by far the most important confirmation of Senora Duran's testimony, however, had been supplied by confidential sources of extremely high reliability available to the United States in Mexico." Unfortunately, as the CIA and Warren Commission concluded, "the identities of these sources cannot be disclosed," not even to the members of the Warren Commission.

The most relevant report about the meeting at which the CIA presented its carefully constructed legend to Warren was written by Melvin Aron Eisenberg, an assistant counsel to the Warren Commission. On January 20, 1964, the commission held its first conference with its staff. On February 17, 1964, Eisenberg wrote a top secret internal commission memorandum entitled "First Staff Conference—January 20, 1964."

That memorandum does not appear in the Warren Commission Report. Eisenberg's name does not appear in the body of the report; it is present only on introductory page where the members of the commission, its counsel and its staff members are listed. In a document never intended for public disclosure he wrote that Warren, soon after he had been briefed by the CIA and President Johnson, met with his staff and counsel and explained his new approach to the case. The president wanted Warren to destroy "rumors" that "were circulating in this country and overseas." Warren was committed to do so for reasons that he soon explained to his astonished colleagues. This pronouncement was made before the commission had taken any evidence and, therefore, before it was able to know if the "rumors" on the agenda for elimination accurately presented the facts.

Warren then stressed the urgency and gravity of the new mission. This evidence, or body of "rumors," was so dangerous that if not suppressed the result might be the deaths of millions of Americans. Warren told those who were required to follow his instructions that the "rumors" were so potentially explosive that, "if not quenched, [they] could conceivably lead the country to war which would cost forty million lives." Warren had accepted the CIA's legend and its possible consequences, even utilizing the same figure of deaths that the CIA had manufactured.

The internal memorandum, a form of annotated minutes of the first staff meeting, stated that Warren had made it clear that "No one could refuse to do something which might help prevent such a possibility."

When I first read the Warren Commission Report about forty-five years ago, I had doubts about the veracity of the conclusion that Oswald had been to Mexico City. After studying the twenty-six selected volumes of testimony and evidence later published by the commission, I was almost certain that the CIA had contrived the story and that Dulles had misled his fellow commissioners. Later, when the government was compelled to produce many of its files that had been designated top secret, it became clear that the CIA had established a legend for Oswald attributing to him a series of actions in which he had not been involved. Although Oswald had been silenced, his wife, then in custody and under the control of the U.S. Secret Service, continued to state that Oswald had not been to Mexico City.

I was puzzled about why the CIA, having insisted that Oswald had acted alone and that there had been no conspiracy to assassinate President Kennedy, had also created the challenging and mutually exclusive story that Oswald had met with Russians and Cubans at their embassies in Mexico just two months before, according to the CIA, he assassinated the president. The two notions seemed at odds with each other especially when the CIA also specifically stated that during the journey Oswald met with the KGB officer responsible for plotting assassinations in the Western Hemisphere for the Soviet Union. Their "lone assassin," they concluded, had traveled to Mexico City for the purpose of conferring with the one person present in the Western world who had the unique ability to provide expert advice, funds, logistical support and technology. To an uninformed observer it appeared that the CIA was presenting information that was devastatingly counterproductive to its lone-assassin theory. The CIA stated that Oswald's trip to the Cuban embassy comprised evidence that after the assassination he planned to return to Mexico City, change planes there and escape to Cuba. A putative assassin engaging the cooperation of two Communist countries, each in a position to provide considerable help to advance his murderous scheme, tends not merely to detract from the CIA Party Line of a "lone assassin." It presented an entirely competing theory. Either one concept or both were off the mark. At best, only one of them could have been valid.

The relevant question was why had the CIA sought to uncomfortably ride two horses at the same time while they were going in opposite directions? The answer to that question provided not just a clue, but evidence as to the identity of those who killed John Kennedy. Of course the CIA was aware that the two stories it was so assiduously promoting were contradictory, but its plan was to share each story exclusively with different audiences. The Oswald Legend of the Mexico City adventure was presented to Warren as for-your-eyes-only report. It effectively froze him into inaction as was its intent.

The lone-assassin concept, with no reference to the implications of the fabricated Mexico City story, was for public consumption. It came with assurances from Dulles to his colleagues on the commission that no one would look beyond their assurances for many years. That prediction proved that the former director of the CIA had become no more proficient as a soothsayer than he had been when he confidently predicted an important and speedy victory at the Bay of Pigs since he was certain that the Cuban people were ready to pick up arms to support the American invasion. He was right about the immediacy of their response and that they would have weapons; just wrong about whom they would be aiming at and who would prevail.

Once the legend was in place, the ultimate sting began. Oswald was dead. Law enforcement officers who discovered inconvenient facts were ordered to remain silent, fired from their positions, and suffered greatly. Others were also silenced, including an employee of the Cuban embassy in Mexico City who was arrested upon the direct orders of the CIA when she answered truthfully that Oswald had not visited the embassy. Marina Oswald, who knew that her husband had not visited Mexico City, was threatened with deportation to the Soviet Union. The only obstacle to the realization of the plan was Earl Warren, the titular head of the investigating team. He became the mark in the sting.

The most important living person who could corroborate the legend was Silvia Duran. The CIA produced a statement signed by her stating that Oswald had visited the Cuban embassy and then assured the commission that her statement was confirmed by other sources. The members of the Warren Commission relied upon those representations, and she was not called as a witness. No member of the commission, no one associated with the commission, no staff employee, neither the general counsel nor any of the numerous assistant attorneys ever sought to contact Ms. Duran in person or even by letter or telephone, although her written statement was the only evidence that Oswald had been to the Cuban embassy.

During August 1963, a vacancy was created by the death of a Mexican national who worked at the Cuban embassy in Mexico City. The employee had been killed in what had been described as an "automobile accident." Although the Mexico City police considered it to be a suspicious death, the local police never investigated its cause. The vacancy was filled by another Mexican national, Silvia Duran, who was a twenty-six-year-old woman without experience and from a family without power or political connections. When Duran was first questioned about her interaction with Oswald at the Cuban Embassy, she stated that she had never seen him there. The CIA then directed its assets in the police department of Mexico City to arrest her. The director of the CIA sent a cable to the CIA office in Mexico City that read, "Arrest of Silvia Duran is extremely serious matter which could prejudice US Freedom of Action on entire question of Cuban responsibility." The cable also directed that the CIA's Mexican police assets isolate Duran so that she could not be heard by anyone while in the Mexican prison. The local police were also ordered by the CIA to prevent Mexican officials from learning about Duran's arrest and the role of the CIA in having her arrested and being placed in solitary confinement pursuant to the orders of the director of the CIA. That cable revealed the extent of CIA control over Mexican police officials. Many of those officials had been trained by the CIA, and many actually worked for the CIA at the same time they theoretically were working for the Mexican police. After a period of solitary confinement, Duran agreed to sign a statement prepared by the CIA that identified Oswald as the person in the Cuban embassy.

She was then released from prison but ordered never to speak about the matter. Of course, she had no idea that the CIA was responsible for her arrest, and her outrage was directed at the Mexican police. She began to speak about the incident. In a cable marked "priority," the CIA ordered the Mexican authorities to rearrest her and "to be certain that there is no misunderstanding between us, we want to ensure that Silvia Duran gets no impression that Americans are behind her rearrest. In other words, *we want Mexican authorities to take responsibility for the whole affair.*" [Emphasis in the original.]

Regarding Oswald's presumed visit to the Soviet embassy, the CIA told Warren that it had a plethora of unquestionable documentation. The CIA intrigued Warren with war stories about their incursions into the Soviet telephone system so they could hear and record all conversations and their clever installation of motion picture cameras, unseen by the Russians, yet filming all entrances and exits to and from the embassy so that a filmic record was established of all visitors. All this information was dramatically provided to Warren with the CIA's firm conclusions and suggestions about the future course that the inquiry must take.

Warren was told that the CIA had examined all of the evidence and had concluded beyond doubt that Oswald had been the assassin and that he had acted alone, thereby obviating the need for further inquiry by the commission. That conclusion merely restated the position taken by Hoover, the FBI and the Dallas authorities hours after the murder in Dealey Plaza and before any investigation had begun. Since the commission had previously decided not to retain its own independent investigators and to rely primarily upon the CIA, the FBI, and the Dallas Police Department, an additional investigation would have been redundant, he was informed.

The CIA warned Warren that a further inquiry into the facts was not only unwarranted and superfluous, but would imperil the security of the nation and might lead to the death of many Americans. That prediction was contrived to alarm the pragmatic Chief Justice. The CIA told Warren that Oswald's journey had been established by numerous incontrovertible facts.

Subsequently, when it was established beyond doubt that Oswald had not been in Mexico, the CIA's elaborate series of charades provided evidence that it had been involved in planning the assassination for at least two months before it had taken place. One small indication of the flawed scheme is that the name of the Cuban consul at the relevant time was Eusebio Azque, not Ascue, a fact well known to Duran, who had not in fact written the statement with the incorrect spelling of the name of the consul to whom she regularly reported and saw on a daily basis. That report was written rather carelessly by the CIA, the agency that demanded that she sign it.

When some members of the Warren Commission became suspicious about the legend and asked for the CIA cables, then–CIA director Helms admitted that the CIA had censored the evidence before allowing the Chief Justice and other members of the president's commission to review it. The CIA continued to refuse to show its cables, dispatches, and other documents in its possession to the Warren Commission claiming that "they contained code words and digraphs which would be unintelligible to a person not familiar with them." Later I was able to examine all of the original cables. They contained no code words. After consulting the dictionary, I discovered what a digraph was: "A pair of letters that represents a single speech sound, such as *ph* in pheasant." "I was of the impression that the Chief Justice and the other members of the commission would not be puzzled by the spelling of pheasant."

The entire story about Oswald being in the Cuban embassy was a fiction created by the CIA. Oswald had never been to Mexico City. The photograph provided by the CIA of the man at the entrance to the

Soviet embassy was not a photograph of Lee Harvey Oswald, as even
the CIA was later to concede. Seven different FBI agents interviewed
Oswald on November 22nd and 23rd. They obtained a copy of the
CIA recording of the man who identified himself as "Lee Oswald"
while talking to the Soviet embassy. According to an FBI report, they
all agreed that the person on the tape recording "was NOT Lee Harvey
Oswald." While not one shred of evidence connected Oswald to the
Mexico City scenario, there was substantial evidence demonstrating
that he had never been to Mexico City. His widow, at that time a
cooperating witness with the FBI and Secret Service, who held her
in custody along with her children, said that Lee had never been to
Mexico City, and could not have been there without her knowledge
while she was living with him.

A Trip to Washington

In 1975, I moved to Washington, D.C., to organize the Citizens' Commission of Inquiry (the successor to the Citizens' Committee of Inquiry established in New York in 1964) to urge congress to investigate the assassination of the president and the resultant cover-up of the facts by the FBI and the CIA.

I rented a suite of rooms in a residential building on Capital Hill and I rented an apartment to live in around the corner on Constitution Avenue. Since the residential building banned dogs and my best friend was a collie, Sean was temporarily required to sleep in the office at night on those occasions when I was unable to have him surreptitiously enter my sixth-floor home up the back stairs.

Our office organized a series of lectures at colleges, universities and law schools throughout the country. I averaged almost a talk every other day for months. Speaking fees paid by the schools went to our committee. The fees covered the rent, the salary of the one paid staff member and printing and mailing costs, as we published a newspaper and contacted members of Congress through the mail, and, in numerous districts, their constituents as well.

There was ample evidence that the subject had not been abandoned by the American people and that interest in the unsolved mystery was greater than ever. At many of the schools the audience comprised the largest group ever to attend a lecture there. In Madison, Wisconsin, the university rented and filled a large downtown theater. In Monroe, Louisiana, more than four thousand students and others attended. At

Purdue more than 6,000 attended and more than 5,000 said they would support our request for a congressional committee.[118]

And so it continued week after week in almost every state in the continental United States. We announced our presence on May 23, 1975, in a feature story published by *The Washington Post*.

We organized 180 chapters of the CCI; almost every state was represented. It soon became clear that our office space was inadequate. Our paid staff had increased and numerous volunteers offered their services. I obtained a loan and bought a row house near our office. It had been functioning as a rooming house and was quite dilapidated, and therefore, in spite of its location, remarkably inexpensive. My collie and I moved into the top floor and the other three floors became our office.

At each school after each talk I met with students who either organized a local chapter or asked existing campus student groups to assist. The chapters contacted their representatives in Congress. Within months we had built a national campaign.

I prepared a resolution calling for the establishment of a Select Committee and began to call upon members of the House of Representatives. The first congressman I visited was Herman Badillo. He had been a volunteer in my campaign for election to the state legislature in 1960, remained active in politics and was a friend. Ten years later he was elected to the House. He greeted me warmly and was happy that I had moved to D.C. He said that Congress would never conduct an investigation into the two murders and that he doubted that a single member of the House would sign on. I asked him if he would. He said "of course" and he became the first sponsor of the resolution I had drafted.

The following week, I invited three first-term Democrats to dinner that I cooked at my apartment. It was as close to a Chinese banquet as I could come. After the last course I suggested discussing the resolution. One of them said that they had all read it and added jocularly that the food was so good they would rely upon my judgment. All three signed the resolution while still at the dining room table.

One morning I walked from my office to meet with Andrew Young in his congressional suite. He took me into his private office and said that he would sign the resolution. He suggested that I consider

---

118. *Lafayette Journal and Courier,* Indiana, April 19, 1975.

amending it to include an inquiry into Dr. King's assassination. I met with those few who had already joined the effort and all favored the amendment. Andy arranged a meeting for me with the leader of the Congressional Black Caucus, Yvonne Brathwaite Burke. She had been the first African American woman elected to the California Assembly and the first to be elected to Congress from that state. She was also the first woman elected to lead the caucus. She agreed to enthusiastically endorse the resolution and to seek the support of the caucus.

While support for the resolution was growing, one white member of the House from a Southern state raised questions about why a black minister should be in the same resolution with a former president. My answer—because they were both assassinated and because there remain unanswered questions about their death—did not really satisfy him, but he remained a loyal and important supporter of the amended resolution.

We filed a lawsuit under the Freedom of Information Act [FOIA] for the declassification and release of hundreds of thousands of documents related to the assassination of President Kennedy. We were supported in that effort by the American Civil Liberties Union; Morton Halperin, former Deputy Assistant Secretary of Defense; and the Center for National Security Studies.[119]

---

119. The old FOIA had basically prohibited the release of documents in spite of its grand name that held out a promise of transparency in government. After the excesses of the Nixon administration during Watergate, which led to Nixon's resignation under the threat of impeachment (in my view those acts did not rise to the level of impeachable crimes and in retrospect, they were minor compared with what was to follow at the start of the new century), the one prospective reform was the amendment to make the act as effective as its name implied. President Ford made it clear that he wanted to lead that effort. But two of his advisors, Donald Rumsfeld, his chief of staff, and his deputy Dick Cheney, warned him about "leaks" and insisted that he abandon the effort. One government lawyer, Antonin Scalia, assured Ford that the bill was unconstitutional. Some names follow us through the decades like a song we did not want to hear in the first place. Congress passed the bill and Ford vetoed it. Congress then passed it over the veto and it became law. By 1976, the availability of documents was restricted by new amendments. FOIA access was further limited starting in 1982 by executive orders issued by President Reagan. In 1995 President Clinton restored some of the act's reach. But on November 1, 2001, Executive Order 13233 drafted by Alberto R. Gonzales was signed by President George W. Bush severely limiting the impact of the FOIA.

The Department of Justice opposed the lawsuit we had filed in the United States District Court for the District of Columbia. Its lawyers told the federal judge that the publication of the documents would violate the nation's security. I argued that since the government had said that one man, Lee Harvey Oswald, had acted alone, I could not imagine how there could be a national security problem. That is, unless the government would like to confess that there had been a conspiracy and there was an ongoing investigation.

The judge agreed with me, and over the heated objections of the Department of Justice, the CIA and the FBI, he ordered that copies of the documents be delivered to our office. It was one of the first major court victories regarding the release of documents under the newly amended Freedom of Information Act and it was celebrated in a novel written by Robert Tanenbaum.[120]

I soon learned the wisdom of the advice that you should be careful what you wish for, since it may be granted. The court gave the intelligence agencies a deadline for the production of the documents. Neither the CIA nor the FBI had enough experts in the subject matter since they had shared their awful secrets only on a need-to-know basis, which had been strictly adhered to. They were obligated to allow clerks without specific knowledge of the complex case to review the material and to decide what should be redacted. Admissions of blatant CIA or FBI misconduct were initially removed, for the most part. Later we demanded and received some of those documents as well.

The first production took place one afternoon when a huge truck filled with file boxes of material was unloaded at the curb outside of our office. It was soon followed by another. At first we estimated that approximately 100,000 documents had been delivered. We were surprised by the volume and almost, but not quite, overwhelmed as we had prepared to the best of our ability. Many very bright and dedicated volunteers had joined us. One college and one university gave a semester of credit for those who spent five months with us. I had participated with others in teaching classes to the students as to what type of documents might be useful. They were far more expert in the subject than the government employees who had made the decision as to what should be produced. The kids worked through the night,

---

120. Robert K. Tanenbaum, *Corruption of Blood*, (Dutton, 1995).

sometimes fifteen or twenty at a time, dividing the reports and reading every page. It was an exciting time, for often the silence was broken by a student holding a document and shouting, "Look what I found! Listen to this!" The reading aloud was often concluded with enthusiastic applause. They were not just learning about American history; they were writing it. Many of their discoveries were subsequently provided to members of Congress.

Among the hundreds of thousands of pieces of paper we plowed through was a ten-page, single-spaced group of three documents, the first one dated August 2, 1966, which was a CIA review of *Rush to Judgment* written two weeks before the book was published. It bears the hand-printed legend "ONLY COPY." Well not anymore; some assurances have less staying power than others. The second document, dated January 4, 1967, attacks every author who raised any question about the Warren Commission Report. It sought to dismiss Joachim Joeston who fled from Germany to warn the allies about Hitler's intentions to wage war, by stating that he was politically unreliable. Its source, the CIA wrote, was "a Gestapo document of 8 November 1937 among the German Foreign Ministry files." Hitler may have been a mass murderer, perhaps the CIA reasoned, but no one ever said he was a poor judge of his fellow man.

The third document was a top secret "DISPATCH" advising the CIA "Chiefs, Certain Stations and Bases" to "employ propaganda assets to answer and refute the attacks of the critics."[121]

It set forth in detail the questions and assertions interviewers, book reviewers and writers of feature articles should be told to utilize when interviewing or discussing me or any other critic of the Warren Report. Throughout the first part of my investigation into the Kennedy assassination, as I traveled to speak about the assassination and as I wrote and tried to publish and then publicize *Rush to Judgment,* I had not known that the CIA was engaged in an organized campaign to discredit me. The CIA, expecting that its memorandum would never be seen by non-officials without high-level clearance, had written regarding the murder of President Kennedy:

---

121. These three formerly top secret documents are published in their entirety in this book in the chapter entitled "The CIA and the Media."

"Our organization itself is directly involved: among other facts we contributed information to the investigation."

I believe that they had indicated responsibility for the cover-up and had not excluded "among other facts" their direct "involvement" in the assassination.

The CIA instructed its officers to discuss this effort with "liaison and friendly elite contacts (especially politicians and editors)" and tell them that doubts about the FBI conclusion that Oswald had acted alone, a view held by most Americans, "appear to be deliberately generated by Communist propagandists."

I had always been baffled by the report of the huge sums of money I received for writing *Rush to Judgment*.[122] The memo cleared that up for me as well. In the section instructing what information to use to attack Warren Commission critics, the memo states: "Another factor has been the financial reward obtainable for sensational books," and then proceeds to recount the success of "Mark Lane's *Rush to Judgment*." The CIA had sent written instructions to its assets in the news media stating that I had written the book in exchange for huge sums. The media ran incessantly with that story.

The CIA proclaimed to its "assets" in the news media, including reporters, editors, and publishers who were paid or given other benefits to present the CIA view, that the Warren Commission and its helpers, investigating on behalf of America, were "men of integrity, experience and prominence," getting two out of three right. The CIA memorandum accused me of being unpatriotic and un-American. In fact, the commission members were all elderly white men (no women, no African Americans, no Hispanics), most with flawed backgrounds, including directing assassinations, arranging the odd coup or so in foreign countries and usually covering them up, or excusing war crimes or unlawfully withholding information in order to convict innocent victims.

The major news media, all television and radio networks and national newspapers, acted in accordance with the directives from the CIA for a protracted time. No doubts about the accuracy of the FBI or Dulles–Warren Report were permitted and the dark side of the illicit background of the official "chosen investigators" was never mentioned. Walter Cronkite, for one example, used his stentorian voice to demand

---

122. After the book had been rejected by almost all publishers in the United States, one offered $13,500 to me as an advance for world wide rights. I agreed but the publisher later withdrew the offer.

that we "have faith" in these men of unquestioned integrity, rather than suggest that we look at the evidence.

Our office was located on Second Street across the street from the United States Supreme Court and just down the block from the Library of Congress, a virtue that was of enormous importance in that ancient time before the Internet and Google. It was also a short walk to the House and Senate office buildings that flanked us and that convenience was even more relevant.

One night, a staff member was having her friend, Peter Jennings, over for a private dinner in our office. She had purchased two frozen game hens, each wrapped in heavy-duty plastic that had been secured by large staples. She imprudently left them on a kitchen counter to thaw as she left to purchase some wine. Peter, Kathy, and the wine arrived at the same time to discover that the plastic and staple survived but the hens were gone. Sean, my collie, had eaten them, still almost frozen, as dessert. Kathy was furious as her new relationship was secret and the nearby restaurants were off-limits. Even a thank-you note left the next morning and signed by Sean, albeit with a suggestion that he hoped in the future the hens might be better cooked, did not mollify her. In most other respects, our efforts in Washington were a success.

One morning I received a call from a man who identified himself as Dick Schweiker. He said that he was interested in my work and asked if I could visit him. He gave me the name of the Senate building and the room number where I could find him. Richard S. Schweiker, Republican, was a United States senator from Pennsylvania. He was the chairman of a subcommittee of the Church Committee,[123] which was charged with the responsibility of reviewing and investigating the role of the CIA and the FBI in providing information and conclusions to the Warren Commission. This was the first federal inquiry into a matter related to the assassination since the publication of the Warren Report.

---

123. The Church Committee was chaired by Senator Frank Church, a former army intelligence officer. It concluded that the CIA had violated the law by attempting to assassinate foreign leaders, referred to the CIA as a "rogue elephant rampaging out of control," and identified fifty American journalists directly employed by the CIA and many others who were affiliated with that agency and paid by it. It also concluded that the CIA withheld from the Warren Commission critical information about the assassination of President Kennedy and that the FBI had conducted a counterintelligence program (COINTELPRO) in an effort to destroy Dr. Martin Luther King, Jr.

Later that day we met in his office, the first of a number of meetings comprised almost exclusively of my answering his probing questions and providing documents to him. "Mark, please don't think of me as someone who only seeks information about things you can prove. Use my office for any leads you have. Our staff will investigate. I know that all leads will not check out. I will not judge you if they don't; I will thank you for the effort."

I was impressed by his grasp of the complex material and was not surprised to learn that he had graduated Phi Beta Kappa, was elected to the Senate in 1968, and was reelected in 1974 in the midst of a strong Democratic Party showing nationwide. I was hesitant to accept his invitation to submit untested data out of a concern that it might later be said that I had made claims that could not be substantiated. I had become aware and wary of unfair attacks. As I came to know him, I became convinced that he was a man of his word and I offered numerous areas for inquiry, almost all of which, but not all, proved to be useful. Sen. Schweiker and his staff never made any public or private comment about me that was less than gracious.

The Schweiker Committee Report asserted that it "has developed evidence which impeaches the process by which intelligence agencies arrived at their own conclusions about the assassination, and by which they provided evidence to the Warren Commission." It added that "the evidence indicates that the investigation of the assassination was deficient." Sen. Schweiker said that the Warren Report "had collapsed like a house of cards." He concluded that the investigation into the death of the president was "snuffed out before it began" by "senior officials who directed the cover-up." His findings became the basis of a media campaign against him led by *TIME,* which reported in an article entitled "The Road from Slippery Rock," that "A student of the John Kennedy assassination, Schweicker embarrassed himself" by "impetuously calling previous investigations of the murder 'a coverup.'" Since the article was unsigned it is difficult to know if it was written by any of the CIA's full- or part-time owned journalists. Schweicker declined to run for reelection in 1980 and was appointed as the United States Secretary of Health and Human Services. He was succeeded in the Senate by Arlen Specter, the creator of the Magic Bullet Theory.

During 1975, I also met with Representative Don Edwards of California. He had been a special agent of the FBI in 1940 and 1941.

He was the chairman of the House Judiciary's Civil and Constitutional Rights Subcommittee. The Edwards Committee had been given oversight duties of the FBI. I spent many days with him and with his excellent staff. It was decided that the committee had jurisdiction over FBI record keeping; we discussed the FBI treatment of records relating to the assassination. Edwards held public hearings on the subject and uncovered facts about the note that Oswald had left for FBI agent James Hosty on November 6, 1963. It had been destroyed by Hosty upon instructions from his superior, Special Agent in Charge J. Gordon Shanklin. These and other revelations were helpful in getting to the truth and were a significant contribution to educating his colleagues about the unanswered questions about the previous government investigation.

Finally, during 1976, we had more than one hundred congressional sponsors of the resolution. Among the other stalwarts were Christopher Dodd, later a Senator, then a representative, Richardson Preyer, Mervyn Dymally and Bella Abzug. A date for the vote was set, and we began to contact our supporters nationwide with the urgent request that Congress hear from them. Texts, fax machines and e-mails were not available. In their stead were telephones, telegrams and the U.S. mail.

I continued to organize at colleges and at meetings in places chosen for congressional districts where opponents to the resolution were located. We were able to circulate petitions and encourage letters to numerous members of Congress, sometimes as many as four thousand messages to a representative within one week. More than one million letters, telegrams and signatures on petitions were sent to members of Congress by their constituents, in addition to countless telephone calls that we could not, by definition, count.

The resolution was set for a vote. I was in the first row of a gallery seat next to my associate, April Ferguson. On the floor voices against the proposal were raised, and when the votes were cast it seemed for a short time that it was going to be defeated. I gave April my wallet and the keys to my apartment and car. If the resolution was rejected, I had decided to tell our representatives that they had acted shamefully in turning their backs upon both their late president and hopes for the truth. I knew if I spoke I would be arrested within moments.

The bill passed. Rep. Don Edwards looked toward me, held the resolution in his hand and said, "This should be called the Mark Lane resolution." April handed the keys and wallet back to me and I sighed with relief. I had never liked the D.C. jail even when I visited it to represent Dick Gregory every Christmas day when he was arrested for protesting at the South African embassy during the long apartheid nightmare.

The Gallup Poll taken in 1976 revealed 81 percent of Americans believed that there had been a conspiracy to murder President Kennedy. And ABC News confirmed it was still 81 percent in 1993. Frank Newport, editor in chief of the Gallup Poll, appeared on the *Jim Lehrer News Hour* on November 20, 2003. When asked why 81 percent believed there was a conspiracy in 1976 and whether it tied "in to any particular event," Newport replied, "not that I am aware of," and that "we just came back into the field and *lo and behold* discovered that it had gotten high at that point and stayed that time [sic] every time we decided to ask it since, it remains at that height." On one of their trips into the field, Gallup might have asked the question and then have been in a position to provide a more scientific and precise answer than *lo and behold*; people probably knew the basis for their beliefs.

The House Select Committee on Assassinations (HSCA) was authorized and given a down payment for its budget, but it had not retained someone to lead. Two members of the committee suggested that I become the counsel. I said that even I would object since my objectivity had long since evaporated in view of the undeniable evidence. The committee was moribund and finger pointing had begun.

Two of the members asked me for recommendations for staff director and general counsel. I thought of Ed Ennis, the former Justice Department official who during World War II had opposed the internment of Japanese residents who were innocent civilians. He later became chairman of the ACLU. He was a friend and a scholar of unquestioned integrity. A colleague of mine reminded me that we were in need of a tough prosecutor who did not have a liberal background. He suggested Richard Sprague. I immediately looked into Sprague's legal accomplishments and discovered that he was a brilliant lawyer, had served as a prosecuting attorney and had prosecuted and convicted all those complicit in the labor union–organized criminal conspiracy to murder the Yablonski family.[124] Sprague was praised by judges, defense lawyers, prosecutors and the press for his ability and integrity.

---

124. Tony Boyle, the president of the United Mine Workers, was afraid that Joseph (Jock) Yablonski might bring democracy to that union, and hired hit men to kill Yablonski and his family.

I called Richard Sprague and asked him if he would take the job if it was offered. He asked if I had the authority to make an offer. "No, no authority at all, just an abiding interest." He invited me to meet with him in his office in Philadelphia. We discussed the case and I warned him that if he conducted a fair investigation he would suffer unfair and continuing attacks. He smiled and said that his record precluded that possibility.

We traveled together by train to Washington, and took a cab from Union Station to a House office building where I introduced him to members of the HSCA, staying only long enough to shake hands with the committee members. They talked to him and then hired him.

The FBI and the CIA acted at once. They asserted that *they* would investigate those Sprague wanted to employ and decide what documents they would make available. Sprague rejected their offers and stated that "We must get every relevant document from the FBI files here in Washington and from the CIA vaults in Langley, Virginia." When asked by a reporter how he could hope to get classified documents that the FBI and CIA had denied to Senate and House Intelligence Committees, Sprague responded, "We are a congressional committee in form, but in substance we are investigating two homicides."

Gaeton Fonzi was a dedicated and talented investigator working for the HSCA. He wrote, "After talking with Sprague I was now certain he planned to conduct a strong investigation and I was never more optimistic in my life." He described the scope of the forthcoming efforts and concluded, "The Kennedy assassination would finally get the investigation it deserved and an honest democracy needed."[125]

The implicated intelligence agencies apparently reached the same conclusion. The CIA refused to make information about its Mexico City story available and then insisted that Sprague sign an agreement with the CIA committing him to silence. Sprague said that House Resolution 222, which established the HSCA, authorized the committee to investigate the agencies of the United States government. He said that signing a secrecy agreement would be in direct conflict with the resolution. Sprague asked how he could "possibly sign an agreement with an agency I'm supposed to be investigating."

The CIA–drafted agreement was the most onerous of the species. The signer is prevented from revealing *any* information he has become

125. *The Third Decade Journal,* November 1984.

aware of *in perpetuity*. If he violated that agreement, he faced legal action against him and he would be required, after losing the case, to pay the cost of the legal action against him. Sprague declined and said that instead he would subpoena all relevant CIA records.

A campaign to remove Sprague was undertaken. Jeremiah O'Leary of the *Washington Star,* revealed to be one of several reporters on the asset list of the intelligence agencies, together with other CIA and FBI assets in the news media, led the charge. The FBI hired former agents to lobby with congress to fire Sprague. Some conservative members of congress demanded that if Sprague was not removed they would prevent any funds from being allocated to the HSCA. The committee was a select committee, not a standing committee, meaning that it was not financed annually or bi-annually, but sporadically. The CIA and the FBI targeted Sprague because he was moving in on the culprits. If he could be removed, the committee could be tamed.

One influential member of congress called me to explain the dilemma. She said if they did not fire him there would be no funding. She said that I had worked harder than anyone to form the committee. She said that no one wanted to fire him, but that they had no choice. She asked, "Can I say you agree?" I said that Sprague was a man of honor, which is why the CIA and FBI were afraid of him. I said that the members should stand up on the floor of congress and tell the American people the truth. I had hoped that they had once seen *Mr. Smith Goes to Washington.* I said, "You can say that I am certain that if you fire him you will replace him with a government agent who will sign a secrecy agreement, who will clear the FBI and CIA and who will not explore the Mexico City Scenario." She said, "Mark, you just don't know how things work here." I said I knew how they worked; I just didn't like it and I did not understand their fear.

That year another matter also occupied me. Jose Ramos-Horta, a founder of the Revolutionary Front for an Independent East Timor (FRETILIN), was in New York. He was going to address the United Nations Security Council about the brutal Indonesian occupation of East Timor. Later reports indicated that more than 100,000 East Timorese had died. He had recently been appointed Foreign Minister of the Democratic Republic of East Timor at the age of twenty-five. Indonesian troops invaded and began an indiscriminate slaughter of civilians. Ramos-Horta asked if I could meet with him to discuss the matter, including his efforts at the UN. I met the penniless young man. His passion and determination were obvious. I had not the slightest indication then that within a decade, he would become a Nobel Peace Prize recipient and later the president of his country. After several discussions of his forthcoming work at the UN, he called upon me again for another mission.

He explained that his country was suffering and that a dramatic act was required. I was intrigued and he had my full attention. He explained that there was a man in Australia who owned a schooner that he was making available for the trip. The trip was from Australia to East Timor through an Indonesian blockade. "To deliver supplies?" I asked. "No," he replied, "to have on board distinguished people known for their commitment to humanity and their courage." Dr. Benjamin Spock, he said, would probably be on the ship. "And," he added, "perhaps you?" It was an honor to be asked, yet I had a few questions of my own. It was about the "courage" part. Well, it was really just one question. "What does the Indonesian government say about the voyage?" He answered quite calmly, "Well, of course they say they will blow the ship out of the water." He paused and said, "We think they probably will not do that, it would be too embarrassing for them." And, I thought, also somewhat inconvenient for those of us on the ship. "Us?" I asked myself. My only explanation for agreeing is that I was much younger at the time.

I did make plans, made sure my passport was in order and flew to San Francisco for a flight to Australia. The press in Australia evidently thought it was an event worth reporting. In looking through my files the other day I found a clipping from *The Australian*[126] dated May 12, 1976. Stapled to it was a note saying "Jose (Jose Ramos-Horta) asked me to request that you let Mark Lane have a copy of the enclosed clipping." The four-column headline read "Crusader fights to save Timor." It began, "The crusading American lawyer Mark Lane has pledged his immediate future to the Timorese, a people he had not heard of six months ago." It continued, "He has no qualms about facing a potentially dangerous situation in East Timor." What could I have been thinking, I wondered as I recently read the article.

---

126. A recent trip to the Internet informs that *The Australian* is the most widely read national publication in the country and that its politics are decidedly conservative.

Perhaps there are some forces in the universe that protect people who have made reckless decisions. The first guardian angel in this case was the government of Australia, which was more concerned about a good relationship with the genocidal government of Indonesia than it was about those dying in a powerless little country. The government announced that it would not grant a visa to me to enter Australia. That became a major event since it led to a battle on the floor of the parliament. Threats of a vote of no confidence prevailed, the government relented, and the trip was on again.

Apparently the only person with a substantial financial stake in the matter, the owner of the schooner who had never volunteered to be a passenger, decided to withdraw his offer of the vessel. He had determined that if his ship was blown out of the water, his insurance company would not have considered it to be an "accident" as defined by the policy. With no alternative transportation available, the trip was off again.

Back in the slightly less frightening confines of the nation's capital I met with Sprague over lunch at the Market Inn, a wonderful old Washington seafood place located close to the humble offices assigned to Sprague and his staff. He told me about Robert K. Tanenbaum and asked if I knew him. He added that he was going to ask Tanenbaum to run the investigation into the assassination of President Kennedy. I said that I knew he had a fine reputation and that I had never tried a case against him. Since then I have had the opportunity to learn about Tanenbaum.

Two young women, Janice Wylie and Emily Hoffert, were murdered in their Upper East Side apartment in Manhattan. Eight months later, police officers in Brooklyn, after a lengthy interrogation, obtained a sixty-three-page confession from George Whitmore and celebrated the fact that they had solved a case with great media attention and concomitant political pressure.

A young assistant district attorney in Manhattan, Melvin D. Glass, doubted the validity of the confession and conducted his own investigation causing anger among the police for seeking to open a closed case and to impugn their methods. Mel Glass persisted. The confession was proven to be false and eventually the real murderer, Ricky Robles, was arrested and convicted. That false confession was cited in the case establishing what is now called the Miranda Rule, requiring those in custody to be warned that statements they make may be used against them at trial, that they need not talk to authorities and that they are guaranteed the right to counsel. Mel worked for the legendary Frank Hogan. The modus operandi at that office was to seek justice, not merely to convict.

When Robert Tanenbaum joined the District Attorney's Office, Mel Glass took him on a tour of the Tombs, a cramped, rancid-smelling prison attached to the courthouse. He told Tanenbaum if he ordered the arrest of a person, the prisoner, unless he could post bail, would likely end up there for a long time even before trial. He said be sure, not just beyond a reasonable doubt, but absolutely beyond any and all doubt that he is guilty and that you have admissible evidence to prove it. He also advised Tanenbaum not to request bail that was beyond the means of the prisoner.

Tanenbaum later became chief of homicide and bureau chief of the criminal Court where he was responsible for the intake of all cases, approximately 250 per day. Neither he nor Glass ever wavered from the high ethical standards established by Mr. Hogan. In the many years I practiced as a defense lawyer in Mr. Hogan's courthouse, I never heard of even a hint of district attorney corruption nor did I see that office yield to political pressure. Those high and immutable standards were rarely shared by prosecutors in the other boroughs or elsewhere in the state or nation where I tried many cases.

Both Sprague and Tanenbaum were honest, intelligent and skillful lawyers committed to learning and publishing the truth. When both the CIA and the FBI, aided by powerful media allies, began the campaign to have Sprague fired, Rep. Harold Ford, a member of the HSCA, stated that "the FBI has hired former agents to lobby with Congress against the continuation of the Select Committee."

Later I talked with Tanenbaum about George De Morhenschildt. I said that I had long believed that he was a viable suspect who had never been adequately questioned and whose testimony might be the Rosetta stone placing other relevant evidence in context. Sprague and Tanenbaum dispatched Gaeton Fonzi, their most experienced investigator, to meet with De Morhenschildt.

Events were moving quickly as Sprague and Tanenbaum were getting close to the truth. Phillips was on the verge of confessing that the entire story the CIA had told to the Warren Commission was a fabrication, that in fact Oswald had never been to Mexico City and that the story was created by the CIA to prevent Warren from conducting an honest investigation. Phillips later made those specific admissions in public. His confession demonstrated conclusively that the CIA, in September 1963, was falsely creating a fiction that could and would be used to implicate Oswald in a crime that would not be committed until November 1963; this guilty foreknowledge, known at the law as scienter, clearly demonstrated the CIA's complicity, not merely as accessories after the fact, but as accessories before the fact. That difference is most significant.

In addition, De Morhenschildt was about to be seriously confronted with evidence of his involvement as the CIA agent assigned to control Oswald, his pre-assassination moves, as well as his previous efforts on behalf of the CIA and before that, his actions for foreign governments in assisting assassination plans against other heads of state.

Sprague and his inquiry and De Mohrenschildt were loose ends. De Mohrenschildt had expressed remorse in his role and stated that he had been unfairly used by the CIA since that agency had originally assured him that his control of Oswald was not going to place Oswald in harm's way.

Tanenbaum put it succinctly, "That was some evening. Fonzi was on his way to see De Morhenschildt; De Mohrenschildt was found dead. A shotgun blast had blown his head off in Florida. At the same time, Sprague was being told that the committee was dead if he remained."

Early on, as the Kennedy investigation began, Tanenbaum received a phone call from Senator Richard Schweiker, asking to meet with him. Tanenbaum brought with him to the meeting Cliff Fenton, an African American police officer who had served as a mentor for Tanenbaum in the district attorney's office and had accompanied him to Washington to assist with the investigation into the murder of JFK. With Senator Schweiker, were two members of his own staff. Schweiker asked Fenton and his own staff members to leave the room so that he could have a private talk with Tanenbaum. When they were alone Schweiker said, "I have a file I want you to read, and keep it in a secure place. All of the intelligence agencies will fight you tooth and nail during your investigation and they will also claim that they are cooperating." Schweiker handed the report to Tanenbaum and said, "I believe the

CIA was involved in the assassination of the president." The two men shook hands and Tanenbaum and Fenton left.

They studied the report until 3:00 AM and Tanenbaum was stunned by its contents. Fenton was silent for a period. Then he turned to his friend and said, "Tanny, we're in way over our heads here and there's no Hogan here to protect you."

The Hoover Memo

When I first met with Sprague, he asked two questions. "What is the single most important issue we should look at and who are the most important witnesses?" I suggested that an interview with George De Mohrenschildt, who apparently was Oswald's babysitter for the CIA, would be a good place to start since De Mohrenschildt had been engaged in assassination planning in other countries. I also said to Sprague that crucial to the cover-up by the CIA was the false assertion by David Atlee Phillips about Oswald's apocryphal trip to Mexico City. I suggested that David Atlee Phillips be called to testify about that matter.

The rivalry between the FBI and the CIA has been well documented. Hoover did not fully understand why he had been surreptitiously provided with information from other intelligence forces allowing him to be the first to declare that Oswald was the assassin and that there had been no conspiracy, but he had solved the case and he was eager for the credit. It was not unusual for him to rush to the press with pronouncements of guilt without adequate factual support and in this national crisis he thought it would escape notice that he had certified that Oswald had acted alone even before his investigation had begun. His judgment was largely vindicated when the news media offered his proclamations without critical comment or inquiry.

Hoover knew how to keep a secret. His undisclosed files were proof of that talent as he used that material to extort support even from his critics to ensure his record-breaking longevity as Director of the FBI for Life. He felt sufficiently secure to name his office SOG claiming that it was the permanent "Seat of Government" which remained constant while presidents and their administrations, considered to be transients by him, came and went.

He was outraged when evidence of the FBI contacts with Lee Harvey Oswald became known and he took immediate action against special agents of the FBI who had not adequately covered those tracks.

The agents were sufficiently terrified and took no action that might cause problems for them. Years ago, one special agent of the FBI confided in me that while driving through Los Angeles and in the company of another agent they saw a bank robbery taking place. They quickly analyzed their options. Call it in to local police or the FBI, charge into the scene to confront the criminals, or just drive by. They chose the non-involvement plan, reasoning that if some civilian was hurt or killed as the result of any action on their part, however reasonable, they would have committed the unforgivable sin of "embarrassing the bureau." Funds maintained at banks are federally insured.

Of course, the agents never were sure what Hoover meant when he issued an order. He often would respond to a memorandum submitted to him by scrawling a hand-written statement with a fountain pen across the document. In one instance a document regarding some criminal activity was enhanced by his demand that they "watch the borders." The intimidated agents increased security at crossings from the United States to Canada and Mexico. Later, they realized that the director meant "margins" not "borders" and that he was incensed because there was not a space large enough for him to write a response on the memorandum.

Our small group of volunteers, mostly students, some, but not many, receiving credit from their university or college for their experiment in democracy or government, was inadequate to keep track of the hundreds of thousands of documents which we received and the newly declassified documents at the National Archives that were placed along with the previously available documents. I was a regular visitor at that building and often walked there from our office on Capitol Hill. Employees at the archives, one or two in leadership positions, called me from time to time to inform me that the document that I had requested was then available. I had not requested any specific document but I hurried to the building to see what was there. An archives assistant brought over a number of files, some several inches thick, and placed them on the desk I usually occupied. All the papers were interesting, but only one was of great significance. I never could credit those federal workers and leaders at the National Archives who had served their nation in this matter. Of course, they had violated no law, they never revealed any secrets to me of the many they must have seen; but I feared that their generous advice, if known, would have led to disciplinary action against them. In that spirit I now thank them for their service to our country.

A memorandum signed by J. Edgar Hoover asserted that seven special agents of the FBI had interrogated Oswald starting just after his arrest. The agents, frightened by their director who might have been critical of their performance, or more likely, just following orders, had claimed that no verbatim notes had been made and Oswald's responses were not recorded on tape. That Hoover memorandum, nevertheless, when analyzed in conjunction with the case being developed by Tanenbaum and Sprague, provided evidence of the CIA's complicity in the assassination and led to the destruction of the House Select Committee on Assassinations.

The special agents of the FBI, having talked with Oswald for many hours, could recognize his voice. They also had been provided with the CIA's tape recordings of Oswald in Mexico City. Possibly to impress Hoover so that he could secretly tweak the CIA, the agents all truthfully stated that it was not Oswald's voice on the CIA recording.

Hoover then wrote a secret memorandum, which he may have thought he was directing at some CIA mix-up or filing error, in which he said that Oswald's voice was not recorded by the CIA in Mexico City and that all seven FBI agents who were familiar with the sound of his voice all agreed that it was not Oswald.

I was not an official member of the team conducting the congressional investigation. Although I shared with the committee counsel much of what I had learned during the previous several years I had no expectation that I would be regularly briefed about their progress. However, on occasion, I was told about important events especially when they took place after I had briefed them on the subject matter.

One of those events concerned David Atlee Phillips. Sometime after Phillips testified about the Mexico City affair, counsel told me that Phillips had sworn that the CIA had proof that Oswald had been there, that he had met with an official at the Soviet embassy and had also visited the Cuban embassy in that city. These events all supposedly took place in late September and early October in 1963. They were proof, according to Phillips, that Oswald had been planning the assassination for almost two months before he murdered the president. That proof was the CIA's often repeated assurances that it had surreptitiously recorded Oswald as he talked to his contacts and photographed him as he entered and left the Soviet embassy. That indisputable evidence of Oswald's presence in Mexico City and his mind-set were the tape recordings with Oswald's voice and the photographs of him at the embassy.

Of course, Tanenbaum asked if Phillips had brought the evidence, since that was the basis for his appearance before the investigators. He had not, said Phillips and then he swore that the camera had malfunctioned and the picture was of a man other than Oswald. There was no picture of Oswald in Mexico City, much less of Oswald at the Soviet embassy.

That left only the tape recordings. However Phillips also swore that the tapes had been destroyed by the CIA in the regular course of business. How could the best evidence, the historic documents, be destroyed, why had copies not been made, why were there no transcripts of the recordings and numerous other questions came immediately to mind.

The sole explanation by Phillips was his sworn statement that they would have been preserved if Oswald was a suspect but they had been destroyed before November 22, 1963. That assertion was at best quite dubious. Oswald had been, according to the CIA, talking to the KGB agent in charge of assassinations in the Western Hemisphere, the same geographic area that was Phillips's jurisdiction. After the CIA had learned of Oswald's interest in murdering the president why were the FBI and the Secret Service not notified in September that Oswald was a suspect? Why was there no concern when the intelligence authorities learned that Oswald, having met with the Soviet agent responsible for assassinations in our country, was working at a building that overlooked the presidential motorcade when the president's limousine would be proceeding at its slowest speed to make a very sharp turn in front of that building, the Texas School Book Depository? Of course, there were no answers, and could be none, since Oswald had never been to Mexico City.

After I learned of the Phillips testimony I spent some time alone in my office conducting mental research in an effort to remember what document I had seen some long time before, of the literally tens of thousands I had read, that might cast a light on the matter. I recalled my trips to the National Archives. And I remembered the Hoover memorandum. The tape recording had not been destroyed before Oswald was arrested. Phillips had committed demonstrable perjury and obstruction of Congress. Later, baseball legend Roger Clemens was indicted for having made false statements to Congress, perjury and obstruction of Congress. Clemens had merely denied that he had knowingly used steroids, a matter where the Congress had little or no jurisdiction. Phillips had lied about planning the assassination of the president of the United States and the Congress was conducting the first serious investigation into the facts.

I called the offices of the Select Committee to inquire if Tanenbaum was there. He was and I walked to the committee's office. Tanenbaum, whom I did not know very well, although I now count him as one of my most respected and admired friends, stood up when I walked in, which surprised me. He asked me to be seated and I told him that I had just come to deliver a document to him. I handed him an envelope with the Hoover memorandum in it. He asked what I thought he should do with the document once he read it. I said that once he read it, he would know and that I was confident that he would do what was right.

Tanenbaum directed Phillips to return for further questioning. When Phillips walked into the committee room for his second encounter with counsel he appeared, as he often did, confident and somewhat arrogant. He had already told his story, explained why it could no longer be proved since the evidence to accomplish that was unfortunately gone and irretrievable. He was sanguine about his testimony and expected to be there but a short time to restate his previous position.

Counsel asked him to again state the facts and he responded by repeating his previous false testimony. There was a pause while Tanenbaum took a document from his file and handed it to Phillips. It was, of course, the Hoover memorandum. The tapes had existed after Oswald had been arrested; they had not been destroyed weeks before as Phillips had testified. The memo not only existed, it offered proof that the CIA legend had been fabricated. Oswald had never been to Mexico City and Phillips knew that to be the case when he offered false testimony to the contrary.

There was a pause while Phillips read the document and then slowly folded it up and put it in his pocket. He then rose and silently left the room. He was a witness before a committee of Congress and had not been excused. He was at that moment guilty of obstructing Congress and numerous counts of perjury and uttering false statements. If the Congress acted in accordance with its rules the case would have been referred to the Department of Justice for a perjury indictment on many counts and for obstruction of Congress and for making false statements. Congress itself could act, was required to, by citing Phillips for contempt. Phillips could not speak at that moment since he knew that his life had changed. The Hoover memorandum should have been located and destroyed by CIA moles in the FBI. Phillips had failed and his meticulously fabricated legend was in tatters. He faced public disgrace as well as a substantial prison term and the destruction of the life he had known.

Whether he fled to meet with counsel or his superiors in the CIA is not known. As it turned out he had become a broken man, unable to function any longer in the CIA and finally willing to tell some semblance of the truth. Some years later, quite coincidentally, a debate between CIA officials and those who questioned their methods and goals had been set at the University of Southern California (USC). I was to debate Phillips; he did not know that I was privy to portions of his testimony before the committee.

Early in our exchanges I pointed out that in the most recent work published by Phillips, he stated that Oswald had sent a note to the FBI in which he threatened to "blow up the FBI and Dallas Police Department." Thus Oswald was again demonized as a violent radical. The note Phillips was referring to was sent by Oswald to Special Agent James Hosty. Oswald was concerned that Hosty was bothering his wife, Marina. He wrote, "If you have anything you want to learn about me, come talk to me directly. If you don't cease bothering my wife, I will take appropriate action and report this to proper authorities." No threat, no bomb, no blowing up anything. It was a letter respectful of authority and was moderate, not radical, in tone. If a lawyer had written it for him it could not have been more appropriate while still making the point. Phillips had lied yet again; his response was conciliatory but devoid of an explanation for the fabricated "quotation." He said, while addressing me, "About my book, and the statement that Oswald had threatened to blow up the FBI building, I appreciate your clarification on that. I'm glad to get it straight."

At the debate I revealed some of his misconduct before the congressional committee. He was both surprised and furious but he was careful not to deny the import of his testimony. Present in the audience was Abby Mann, a dear friend and the talented screenwriter of *Judgment at Nuremberg,* the great film of World War II. Abby asked Phillips why he and the CIA had tried to destroy me and if he did not agree that such a strategy was unfair. In essence Phillips said that it was a CIA strategy since I was raising questions about the assassination of President Kennedy that the CIA did not want the American people to be informed about.

He added, "There are certainly a number of things I regret, and I regret the attempts to destroy Mr. Lane. There are a number of things for which intelligence officers should go to jail if they violate the law. Sure, I regret a lot of it."

As Phillips went on about how difficult it was to be a CIA officer, a student in the audience interrupted to call out a question. "Mexico City, Mr. Phillips. What is the truth about Mexico City?" Phillips began his response by saying, "I am not in a position today to talk to you about the inner workings of the CIA station in Mexico City." He could have then turned to another subject since he said he was not permitted to answer the question. Instead he volunteered to continue, "But I will tell you this, that when the record comes out, we will find that there was never a photograph taken of Lee Harvey Oswald in Mexico City. We will find out that Lee Harvey Oswald never visited, let me put it, that is a categorical statement, there, there, we will find out there is no evidence, first of all no proof of that. Second there is no evidence to show that Lee Harvey Oswald visited the Soviet embassy."

Phillips had confessed that the entire CIA-fabricated legend that it so assiduously sold to the Warren Commission was untrue. In addition, most troubling to him, and startling to those familiar with his testimony before the congressional committee, he had just confessed to having committed several counts of perjury and obstruction of Congress.

William Colby, the former director of the CIA, missed my debate with Phillips. When he arrived reporters asked him several questions about Oswald that had no reference to Mexico City. He responded, "All I know about Lee Harvey Oswald is that he visited the Soviet embassy in Mexico City. Ask David Phillips about that. He's the expert. Thank you, gentlemen."

Apologists for the CIA and the Warren Commission who based their conclusions upon the Mexico City Legend were hardpressed to find a reasonable response. One, who had admitted that he received payment to argue that Oswald was the lone assassin, even before he had examined the facts, wrote a book comprised of more than 1,600 pages which attempted to reinvent history, but could not find room in it to present a credible explanation for the Phillips confession.

Robert G. Blakey, who later derailed the congressional committee, sought to explain away the Phillips confession. He wrote that I must have upset Phillips by my cross-examination of him about Mexico City. As we have seen I did not even inquire about the matter; a student seated in the audience asked the question. In addition, Blakey, a Justice Department bureaucrat, betrayed his lack of knowledge about trial procedure. Cross-examination is the engine that runs the system of due process and often brings forth the truth after a rehearsed and unrevealing direct examination. In any event, my questioning of Phillips about other matters never rose to the level of cross-examination; it could not have done so given the circumstances. There was no judge ordering Phillips to answer; he had not been present due to the process of law, that is, he had not been subject to subpoena. He was not in a courtroom. He was a volunteer who came to a university to speak, and he knew that he could at any moment invoke the "well, I can't talk about that" phrase, which in fact he had done. While the debates were educational, it is our system of justice that requires that wrongs be addressed. Compared to that mandate we had engaged in useful theater.

Tanenbaum and Sprague knew that their committee was obligated to act. Tanenbaum had specifically been guaranteed by the members of Congress that there would be no political interference with their work. Yet when presented with the facts and the need to vote to hold Phillips in contempt and to recommend that he be indicted, the members of congress cowered. The intelligence organizations counterattacked, knowing that Phillips was vulnerable, and therefore their weakest link. Massive lobbying efforts were organized with FBI agents instructing representatives about what was at stake. Old debts were called in and old embarrassing files utilized. The media assets were again activated. Those who had regularly made false statements about critics of the Warren Commission Report were enlisted to demean and defame Sprague.

Tanenbaum briefed the chairman of the congressional committee about the opportunity to take a major step to resolve the issues about the assassination, the stated purpose of the resolution that established the committee. He knew that it would take a measure of courage and suggested that the facts be presented to the president so that the Department of Justice, armed with the facts, could take effective action. The plan was sound but the needed courage was absent. Congress, in the face of the intelligence-directed onslaught, suffered a failure of nerve.

Tanenbaum had been regularly meeting with members of the House of Representatives to explain to them why the investigation was important and to provide information to them as to why they should vote for the funding. At the end of March 1977, the day before the vote on the funding, Tanenbaum met with Representative Louis Stokes, the chairman of the committee. Stokes said that he would not vote for funding if Sprague remained.

Tanenbaum and Sprague met later and Tanenbaum suggested that they both resign, as they did not wish to be part of an ineffective effort that was turning toward becoming a cover-up. Sprague said that he would resign but urged Tanenbaum to stay on. Tanenbaum was concerned that the media had been manipulated so that it would be said that Sprague, not the intelligence organizations, would be held responsible for the committee's failure. He also stated that they could no longer remain in leadership positions with a committee that operated politically and had abandoned its search for the truth. Both men resigned; Tanenbaum stayed on for a short while to help with the transition.

Tanenbaum met G. Robert Blakey, the newly appointed general counsel for the committee. Blakey showed Tanenbaum a booklet he had prepared about how to investigate the case. It was called "Means, Motive and Opportunity." Tanenbaum laughed and advised Blakey that if he had any concern for his reputation, he should never show that booklet to anyone else. Tanenbaum explained that the elements of the crime do not include means, motive or opportunity, and that television concepts are totally unrelated to the real world. Factors to be considered, he said, include witness credibility, and matters of that kind.

Tanenbaum's last words to Blakey were, "I take it you have never tried a case, is that correct?" Blakey admitted he had not.

Sprague told me that his position had become untenable because he insisted on asking questions about CIA operations in Mexico City and that he had demanded total access to the employees there and all documents about photographs, tape recordings and transcripts. I told him that I was sorry that I had invited him into what turned out to be a most unpleasant experience for him. He was gracious and thanked me for his very interesting sojourn.

Unlike Sprague, who had insisted upon using the power of subpoena to obtain documents and testimony and who had assembled a group of talented and brilliant counsel, Blakey relied upon the judgment of the CIA and the FBI, who placed their operatives on his staff and who provided only those documents that they wanted the Congress to see. The congressional committee had been captured.

Blakey signed the secrecy agreement and required that all those who worked for him do the same. He opposed the use of subpoenas; he cleared the FBI and the CIA of complicity in the murder, and he refused to explore the CIA's activities in Mexico City.

I met with him one time to present that evidence. He seemed uninterested, and he could not respond since I had not signed a secrecy agreement. What was not a secret is that the CIA had prevailed once again.

Blakey favored the concept that Oswald had acted alone, but the committee members were facing an election and could not return to their districts with a story that few of their constituents would accept. The House Select Committee on Assassinations concluded that the assassination of President Kennedy was likely the result of a conspiracy to commit murder. That finding by the government was the figurative stamping across the cover of each copy of the Warren Report the words, *No Longer Valid*. If you have a copy you might want to ask the Government Printing Office for a refund.

Blakey then moved toward the second CIA option. He would blame it all on organized crime and bar all evidence that led to contrary conclusion, especially if it seemed to implicate the CIA.

Perhaps the most egregious example of Blakey's misconduct was the person he appointed to act on his behalf to secure information from the intelligence agencies. That person, George E. Joannides, became crucial to Blakey's operation. Joannides was brought in to guide Blakey and to provide him exclusively with documents that the CIA wanted him to see and above all, to be certain that documents that implicated the CIA were never produced or even referred to. Joannides was chosen by the CIA for that post.

Joannides was living in official retirement in 1978 when the CIA assigned him to Blakey. The agency had access to hundreds of active duty experts and document researchers on its payroll. But Joannides was perhaps the only one with specific knowledge of where the bodies were buried. He knew; he had buried a few of them. His job was to make certain that the unwitting Blakey never found them.

In 1963, Joannides was a secret member of the CIA's Special Affairs Staff. His assignment then was to provide funds and advice for the anti-Castro group "Directorio Revolucionario Estudiantil" (DRE) based in Miami. The CIA referred to the group, the most militant of all the exile organizations, as the "Cuban Student Directorate," and all of the American news media followed suit in hundreds of reports about the violent group.

The leaders of the DRE were quite open about the goals of their CIA-directed media campaign. They wanted to create panic in Havana and build a wave of public support in the United States to attack Cuba. Castro was knowledgeable and concerned about the effort. The Cuban military was placed under its highest alert. On the evening of November 23, 1963, Fidel Castro addressed the people of his nation. He specifically discussed the DRE and its false claims and unequivocally stated that it was a CIA-directed provocation. Too bad Blakey had not tuned in to the broadcast.

Joannides was based in Miami and was the chief of the Psychological Warfare branch of the CIA's station there. He had twenty-four staff members working for him and a budget of $1.5 million. Working under the CIA's program called AMSPELL, he provided regular monthly payments to Luis Fernandez Rocha, the directorate's leader.

Almost immediately after the shots were fired in Dallas, the Joannides-guided group launched a media campaign to connect Fidel Castro to the murder. This was the first public result of the Mexico City fabrication created by the CIA. The members of the DRE had been well prepared for that moment. One DRE leader called Clair Booth Luce[127] and assured her that the directorate knew that Oswald was part of a Cuban hit team organized by Castro. Similar allegations were simultaneously made to a reporter for *The New York Times.*

Another DRE officer told Paul Bethel, who had been an officer at the State Department leading the campaign against Castro, that Castro was involved with Oswald. Likely many other media contacts were approached but the CIA refuses to release those documents.

The DRE began to assemble documents to support the false charges that they released to the news media on November 23. They included photographs of Oswald and Castro under the headline "Presumed Assassins."

Thus it was the CIA and Joannides that paid for, organized and published the very first conspiracy theory about the assassination of President Kennedy. And all along, the CIA and the FBI and their assets in the media had repeatedly awarded me that honor.

After Joannides died, his role as the secret hand, mind and financier of the DRE and its theories became known. Blakey was outraged, or so he said. "I am no longer confident that the Central Intelligence Agency cooperated with the committee." Oh really, and just after you exonerated them from any misconduct in the murder of our president.

He continued, "I was not told of Joannides's background with the DRE, a focal point in our investigation. Had I known who he was, he would have been interrogated under oath by the staff or by the committee." Interrogated? Blakey had waived his right to subpoena power. He could not have deposed Joannides without his agreement.

"He would never have been acceptable as a point of contact with us to retrieve documents." Documents are not "retrieved" by "a point of contact." Lawyers obtain documents through legal process, motions, formal demands, and the exercise of subpoena power. The rules are clear. We have been engaged in this practice for two centuries.

"In fact," Blakey continued, "I have now learned that Joannides was the point of contact between the agency and the DRE during the period Oswald was in contact with the DRE. That the agency

---

127. Luce was an influential conservative with high-level media connections. Her husband, Henry Luce, was the publisher of *TIME, Fortune,* and *LIFE* and the editor in chief at *TIME.*

would put a 'material witness' in as a 'filter' between the committee and its quests for documents was a flat out breach of the understanding the committee had with the Agency that it would cooperate with the investigation."

And so we are left with this question. What did Blakey know and when did he know it? Is he now haplessly relying upon the excuse that he was so inept an investigator that he could not even discover who was his own main source?

Blakey met his commitment to those who hired him. While he could not discover the names of all those who did participate in the murder he was able to state with absolute authority that he knew who did not. He declared that the CIA and the FBI were innocent.

The Department of Justice was directed to conduct a further serious investigation. It declined.

BOOK FIVE

THE INDICTMENT

Introduction

One month to the day after the assassination of President John F. Kennedy, an article written by former president Harry S. Truman was published in *The Washington Post*.[128]

It was during Mr. Truman's presidency that he organized the Central Intelligence Agency to operate as an arm of the president and to coordinate intelligence reports. He was disturbed by the manner in which the CIA had expanded its role into areas that had never been contemplated by him. He objected to the fact that the CIA had become an operational and policy-making body of the government. As we explore the excesses of the Central Intelligence Agency, a group that now has its own air force and an agency which has committed murder and has planned the assassinations of heads of state with whom it disagreed, it is appropriate to read the words of President Truman as an introduction to this portion of *Last Word*.

---

128. Harry S. Truman, "Limit CIA Role to Intelligence," *The Washington Post*, (December 22, 1963), p. A11.

Harry Truman Writes: Limit CIA Role to Intelligence

By Harry S. Truman
Copyright, 1963, by Harry S Truman

INDEPENDENCE, MO., Dec. 21—I think it has become necessary to take another look at the purpose and operations of our Central Intelligence Agency—CIA. At least, I would like to submit here the original reason why I thought it necessary to organize this Agency during my Administration, what I expected it to do and how it was to operate as an arm of the President.

I think it is fairly obvious that by and large a President's performance in office is as effective as the information he has and the information he gets. That is to say, that assuming the President himself possesses a knowledge of our history, a sensitive understanding of our institutions, and an insight into the needs and aspirations of the people, he needs to have available to him the most accurate and up-to-the-minute information on what is going on everywhere in the world, and particularly of the trends and developments in all the danger spots in the contest between East and West. This is an immense task and requires a special kind of an intelligence facility.

Of course, every President has available to him all the information gathered by the many intelligence agencies already in existence. The Departments of State, Defense, Commerce, Interior and others are constantly engaged in extensive information gathering and have done excellent work.

But their collective information reached the President all too frequently in conflicting conclusions. At times, the intelligence reports tended to be slanted to conform to established positions of a given department. This becomes confusing and what's worse, such intelligence is of little use to a President in reaching the right decisions.

Therefore, I decided to set up a special organization charged with the collection of all intelligence reports from every available source, and to have those reports reach me as President without department "treatment" or interpretations.

I wanted and needed the information in its "natural raw" state and in as comprehensive a volume as it was practical for me to make full use of it. But the most important thing about this move was to guard against the chance of intelligence being used to influence or to lead the President into unwise decisions—and I thought it was necessary that the President do his own thinking and evaluating.

Since the responsibility for decision making was his—then he had to be sure that no information is kept from him for whatever reason at the discretion of any one department or agency, or that unpleasant facts be kept from him. There are always those who would want to shield a President from bad news or misjudgments to spare him from being "upset."

For some time I have been disturbed by the way CIA has been diverted from its original assignment. It has become an operational and at times a policy-making arm of the Government. This has led to trouble and may have compounded our difficulties in several explosive areas.

I never had any thought that when I set up the CIA that it would be injected into peacetime cloak and dagger operations. Some of the complications and embarrassment I think we have experienced are in part attributable to the fact that this quiet intelligence arm of the President has been so removed from its intended role that it is being interpreted as a symbol of sinister and mysterious foreign intrigue— and a subject for cold war enemy propaganda.

With all the nonsense put out by Communist propaganda about "Yankee imperialism," "exploitive capitalism," "war-mongering," "monopolists," in their name-calling assault on the West, the last thing we needed was for the CIA to be seized upon as something akin to a subverting influence in the affairs of other people.

I well knew the first temporary director of the CIA, Adm. Souers, and the later permanent directors of the CIA, Gen. Hoyt Vandenberg and Allen Dulles. These were men of the highest character, patriotism and integrity—and I assume this is true of all those who continue in charge.

But there are now some searching questions that need to be answered. I, therefore, would like to see the CIA be restored to its original assignment as the intelligence arm of the President, and that whatever else it can properly perform in that special field—and that its operational duties be terminated or properly used elsewhere.

We have grown up as a nation, respected for our free institutions and for our ability to maintain a free and open society. There is something about the way the CIA has been functioning that is casting a shadow over our historic position and I feel that we need to correct it.

The CIA Today

J ust moments before this manuscript was sent to the publisher, the CIA was involved in adventures that would demonstrate that President Truman was correct; the agency had abandoned effective intelligence analysis and had focused instead upon policy making and overt operations activity.

On Sunday, February 20, 2011, *The New York Times* featured on its front page a story about the government's effort to hide details about one of the great alleged swindles of modern times. Following the September 11 attack, a recent Pentagon study found that it had paid $285 billion in three years to enterprising but apparently crooked entrepreneurs for programs to prevent future aggression. The payments were made to individuals or groups that were accused of fraud or other wrongdoing.

The article featured the machinations of Dennis Montgomery, who had been paid many millions of dollars for computer codes that were fake. Montgomery's former lawyer, Michael Flynn, now describes Montgomery as a "con" man. CIA officials had previously said that Montgomery's codes comprised "the most important, sensitive" tool that the agency possessed. President Truman had established the CIA for the sole purpose of evaluating intelligence-related data. Apparently the agency is ill-equipped to even do that. The Montgomery group had been paid $20 million by claiming that his software could stop the next Al Qaeda attack on the United States. In December 2003 Montgomery claimed that he had decoded messages revealing that specific planes, headed toward the United States from France, Mexico and Britain, were targets of identified terrorists. There was discussion about firing on the planes, but the Bush administration instead ordered them grounded, causing a major international incident. The French government commissioned a secret study that found that the Montgomery technology was a fabrication. Perhaps the French experts could be retained after the CIA "experts" have been fired. Or even better, how about hiring the sharp-eyed business experts who supervise the Las Vegas gambling establishments. Montgomery is set for trial in Las Vegas for attempting to pass $1.8 million in bad checks at casinos.

Meanwhile, our government has declined to charge him with any wrongdoing or even attempted to have any of its, rather our, funds returned. The government has covered the events with a dense cloud of mystery and has even adopted a technique we last saw when I tried the E. Howard Hunt case. During that trial, two persons who never spoke on the record and declined to reveal their names or their association with any group were present when I deposed two highranking former CIA officials, each additionally protected and represented by his own counsel. The deponents both said that they would leave unless the two nameless suits were allowed to stay. Of course, they had no right to be there, and I was concerned that a bizarre precedent was being established. I expected to appeal the case and try to have the rule of law established. However, since we won the case an appeal was neither necessary nor possible.

In the Montgomery case *The New York Times* reported:

> The secrecy was so great that at a deposition Mr. Montgomery gave in November, two government officials showed up to monitor the questioning but refused to give their names or the agencies they worked for.

The relationship between our government and an ally, Pakistan, appears to have become more complicated and more imperiled due to the actions of the CIA, as reported in *The New York Times* on February 22, 2011. An American arrested in Pakistan, Raymond A. Davis, according to Pakistan officials, has murdered two men; and a third person was killed as an unmarked vehicle, driving at speed the wrong way on a one-way street, was rushing to prevent the arrest of Davis. In spite of requests by the Pakistani that the driver be turned over to local authorities, our government has refused to do so. A similar act in the United States would likely be considered vehicular homicide.

Davis claims that he was resisting two men who he thought were about to rob him and that he had acted in self-defense. The local police, after questioning Davis, who had fled from the scene to avoid arrest, discovered that Davis, using the powerful Glock pistol that he always carried, had shot the men through his windshield, then left the car to shoot them several times in the back.

Davis was employed in secret activities by the Central Intelligence Agency. Since Pakistan is not an enemy, the laws of both the United States and Pakistan were regularly violated as he carried out his assigned tasks. After killing both men, Davis photographed them and then called the United States Consulate for assistance. Likely the response was dispatching a vehicle to the scene to spirit away Davis and prevent his arrest. That attempt resulted in another loss of life when the rescue vehicle struck a motorcyclist. The widow of one of the men, overcome by the death of her husband, then committed suicide.

The *Times* now states that it was aware of the fact that Davis worked for the CIA but had withheld that information from its readers at the request of the United States government. That call was a difficult one to make with the possible life of an American prisoner in a foreign land at stake. However, as the facts now reveal, the local authorities had strongly suspected that Davis was CIA. The American government should not have asked the *Times* and other media outlets to suppress that aspect of the story.

Since the United States is not at war with Pakistan and prevented from carrying out operations in that country, the CIA has been granted authority by the United States to operate armed drones that kill presumed militants in Pakistan and carry out other covert operations of an undisclosed sort without the knowledge of the Pakistan authorities.

The exposure of these public actions and the four deaths of local civilians have placed the government of Pakistan in a difficult and tenuous position. The CIA, through its spokesman, George Little, refused to discuss the matter but issued a statement claiming that their "security personnel" provide security for American officials, but "they do not conduct foreign intelligence collection or covert operations." Those blatantly misleading words placed the authorities in Pakistan in a more difficult position. Again the CIA was making policy, conducting operations and issuing transparently false information.

On May 2, 2011, President Obama, declaring "justice has been done," announced that Osama bin Laden had been killed in Pakistan by military forces of the United States. For many months the president had reviewed intelligence reports by the CIA and others before deciding that the evidence that the person who had been located was in fact bin Laden. He resisted the premature urgings of the CIA to begin the operation until he was quite sure that the gathered intelligence was dispositive.

The CIA's efforts to have its own team, already in place in Pakistan, participate in the planned operation were rejected by Obama. Instead he relied upon a highly trained Navy SEALs unit flown in from a base in the United States. The well-planned incursion was successful. Finally, a president had determined and insisted upon the proper role for the CIA as envisioned by President Harry Truman when he formed the organization. The chief executive alone set the policy and was solely responsible for the operation. The CIA, along with other similar organizations, was relegated to the restrictions of their charter to conduct investigations outside of the United States and offer advice to the president.

Since Obama had not, for reasons of security, shared his plans with the leaders of Pakistan, the relationship between the two countries began to further deteriorate. However, Pakistan's leaders, who had previously been extremely critical of the actions of the CIA in Pakistan, were reassured that its operational activities had been limited. On June 2, 2011, for the first time in many years, the two countries formed a joint anti-terror squad. Pakistan also allowed CIA agents to collect information by examining the bin Laden compound.

The Indictment

The People of the United States

v.

the Central Intelligence Agency

In preparing an indictment, prosecutors examine the criminal statutes to determine if every element of the crime has been established beyond a reasonable doubt. Those who have learned about the law from television programs or mystery novels tend to believe that "motive, means and opportunity" are the sine qua non for a criminal case. In fact none of those considerations has ever been a requirement in a criminal case, although recent "hate crime" legislation has edged a bit closer to motivation by enlarging the concept of intent.

Allegations of previous crimes are often prohibited to prove the character of the defendant. However, the exceptions to that general rule are well-settled law and permit assertions about "other crimes" in many instances. That rule, 404(b) of the Federal Rules of Evidence, also permits evidence, testimony and documents, which establish the defendant's intent, preparation, plan, or knowledge. Many states have adopted the federal rule regarding local prosecutions, and some have admitted evidence if it is similar to the present offense so that it can be said that the acts constitute the "imprint" of the defendant.

Therefore, it is appropriate to inquire, as a prosecutor would be constrained to do, into the "imprint" of the CIA and its officers and agents. For example, had the CIA ever planned, prepared, or demonstrated intent or even knowledge of the assassination of heads of state? The answer to that question is clear. Had it engaged in planning and carrying out specific and selected assassinations of community leaders who were not heads of state? There too, the answer is obvious.

The information set forth below is based upon statements made by former officers of the CIA, including Ralph McGehee, who had been an officer with the agency for a quarter of a century and has since written important books and articles critical of that organization, and K. Barton Osborn, a former Operation Phoenix officer in his testimony before a committee of Congress. It also relies upon the testimony and statements of numerous other eyewitnesses and scholars before committees of the United States Senate chaired by Sen. Frank Church and later by Sen. Edward Kennedy and by admissions made by the CIA in seeking to both minimize and explain the reasons for their criminal actions.

As in any indictment the assertions, while consistent and credible based upon government documents, including some surviving CIA documents, are not proven. The CIA has admitted that it deliberately destroyed numerous documents so that they could not be seen by members of congressional committees charged with the responsibility of oversight. Therefore, their explanations must be considered in that light. If the documents supported their subsequently adopted positions, it is likely that they would have been retained and produced. Those actions may be considered as admissions against interest.

It is well documented that the CIA was responsible for the planning and attempted implementation of numerous attempts to assassinate Fidel Castro. Testimony and documents supporting that conclusion have been available for many years. In addition I have interviewed witnesses and survivors to those bungled efforts. Not as well known are the efforts by the CIA to murder other heads of state.

The CIA plotted the assassination of the first legally elected president of the Republic of the Congo, Patrice Lumumba. The Church committee stated that two CIA officials were asked to assassinate President Lumumba and that Allen Dulles, the director of the CIA, had ordered that assassination as "an urgent and prime objective." Sidney Gottlieb, the director of a then-secret CIA group, designed a poison that he personally smuggled into the Republic of the Congo to murder President Lumumba. Later a Belgian commission stated that there had been both Belgian and United States plans to kill Lumumba. A CIA station chief participated in the capture of Lumumba and his delivery to his enemies in Katanga, where he was murdered. Later a CIA officer admitted that Lumumba's body was in the trunk of his car and that he was involved in an effort to dispose of the body. Today President Lumumba, who had opposed imported ideologies from the West or from the Soviet Union, is considered a prophet in his nation.

The CIA, displeased with the democratic election of Salvador Allende as president of Chile, urged Rene Schneider Chereau, commander in chief of the Chilean army, to lead a coup d'etat to prevent Allende's inauguration. Commander Schneider was a strict constitutionalist who had stated that he intended to continue the Chilean military's history of noninvolvement in political matters. The CIA devised a plan to kidnap him just after he left an official dinner meeting in an official vehicle on October 19, 1970. Schneider, instead, quietly exited in a private car and the kidnappers armed with tear-gas grenades were unable to carry out their mission. The next day a CIA cable was sent from its headquarters in Langley to the local CIA station in Chile calling for urgent action since "headquarters must respond during morning 20 October to queries from high levels." Another effort was made after the CIA had authorized additional payments; that too failed.

On October 22, a third attempt led to the murder of Schneider. He had attempted to defend himself and was shot several times at point-blank range. He was taken to a military hospital where he died on October 25, 1970. The CIA had provided the "sterile weapons" to carry out the operation and the strategy to blame it upon Allende supporters and thereby cause an immediate military takeover. The military investigated and determined that two groups, each armed and paid by the CIA, were responsible for the murder. The groups had been established by the CIA as a "two-track" effort. Henry Kissinger later claimed that he had little confidence in the groups and that he and President Nixon discussed withholding further support since they believed that the attempted coup might fail. Nevertheless, the murder took place. Some of the relevant documents have been classified while others were apparently destroyed. One can fairly assume that the documents destroyed by the CIA or those still classified would not be useful in the defense of the agency, or they would still exist and be available for examination.

The death of Schneider was a major factor leading to the overthrow of the Allende government by members in the military in 1973. The CIA had led efforts to destabilize the Chilean government after President Nixon told the agency that an Allende government would not be acceptable. Ten million dollars were made available for the planned coup, and CIA officers sought to convince and bribe Chilean military officers to participate in that effort. Funds from the United States funneled into political parties opposing Allende, were used to foment and support strikes in major industries. Nixon directed the CIA to "put pressure" on the Allende government.

As the crisis in Chile deepened Allende considered calling for a plebiscite and decided to make that formal request on September 11, 1973. However, the military attacked the presidential palace, La Moneda, that day before the call could be made. Allende's farewell address was broadcast live by radio and was accompanied by sounds of exploding bombs and gunfire. He refused an offer to safely leave the country and indicated that he intended to remain and fight. His body was discovered later that day, and it was officially ruled that he had committed suicide. In 2008, a competition was organized by National Public Television in Chile to determine the Greatest Chilean in History. Salvador Allende was chosen.

The CIA was involved in devising schemes and supporting efforts to assassinate President Trujillo, the leader of the Dominican Republic. The agency had established an assassination training area in Venezuela and transported Dominican exiles to that location. The CIA was not repulsed by Trujillo's dictatorial and oppressive rule—rather it was concerned that Trujillo had no basis of support and that a revolt led by the left might replace him. On May 30, 1961, a group of men assassinated him by automatic weapon. Ultimately Juan Bosch was elected president. However, Bosch stated that he would institute land reform and low-rent housing and consider nationalizing some businesses. The *Miami News* asserted that Bosch represented "Communist penetration." The CIA then decided to utilize its contacts and influence in the Dominican military to overthrow the democratically elected president. In September 1963, the military launched a coup to remove the Bosch government. *Newsweek* stated that "Democracy was being saved from Communism by getting rid of democracy."

Unlike some others who found themselves in the crosshairs of the CIA, Mohammad Mossadegh was relatively fortunate. He was the democratically elected prime minister of Iran in 1951. He had received both his BA and Masters in International Law at Sorbonne, the University of Paris, and a Doctorate of Law in Switzerland.

Prime Minister Mossadegh nationalized the oil industry of his country stating the reasons for his actions on June 21, 1951:

> Our long years of negotiation, with foreign countries . . . have yielded no results thus far. With oil revenues we could meet our entire budget and combat poverty, disease, and backwardness among our people. Another important consideration is that by the elimination of the power of the British company, we would also eliminate corruption and intrigue, by means of which the internal affairs of our country have been influenced. Once this tutelage has ceased, Iran will have achieved its economic and political independence.
>
> The Iranian state prefers to take over the production of petroleum itself. The company should do nothing else but return its property to the rightful owners. The nationalization law provides that 25% of the net profits on oil be set aside to meet all legitimate claims of the company for compensation.
>
> It has been asserted abroad that Iran intends to expel foreign oil experts from the country and then shut down oil installations. Not only is this allegation absurd; it is an utter invention.

The United Kingdom refused to accept that decision and prevented Iran from selling oil through the establishment of an illegal naval blockade. Mossadegh severed relations with Britain. Secretary of State of the United States John Foster Dulles and his brother, director of the CIA, Allen Dulles, arranged a coup to overthrow the elected leader of Iran. CIA Director Dulles arranged for $1 million to be utilized "in any way that would bring about the fall of Mossadegh." The CIA then implemented its plan, and Mossadegh was removed from office in a coup and imprisoned in solitary confinement for three years. He was then placed under house arrest until his death many years later. The CIA flew the Shah to Tehran in clearly identified CIA aircraft to demonstrate its victory. Later, the Shah, a brutal and corrupt dictator, was overthrown by Ayatollah Khomeini, and an Islamic government was installed.

The CIA's mischief in Iran represents a microcosm of its impact during the last half of the twentieth century. Through the use of internationally banned methods it deposed a democratically elected leader and installed a brutal puppet, who was then rejected by his own people, resulting in the establishment of a religious regime hostile to the interests of the United States, one now likely on the verge of becoming a nuclear power. Mossadegh remains today one of the most popular figures in Iran's history although he is not celebrated by the present Islamic government because he was secular, supported democratic reforms, and was open to relations with the United States. Today that history still echoes as relations between the United States and Iran, poisoned by the CIA, remain volatile and a threat to world peace.

Mossadegh was named the *TIME* magazine Man of the Year in 1951 due to his international popularity and his personally tragic struggle for democracy, thus defeating other finalists for that title, the Americans who had destroyed his government, Dwight D. Eisenhower, Secretary of State Dean Acheson as well as General Douglas MacArthur.

Eisenhower, who played a major role in the coup by unleashing the CIA for the destruction of the government of an independent and democratic foreign nation, falsely denied that he had done so and publicly took no responsibility for his actions. However, in April 2000, *The New York Times* published a fact-specific article about the origins of the CIA misconduct. That article was based upon then recently declassified CIA documents.

In March 2000, the United States secretary of state said that she regretted that Mossadegh had been thrown out of office, after having been democratically elected, and then imprisoned until his death. She said that "the coup was clearly a setback for Iran's political development and it is easy to see now why so many Iranians continue to resent this intervention by America."

It had become clear that the CIA, created by President Truman as an intelligence-gathering source, had become an unlawful policy-making and operational unit that functioned as an international murder incorporated. Nowhere was that more pronounced than in Southeast Asia. In Vietnam the CIA planned, organized and carried out more than 25,000 specifically planned assassinations against civilians who allegedly supported the policies of the National Liberation Front and who opposed foreign domination and occupation of their country. An official at the Defense Department stated that 26,369 South Vietnamese civilians had been killed while the Phoenix Program was openly under the control of the CIA. Later the CIA operated the program in a clandestine manner. A former agent for the Phoenix adventure stated that on occasion orders were given to kill American military personnel who were considered security risks.

Scholars who studied the program stated that between August 1968 and June 1971, the CIA killed 40,000 civilians. Others who read the firsthand reports stated that the program was aimed at civilians, not army personnel, and that those who appeared on the lists utilized by the CIA were tortured, imprisoned without trial, or killed without trial.

K. Barton Osborn, a former Phoenix operation case officer, testified before a congressional committee, "I never knew an individual to be detained as a suspect who ever lived through an interrogation." Osborn had witnessed interrogations for one and one half years. Osborn added that the program was a "sterile, depersonalized murder program."

I have read the accounts described above but I have not been able to locate an eyewitness to the events. However, I discovered in unrelated research that a prominent doctor in New York State, Paul Hoch, had engaged in similar activities as a consultant for the CIA in connection with its MKULTRA program. The Church Committee published as "Appendix C, Documents Referring to Subprojects," a two-page CIA memorandum, severely redacted, which is almost certainly related to the Hoch experimentation. It was signed and approved by the "Chief, Chemical Division/TSD," Sidney Gottlieb. He was the chief of the Technical Services Division, a secret group operating within the CIA.

William E. Colby, who had participated in drafting the program and directing it, testified that in less then three and one half years, 21,587 Vietnamese civilians had been killed and that he would not say that Phoenix was never involved in the premeditated killing of a civilian in a non-combat situation. He testified. "No, I could not say that." He added, "I certainly would not say that."

Colby refused to answer questions about $1.7 billion, much of which had been allocated for the Phoenix Program and all of which was unaccounted for. He stated that he did not have the authority to reveal why Congress was not permitted to audit taxpayer funds. He was testifying before a committee of Congress charged with the oversight responsibility for the funding. Later Colby was rewarded for his loyalty: Richard Nixon appointed him director of the CIA.

In April 1973 Colby's only daughter died; she had been painfully ill for sometime. His colleagues considered that her death caused him to rethink his responsibility for past actions. When called before the Church Committee, Colby offered important cooperation providing details of the CIA's operations against the Allende government in Chile. CIA officials made it clear that he had betrayed them and the agency and were fearful of what he might do in the future. Much later, Colby, who was no longer with the CIA, died. The medical examiner said that he had died after he apparently had a heart attack, then collapsed and fell out of his canoe and drowned. Colby had been a strong swimmer. The medical examiner said that no blood clots were found that might have supported the heart attack theory, and speculated that they may have dissolved before his body was found lying facedown in a marshy riverbank near his home in Maryland.

The CIA, probably the greatest threat to American principles of democracy, remains unaccountable to the Congress or to the American people for its transgressions or the expenditure of its burgeoning budget. As the international war on terror continues, and continues to provide a basis for claims by the CIA and its well-rewarded media assets that its organization and methods are necessary, many, some in the United States and millions elsewhere, view it as a leading terrorist entity.

The CIA air force is presently carrying out its own independent bombing missions in Afghanistan and in its characteristic disregard for human life, causing many civilian deaths, resulting in demands by leaders in Afghanistan that the United States withdraw from its country. In many ways the agency has become too costly to continue to operate in a country that prides itself upon its commitment to democracy.

Every nation may be in need of an intelligence-gathering analytical organization of the nature President Truman envisioned. Totalitarian states may enjoy the fruits of specialized military units that are accountable to a dictator and carry out their illegal missions unknown to the people of their own country. The laws of the United States and the concept that our governance rests upon our founding documents, the Constitution and the Declaration of Independence, preclude us from behaving in that manner.

Instead, a decent respect for our nation and our traditions compels us to examine the darkest areas of the CIA's transgressions to determine the actions we are required to undertake. When we prosecuted others for war crimes, beginning at Nuremberg, we assured the international community that we as a nation would apply the same standards to our own leaders should their conduct ever warrant it—MKULTRA and the Phoenix Program are among those operations that should cause us to remember that.

MKULTRA
The CIA's Dark Secrets[129]

During the war in Vietnam, while politicians and other experts in this country were assuring us that American prisoners of war were being uniquely mistreated, a CIA program was taking place in a prison close to Saigon. It was devised and operated by a group of American psychologists employed by the Central Intelligence Agency. During the summer of 1968, at the Bien Hoa Prison, these men were involved in experiments to force Vietnamese prisoners of war, who were suspects not proven to be enemies, to reveal information that they may have possessed. The prisoners, although tortured, did not respond adequately either because they had no information or because they refused to cooperate with those who were inflicting pain upon them. The CIA psychologists then utilized massive doses of LSD, causing serious and permanent damage but still not obtaining the results that were sought.

---

129. It is never pleasant to learn about the depravity of your fellow countrymen. When the practice is organized, continued, and authorized at high levels of government, it is necessary that we examine the facts and take steps to prevent a reoccurrence. Our nation is indebted to John Marks for his scholarship and courage in uncovering the CIA outrages referred to as MKULTRA. His book, *The Search for the "Manchurian Candidate,"* sets forth many of the details. Alexander Cockburn and Jeffery St. Clair, authors of *Whiteout: The CIA, Drugs and the Press,* have also contributed to our knowledge. (Senators Frank Church and the Select Committee on Intelligence and Senator Edward Kennedy with his Subcommittee on Health and Scientific Research properly met the political challenges.) This chapter has drawn many of the relevant facts from those efforts.

Then the furious professionals engaged in techniques that rivaled in barbarity if not in scope the work of the scientists who had conducted experiments at concentration camps under Nazi auspices. Prisoners were operated upon, and portions of their skulls were cut away and their brains exposed. The scientists then implanted electrodes into various portions of their brains.

The prisoners were then moved to a room where knives were available. The CIA psychologists operated the electrodes while watching the prisoners to see what effect their manipulations of the electrodes had upon their subjects. The psychologists were hoping that they might be able to force the prisoners to attack each other. They continued this activity until it became apparent that they could not secure the response that they were seeking. When it was clear that the effort had failed, the electrodes were removed, the prisoners were then executed and the CIA burned the bodies of their victims, likely so that no proof of their conduct might exist. The experiments were part of the CIA's MKULTRA program.

In 1946, Allen Dulles, the director of the CIA, designed and began to implement Operation Paperclip, a program to bring at least 1,000 former Nazi scientists to the United States, including doctors from Dachau who had observed prisoners while they froze to death in tubs of ice water, and chemical weapons engineers who had tested poisonous gases on prisoners. Operation Paperclip then gave birth to Project BLUEBIRD in 1950. Operation Bluebird focused on hypnosis, using North Korean prisoners of war as their test subjects, giving them high doses of amphetamines and barbiturates to see if it was possible to hypnotize them into doing things against their wills. This dubious pedigree of the willful use of human beings as guinea pigs led to Dulles's creation of MKULTRA, a program dedicated to researching differing methods of mental manipulation and their effects on human subjects. The U.S. Army inspector general described it as "concerned with the research and development of chemical, biological, and radiological materials capable of employment in clandestine operations to control human behavior."[130] Under the auspices of MKULTRA, psychiatrists and other researchers used methods such as sensory deprivation, electroshock therapy and psychotropic drugs. Lysergic

---

130. Memorandum from the CIA Inspector General to the Director, 7/26/63. RETAIN?

acid diethylamide, or LSD–25, was the one most commonly used, often on unwitting human beings. The rationalization of these unorthodox and illegal methods to research mind control was to both create agents whose actions could be controlled by outside forces, and to find ways to make enemy agents divulge their secrets.

The man the CIA placed in charge of MKULTRA was Sidney Gottlieb. Gottlieb was a chemist with a clubfoot and a stammer. He was dedicated to research, and was responsible for dosing people with LSD without their consent or even knowledge and devising poisons specifically designed to assassinate undesirable heads of state, that is those who did not share his ethical values. Gottlieb also was behind CIA experiments involving implanting electrodes into the exposed brains of subjects for the purposes of either controlling them or for simple observation. Gottlieb, who received his PhD from the California Institute of Technology, was chief of the Chemical Division of the Technical Services Staff (TSS) in the early fifties, and later the Technical Services Division (TSD). It has been speculated that the initials MK, used to identify several CIA clandestine programs, come from the German *Mind Kontrolle*, leading back to experiments performed in Nazi Concentration Camps by the very scientists recruited through Operation Paperclip. The etymology may or may not be accurate, but the similarities exist.

Richard Helms, who was then the assistant deputy director for plans for the CIA, known in the agency as the Dirty Tricks Department, wrote the original proposal for MKULTRA in a memorandum to CIA Director Allen Dulles in 1953. In it he outlined a program of:

> research to develop a capability in the covert use of biological and chemical materials. This area involves the production of various physiological conditions which could support present or future clandestine operations. Aside from the offensive potential, the development of a comprehensive capability in this field of covert chemical and biological warfare gives us a thorough knowledge of the enemy's theoretical potential, thus enabling us to defend ourselves against a foe who might not be as restrained in the use of these techniques as we are.

After even a cursory study of what Gottlieb and his confederates unleashed on their subjects, it is difficult to imagine how much more unrestrained our "foes" might be.

President Richard Nixon announced in 1972 that Helms would be leaving his post at the CIA to become the ambassador to Iran. Gottlieb decided to resign at the same time; he and Helms would leave together. The fact that we have any information at all on MKULTRA was a mistake. In 1972, Gottlieb, who remained head of the TSS, and Helms, who had become the director of the CIA in 1966, ordered all material related to MKULTRA destroyed. All of the documentary information we now possess regarding MKULTRA comes from seven boxes of financial records found in the Retired Records Center of the CIA, located outside of Washington, D.C., that had escaped the purge.

Nixon replaced Richard Helms with James Schlesinger. Schlesinger, who took the position in 1973, remained head of the CIA for a very short time. While he was there, however, Schlesinger made some unexpected decisions. He felt that the covert operations part of the agency was too powerful and sent out a directive to all CIA employees:

> I have ordered all senior operating officials of this Agency to report to me immediately on any activities now going on, or might have gone on in the past, which might be considered to be outside the legislative charter of this Agency. I hereby direct every person presently employed by CIA to report to me on any such activities of which he has knowledge. I invite all ex-employees to do the same. Anyone who has such information should call my secretary and say that he wishes to talk to me about "activities outside the CIA's charter.

This directive brought forth some startling information, resulting in the creation of the Rockefeller Commission and the United States Senate Select Committee to Study Governmental Operations, or the Church Committee.

In 1977, the seven boxes were found as a result of a Freedom of Information Act application filed by John Marks. Senator Edward Kennedy and his Subcommittee on Health and Scientific Research joined forces with Church's Select Committee on Intelligence to investigate the dark corners of the CIA. The material that follows is the result of those studies, as well as interviews by John Marks, published in his book, *The Search for the "Manchurian Candidate."*

In his 1953 proposal, Helms devised a covert method of funding for MKULTRA, recognizing that the program would be unacceptable for the American public. In a 1963 report, the Inspector General of the

Army, J. S. Earman, showed some discomfort with the nature of the program:

a. Research in the manipulation of human behavior is considered by many authorities in medicine and related fields to be professionally unethical, therefore the reputation of professional participants in the MKULTRA program are on occasion in jeopardy.
b. Some MKULTRA activities raise questions of legality implicit in the original charter.
c. A final phase of the testing of MKULTRA products places the rights and interests of U.S. citizens in jeopardy.
d. Public disclosure of some aspects of MKULTRA activity could induce serious adverse reaction in U.S. public opinion as well as stimulate offensive and defensive action in this field on the part of foreign intelligence services.

But in the early 1950s, no one was trying to temper the program, or its multiple goals. One early document stated:

A portion of the Research and Development Program of TSS/Chemical Division is devoted to the discovery of the following materials and methods:

1. Substances which will promote illogical thinking and impulsiveness to the point where the recipient would be discredited in public.
2. Substances which increase the efficiency of mentation and perception.
3. Materials which will prevent or counteract the intoxicating effect of alcohol.
4. Materials which will promote the intoxicating effect of alcohol.
5. Materials which will produce the signs and symptoms of recognized diseases in a reversible way so that they may be used for malingering, etc.
6. Materials which will render the induction of hypnosis easier or otherwise enhance its usefulness.
7. Substances which will enhance the ability of individuals to withstand privation, torture and coercion during interrogation and so-called "brain-washing."

8. Materials and physical methods which will produce amnesia for events preceding and during their use.
9. Physical methods of producing shock and confusion over extended periods of time and capable of surreptitious use.
10. Substances which produce physical disablement such as paralysis of the legs, acute anemia, etc.
11. Substances which will produce "pure" euphoria with no subsequent let-down.
12. Substances which alter personality structure in such a way that the tendency of the recipient to become dependent upon another person is enhanced.
13. A material which will cause mental confusion of such a type that the individual under its influence will find it difficult to maintain a fabrication under questioning.
14. Substances which will lower the ambition and general working efficiency of men when administered in undetectable amounts.
15. Substances which promote weakness or distortion of the eyesight or hearing faculties, preferably without permanent effects.
16. A knockout pill which can surreptitiously be administered in drinks, food, cigarettes, as an aerosol, etc., which will be safe to use, provide a maximum of amnesia, and be suitable for use by agent types on an ad hoc basis.
17. A material which can be surreptitiously administered by the above routes and which in very small amounts will make it impossible for a man to perform any physical activity whatsoever.

LSD fit the bill for many of these criteria, and as such became the focus of much of the experimentation. The CIA had heard of large doses of LSD that were available from the Sandoz Corporation and made arrangements to procure it. The CIA then began a strange relationship with the drug. According to the Church Committee report, "projects involving the surreptitious administration of LSD to unwitting nonvolunteer subjects 'at all social levels, high and low, native American and foreign' were common." Other sources reveal that many of the "unwitting subjects" were other CIA agents, to the point where spiked drinks were used regularly.

Dr. Frank Olson was a high-ranking and respected scientist with the Special Operations Division (SOD) of the U.S. Army Biological Center at Camp Detrick, Maryland, where the army "assisted the CIA in developing, testing, and maintaining biological agents and delivery systems for use against humans as well as against animals and crops."[131] Olson, who had been the interim head of the SOD, specialized in the delivery of biochemical weaponry through the air and through water systems. He was one of three scientists from the SOD who were given LSD at a conference at an isolated resort in Maryland in November 1953. Also at the conference were three scientists from the TSS, including Gottlieb and his deputy, Robert Lashbrook. It was Lashbrook who surreptitiously doctored Olson's drink with LSD. Olson reacted very badly. Before the conference everyone, including Robert Lashbrook, agreed that Olson was a pleasant and absolutely normal man who was devoted to his family and enjoyed a penchant for practical jokes. After the conference Olson fell into a depression. He became paranoid and was afraid to go home to his family for Thanksgiving because he was afraid he would hurt his children. His colleagues from the agency took him to see Dr. Harold Abramson in New York for treatment. Dr. Abramson was not a psychiatrist; he was an immunologist with no training in psychiatry. What he did have was an interest in how the brain works, and funding from the CIA to experiment with LSD. Gottlieb and Lashbrook thought he might be useful, as well as discreet. Eight days after taking the drug, while Olson was in New York, ostensibly under treatment from Abramson, Olson crashed through the glass of his tenth floor hotel window and fell to his death. His death was ruled a suicide.

The CIA immediately made efforts to make sure Olson's family received death benefits in the form of a pension. Twenty-two years later,

---

131. I spoke to groups of GIs at numerous occasions on United States Army bases, or in front of them, in opposition to the war. After one speech a GI handed me a note and then disappeared into the crowd. After the meeting I read it. It said simply, "Camp Detrick." At a subsequent rally, removed in time and place from the earlier meeting, Barbara Dane, a fine organizer and singer, was given a note by a military officer. It was addressed to me and it said only "Camp Detrick."
A similar occurrence took place weeks later. We were puzzled by the reference. There was no active GI project at Camp Detrick to my knowledge, but I located a couple of anti-war GIs and asked if they knew of any special activity at Detrick. They did not.

after the United States Senate Select Committee to Study Governmental Operations, headed by Senator Frank Church, discovered the real nature of Dr. Olson's death, an act of Congress granted the family $750,000.

Olson's son had his father's body exhumed in 1994, after his mother's death. At that time, forensic studies found that Olson had been knocked unconscious before he went through the window. Olson's son still firmly believes that his father was killed because Dr. Olson was sickened by the work the SOD was doing for the CIA and was thinking of exposing them. He sought to have U.S. attorneys bring an action, but they declined to pursue the matter.

James Stanley was able to bring a case against the CIA. Stanley was an army sergeant who was a volunteer in an LSD drug trial in 1958, although he was unaware of the nature of the drug given to him. He became uncontrollably violent. He was unable to work and his family life was irrevocably damaged. When he was asked to participate in a follow-up study, he discovered that he had been given LSD, and he filed a lawsuit against the United States. His case was dismissed in a 5–4 decision by the U.S. Supreme Court. The 1987 decision upheld the "Feres Doctrine" that states:

"The United States is not liable under the Federal Tort Claims Act for injuries to members of the armed forces sustained while on active duty and not on furlough and resulting from the negligence of others in the armed forces."

Both Justice William Brennan and Justice Sandra Day O'Connor referred to the Nuremberg Code in their dissents in *United States v. Stanley*. Brennan wrote:

> The United States Military Tribunal established the Nuremberg Code as a standard against which to judge German scientists who experimented with human subjects. Its first principle was:
>
> "1. *The voluntary consent of the human subject is absolutely essential.*"

Brennan continued:

> In the 1950's, in defiance of this principle, military intelligence agencies and the Central Intelligence Agency (CIA) began surreptitiously testing chemical and biological materials, including LSD.

O'Connor also recalled Nuremberg:

No judicially crafted rule should insulate from liability the involuntary and unknowing human experimentation alleged to have occurred in this case. Indeed, as Justice Brennan observes, the United States military played an instrumental role in the criminal prosecution of Nazi officials who experimented with human subjects during the Second World War, *post,* at 687, and the standards that the Nuremberg Military Tribunals developed to judge the behavior of the defendants stated that the "voluntary consent of the human subject is absolutely essential . . . to satisfy moral, ethical and legal concepts."

The Nuremberg Code, created in response to the reckless use of human life in experimentation, not only specifies the need for "voluntary consent" of the subjects; it is quite direct about who is responsible:

The duty and responsibility for ascertaining the quality of the consent rests upon each individual who initiates, directs or engages in the experiment. It is a personal duty and responsibility which may not be delegated to another with impunity.

Stanley Glickman was a young man who was pursuing his dream of being an artist in Paris. One night he met a group of Americans at a café. One of them, a man with a clubfoot whom Glickman later identified as Gottlieb, bought him a drink as a peace offering after an argument. Before he was halfway through the drink, he was having problems with reality. He left the café and found his way home, but he continued to have hallucinations. After two weeks, he went back to the same café, where he collapsed. He was taken to a hospital. There, as Glickman stated in an affidavit, he was given electroshock therapy through a catheter in his penis. He made his way back to America and to his family where he was told by psychiatrists that he was insane. His family set him up in a small apartment in the East Village where he became a mild and ineffectual neighborhood character. He never painted again. When he and his family heard of the CIA's LSD operation, the family sued the government. Although Glickman died before the trial, his sister pursued it, but she was unsuccessful. The judge, Kimba

Wood, dismissed the case.[132] It was Gottlieb's responsibility to make sure that Glickman knew about the experiment, consented to it, and was able to handle it; the court system failed to hold him accountable.

Glickman may well have been specifically targeted for his unwilling involvement in the LSD experiments. He had been treated for hepatitis at the American hospital in Paris not long before his dosing. He was brought back to that same hospital when he collapsed at the café. There was some documentation in a report by the Swiss published in 1951 that the effects of LSD were exacerbated in people who had suffered from hepatitis. The CIA did its own report on a study on the effects of LSD on hepatics, a study that started in November of 1952, about the same time Glickman entered the hospital after his encounter with the drug.

Harold Blauer, a professional tennis player, was hospitalized for depression after his divorce in 1953. During his hospitalization, he was given an injection of a "synthetic mescaline derivative." There is some evidence that his physician sat and watched, taking notes as Blauer's condition worsened and he finally died. In the subsequent court case, brought by Blauer's ex-wife in April of 1953, it was discovered that the "mescaline derivative" was supplied by the Army Chemical Corps. The Church Committee Report stated:

> On January 8, 1953, Mr. Harold Blauer died of circulatory
> collapse and heart failure following an intravenous injection of a
> synthetic mescaline derivative while a subject of tests conducted

---

132. The court's ruling engaged in sophistry. The court said that the Statute of Limitations had run and therefore the case was time-barred. However, since the government had concealed the facts, the statute was tolled until Glickman learned about it.

Judge Wood stated that Glickman had a "suspicion" of his injury and its cause. Remarkably, the judge felt that the suspicion demonstrated sufficient knowledge of the facts, which the government was still concealing. A lawsuit based upon a mere suspicion would have been dismissed by the court stating that Glickman had not produced "specific facts indicating that a genuine factual issue existed." In fact, Judge Wood used that very language as a second grounds for dismissing the case citing but not understanding *Anderson v. Liberty Lobby Inc., 477 U.S. 242, 247-50, 106 S.Ct.2505, 91 L.Ed.2d 202 (1986)*. I fully grasp the significance of the Liberty Lobby case since I argued it and won it before the U.S. Supreme Court. The Supreme Court, in fact, reversed the lower court's dismissal and reinstated the Liberty Lobby case, the opposite of the decision in the Glickman case.

by New York State Psychiatric Institute under a contract let by
the U.S. Army Chemical Corps. The Committee's investigation
into drug testing by U.S. intelligence agencies focused on the
testing of LSD, however, the committee did receive a copy of
the U.S. Army Inspector General's Report, issued on October
1975, on the events and circumstances of Mr. Blauer's death.
His death was directly attributable to the administration of the
synthetic mescaline derivative.

Harold Blauer died as a result of experiments done to him by his
own doctors, without his knowledge or consent, as a result of a contract
between the New York State Psychiatric Institute (NYSPI) and the
U.S. Army Chemical Corps, a division of the same Special Operations
Division involved in the death of Frank Olson. The program, known as
Project Pelican, was a subproject of MKULTRA. Its principal leader was
Dr. Paul Hoch, the director of experimental programs for the NYSPI,
who became the Commissioner for Mental Hygiene for the State of
New York. At the time I strongly opposed the actions of Hoch at the
Wassaic State School for Mental Defectives and gained the support
of *The New York Times* and the *New York Post* in that successful effort.
Both newspapers joined me in proving and publishing the facts that
demonstrated that the state had committed serious crimes at Wassaic.
Under Hoch's leadership, children were placed in restraining sheets for
days, held in solitary confinement, beaten, provided with inadequate
food, and denied books, all in violation of the laws of New York State. At
least one child was murdered. Since most of the records were destroyed,
the results of the union of MKULTRA and the State of New York's
psychiatric institutions remain unknown.

The scope of the LSD experiments was huge. During the Church
Committee hearings it was revealed that "44 colleges or universities,
15 research foundations or chemical or pharmaceutical companies and
the like, 12 hospitals or clinics (in addition to those associated with
universities) and three penal institutions" were involved. Ken Kesey,
who helped to glorify the drug, was introduced to it by the CIA in one
of their studies.

It is not possible to determine the long-term consequences of the
use of the chemicals employed by the CIA upon its subjects. There
were no adequate follow-up examinations and in an effort to avoid
detection for the crimes they had committed whatever notes that had

been made were burned. What is known is that the drugs were used to change the mindset and the minds of the subjects.

Dr. Henry Murray designed and conducted the "personality" study in which the subject was psychologically brutalized. The Murray procedure began with each person being required to write a personal, intimate essay focusing on his hopes and beliefs. This surprised the young men as they had been informed that they were merely going to debate philosophy with another classmate. The students were then strapped into a chair and connected to electrodes that recorded physiological responses.

During 1958, one subject was a brilliant young man who had completed high school at the age of fifteen and entered Harvard the next year. At Harvard, Theodore John Kaczynski became a subject of the MKULTRA mind-altering program which took from its subjects the ability to act autonomously and required them to behave in a bizarre manner. Mr. Kaczynski was subjected to three years of that treatment. The initial examination disclosed that he was emotionally stable before being subjected to the "stress interviews."

A few years later Ted Kaczynski became known as the Unabomber. He created and planted sixteen bombs over a period of years killing three people and injuring twenty-three before he was arrested. In his manifesto he called for violent actions as the only method to confront a system "which has robbed contemporary humans of their autonomy . . . and forced them to behave in ways that are increasingly remote from the natural pattern of human behavior."

If one wonders why Kaczynski, with a grade of 98.9 percent, the highest in his class in a course taught at Harvard by the eminent logician Willard Van Orman Quine, would permit himself to be subjected to what appears to be unscientific torture, the answer may be found in the sterling and unquestioned reputation of men such as Murray and Hoch. It would have been difficult at that time to believe that both men were monsters.

In 1927 Murray became the assistant director of the Harvard Psychological Clinic. Later he worked as a lieutenant colonel for the Office of Strategic Services. The OSS was the predecessor to the CIA and provided many of its officers to the newly organized group. Murray returned to Harvard in 1947 where he taught for more than thirty years. He founded the Boston Psychoanalytic Society and when he achieved professor emeritus status he was given the Distinguished Scientific Contribution Award by the American Psychological Association and the Gold Medal Award for lifetime achievement by the American Psychological Foundation. His colleague Dr. Paul Hoch, a German-educated physician, served on the faculty of the University of Göttingen, Germany, where he directed the "brain research" division at the university. Murray and Hoch both worked for the CIA and both were respected by their peers. In New York, Hoch was responsible for the death of at least one patient, Harold Blauer, through CIA-supported experiments he had not disclosed to the patient and injury to many others. As the director of the New York State Department of Mental Hygiene he was responsible for the suffering of thousands of his wards.

It has become increasingly clear that the criminal mischief the CIA imposed upon its victims may continue to haunt us. Thus far, no one, except for the victims, has been indicted.

Sidney Gottlieb also contracted with Harold Isbell, the head of the Center for Addiction Research, later the Addiction Research Center (ARC), in Lexington, Kentucky. The Center was on the grounds of a federal prison. Isbell used the patients in the ARC as his personal guinea pigs. He gave them morphine and heroin, and injected them with LSD. In one "experiment," he injected black heroin addicts with LSD for seventy-seven straight days. Gottlieb believed that African American subjects were more vulnerable to the drug. There is even a record of one mental patient in Kentucky who was given LSD for 174 straight days.[133] In some of the tests the subjects were told what was taking place; in most tests the subjects had no idea of what was happening, increasing their terror to the interest and amusement of doctors or assistants.

Reverend Eugene St. Clair Callender, minister at the Mid-Harlem Community Parish, and I worked together to lessen the impact of heroin addictions upon the community. We opened an informal clinic at his church and raised funds so that those afflicted who wanted more professional treatment could travel to a federal treatment center in Lexington, Kentucky. We were bewildered by the fact that a higher percentage of those who had passed through our unsophisticated clinic remained drug-free than those returning from Lexington.

Many years later we discovered the brutality of the treatment imposed upon the young men and women who had been used as guinea pigs in experiments at the federal facility that severely harmed them and had no scientific basis. Even efforts to restore them to an

---

133. *New York Times*, March 10, 1999.

acceptable life were made impossible because adequate records were not maintained, and when word of the illegal venture became a subject for congressional review, those documents were destroyed.

The United States government did act in one respect. United States attorneys and FBI agents visited our open clinic and then threatened Rev. Callender, me, and the nurses and doctors at our church-run clinic with arrest and prosecution and serious professional sanctions for running an unlicensed free clinic. Eventually we were forced to close the clinic to the dismay of many who sought treatment.

At the same time the United States government, through the actions of the CIA's MKULTRA program, was permitted, in fact, encouraged, to perform atrocities including murder at a federal facility in Kentucky and a state facility for damaged children in New York.

Another of Gottlieb's associates was Major General William Creasy, the chief officer of the Army Chemical Corps. Creasy was a zealous participant in MKULTRA's testing program, although he was disappointed at the limited scale. Where the inspector general expressed concern about placing "rights and interests of U.S. citizens in jeopardy," Creasy complained that he was unable to "test to see what would happen in subways, for example, when a cloud (of psychochemicals) was laid down on a city." His experiment was denied, he said, for "reasons that always seemed a little absurd to me."

Gottlieb was not just an LSD pusher; he also operated as a pimp for the CIA. Operation Midnight Climax started as a way to further find out how unsuspecting people responded to LSD. An operative, often a drug-addicted prostitute, would go to a bar, pick up a customer, and bring them back to the safehouse. The safehouses were whorehouses established by the CIA under Gottlieb's direction in New York and San Francisco. Once there, LSD would be administered to the subject. These safehouses were furnished with two-way mirrors and "recording equipment." Cash transactions of $100, which the CIA admitted were for prostitutes, were found in the records.

George Hunter White was a former OSS officer working with the narcotics bureau when he was recruited by Gottlieb to set up the safehouses. In his diaries, which his wife donated to the Electronics Museum at Foothill Junior College near San Francisco after his death, White spoke of his work with Gottlieb and the CIA: "I toiled wholeheartedly in the vineyards because it was fun, fun, fun. Where else could a red-blooded American boy lie, kill, cheat, steal, rape, and pillage with the sanction and blessing of the All-Highest?"

Barbara Smithe was the young wife of one of White's friends, and attended a party without her husband on one occasion, taking her very young daughter with her. White put some LSD in her drink. Mrs. Smithe left the party, child in tow, about two hours later at the peak of the experience and with no knowledge of what had happened to her. She became terribly depressed, her marriage subsequently crumbled, and she spent the next twenty years in and out of a mental institution. She died in 1978. It was only when her husband heard of the Senate proceedings about MKULTRA that he became aware of what had happened to his wife.

LSD was not the only substance tested in MKULTRA. The Church Committee stated that "Over the ten-year life of the program, many 'additional avenues to the control of human behavior' were designated as appropriate for investigation under the MKULTRA charter. These include radiation, electroshock, various fields of psychology, psychiatry, sociology, and anthropology, graphology, harassment substances, and paramilitary devices and materials."

Although Gottlieb had hundreds of test subjects throughout the United States through contracts with colleges and various medical institutions, he also found a way to expand the program into Canada through Donald Ewen Cameron, a distinguished psychiatrist at the Allen Memorial Institute at McGill University in Quebec. Dr. Cameron served as the president of the World Psychiatric Association and also as the president of the American and the Canadian Psychiatric Associations. Dr. Cameron had a theory that it was possible to clear the mind of all memories and start with a bank slate, thereby curing any mental illness. He called it the "psychic driving concept."

Gottlieb and the CIA found Dr. Cameron's concept quite compelling. They were looking for ways to get enemy spies to talk, and Cameron's work looked promising. Gottlieb, through Cameron, had found a method of psychological torture that could be very effective in extracting information. The Canadian government funded Cameron's experiments while the CIA helped Cameron use potentially harmful, even lethal, pharmaceuticals on the citizens of one of the United States' allies.

Cameron's method was to put the patient into a drug-induced stupor, although sometimes he would go too far and the patient would go into a coma. He would then waken his subjects two or three times a day and blast them with multiple electric shocks, sometimes using as much as thirty to forty times the accepted power. He experimented with keeping his test subjects asleep for weeks and then used either electricity or drugs, among them LSD and PCP, to clean their brains. He used these techniques on hundreds of patients, most of whom had come to him for help for minor complaints.

Gail Kastner was nineteen years old, an honors student, when she went to the Allen Memorial Institute for mild depression. She was put into comas using insulin, among other drugs, and then given multiple electric shocks. At the end of her treatment, she sucked her thumb and used the floor instead of the toilet. Her family would no longer have anything to do with her and she languished in poverty.

In 2004, a landmark decision by a federal court judge in Montreal awarded Ms. Kastner, then seventy, compensation. She was awarded $100,000 for the total loss of a promising life. Although the award was insufficient, the decision did open the door for hundreds of others who had been Cameron's guinea pigs to sue the government. The Canadian government was kinder than our own to Gottlieb's victims.

When Sidney Gottlieb ordered the destruction of the MKULTRA records in 1973, he left behind a wealth of information existing in the human beings involved in the program. But we only see glimpses of a terrifying reality that will remain for the most part unknown. We do know that Sidney Gottlieb authorized the destruction of the lives of innumerable American citizens, as well as the citizens of other countries. In 1972 he described his work as useless. The CIA did not share his opinion; the agency awarded Gottlieb the Distinguished Intelligence Medal.

After his resignation from the TSD, Gottlieb said he devoted his life to good works, spending years looking for atonement. He worked for a time in a leper colony in India, and the last years of his life were spent working with dying patients in a hospice. I would like to believe that as he again surrounded himself with powerless and vulnerable people, it was for pure reasons. Clearly if his conscience wakened it was too late to help many thousands of his victims. Neither he nor any other person involved in the torture or murder of the victims has ever been prosecuted by our government.

Locating the Assassins

We begin with the presumption of innocence, which never was in evidence for Lee Harvey Oswald from the day of his arrest until two days later when he was murdered by an FBI confederate in the Dallas courthouse while he was surrounded by police officers who provided the same quality of protection to him as the Secret Service had for President Kennedy earlier. At least now, in retrospect and with less hysteria, perhaps that legal mandate at the heart of our judicial system may be acknowledged and respected. Those words from a defense attorney are neither unprecedented nor unexpected.

We move to the words of a skilled prosecutor, Robert K. Tanenbaum. His conclusion: "Based upon the evidence that we have seen, Oswald, had he lived long enough to be tried, could never have been convicted of the murder of the president. Simply put, the evidence was not there."

Let us presume, as I do, that Oswald was innocent. Who then was behind the fence and fired the fatal shot from the front? Who placed a weapon and shells on the sixth floor of the book depository building and who fired the shot from the rear that struck Kennedy in the back?

There are then two locations that are crucial to this inquiry and even setting aside legal protections, the laws of nature remain intact, and Oswald could not have performed both actions during the same limited time frame. Then who did?

As we have seen there is undisputed testimony that a Dallas police officer, his weapon drawn, searched for and located a man who had just come from behind the fence that the vast majority of witnesses said was the point of origin for the fatal shot. It appears likely that he was about to arrest the assassin. However, he did not. The man had with him a remarkable document that shielded him from apprehension.

At about the same time two men, strangers to those who worked in the building, were seen hastily leaving the book depository. When asked who they were they displayed the same magic "get out of jail" documents.

All three men in the strategic locations had in their possession authentic credentials of the United States Secret Service White House detail and thus were immune from arrest or even further scrutiny. Later that day the roster of authentic Secret Service agents revealed that there were no agents from that service in the Dealey Plaza area except for those in the motorcade. How had the three men in the most sensitive and suspicious areas of the plaza obtained their credentials? The Warren Commission, relying upon the CIA and the FBI for leads and information, never inquired. We must.

I am indebted to James W. Douglass, a leading author on nonviolence and Catholic theology, for alerting me to the role of the CIA with the Secret Service.[134] Of course, the Secret Service had the capability to print credentials in-house. It is a division of the Treasury Department as is the Bureau of Engraving and Printing, which is responsible for printing millions of documents annually including all of our paper money. However, it did not print the credentials for its own agents of the Secret Service White House detail.

All related documents including gate passes, security passes, emblems for presidential vehicles, and above all, the authentic credentials for Secret Service agents assigned to the White House detail, were manufactured and distributed by the CIA's secret Technical Services Division (TSD) under the direction of Gottlieb who followed the orders of Helms. That information became available for the first time in June 2007 when the CIA, in response to a Freedom of Information Act request, released the documents, including a memorandum prepared and signed by Gottlieb. The application for the information had been made in 1992. The CIA had stalled for a decade and a half. After the assassination the Secret Service withdrew all credentials issued to its agents and provided them with documents printed by its own service. That reform came too late for John Kennedy.

---

134. He and his wife, Shelley, have organized opposition to nuclear-assisted war efforts and have founded a "house of hospitality" for homeless and indigent people who are in need of long-term health care, for which they have earned my admiration and respect.

It is important to recall that the TSD was disinterested in pure research. The objectives of its bizarre experiments were clear and they were universally result-oriented. They did not place electrodes into the brains of prisoners of war and arm them with knives to gain knowledge about the limits of brotherhood but rather to see if they could force their enemies to kill each other. It is in that light that it is appropriate to consider why that unit, one committed to undermining and destroying Kennedy's policies, and planning the assassinations of other heads of state, wanted to control the Dealey Plaza scene. We must also understand its motive and expectations when it distributed authentic credentials to agents who did not work for the Secret Service. In fact, it appears that they provided credentials to the assassin on the grassy knoll and his confederates in the book depository as part of the plan to assassinate the president.

President Kennedy made several statements in the last months of his life, some public and others private, which illuminate the motives for the assassins. His predecessors, starting with Truman, had wielded the atomic bomb as a weapon to coerce the Soviet Union to yield to demands. Truman dared the Russians to try to match the power of the United States, and his counterpart in the Soviet Union responded that the American president had started the arms race. The Cold War became more intense. Kennedy, who had stated that a representative of a new generation of Americans had been elected and had sent a message to friends and foes alike in his inaugural address, had become less confrontational. On June 10, 1963, he addressed the nation from American University. He called world peace "the most important topic on earth." He explained the kind of peace he sought:

> Not a Pax Americana enforced on the world by American weapons of war. Not the peace of the grave or the security of the slave. I am talking about genuine peace, the kind of peace that makes life on earth worth living, the kind that enables men and nations to grow and to hope and to build a better life for their children—not merely peace for Americans but peace for all men and women—not merely peace in our time but peace for all time.

World leaders were cautiously impressed and hopeful.

In his farewell address, delivered a few days earlier, President Eisenhower had warned of the dangers of the military-industrial complex. He urged that "we must guard against the acquisition of unwarranted influence" by that group since "the potential for the disastrous rise of misplaced power exists and will persist."

I believe no one could better summarize these remarks than Jim Douglass did in his book *JFK and the Unspeakable.* He wrote, "what Eisenhower in the final hours of his presidency revealed as the greatest threat to our democracy, Kennedy, in the midst of his presidency, chose to resist."

The negative reaction to Kennedy's remarks at Langley was exacerbated when CIA officers learned of Kennedy's plan to end the war in Vietnam and to consider dissolving the CIA and replacing it with the intelligence-gathering unit that Truman had anticipated when he established it. The possibility of Robert Kennedy becoming the director of that group was terrifying. With the files in his hands detailing the criminal conduct of the agency, including murder, torture and numerous assassinations of political leaders, the repercussions could be feared but not known. Those responsible might be indicted, convictions were possible, and if political expediency became a mitigating factor at the least they would live in disgrace and with the knowledge that their futures were not secure.

With each new proposal for rapprochement, there was cautious optimism in Havana and Moscow contrasted by desperate preparations in Langley. In foreign capitals, plans were being made for the next steps toward peace. Fidel Castro was hoping the relations with the United States might change while in Langley, Gottlieb, at the direction of Helms, was creating a poison pill to assassinate the Cuban leader. The pill was manufactured and taken to Cuba, just as Gottlieb himself had earlier smuggled a similar product to the Republic of the Congo to assassinate its head of state.

The messenger sent to Havana was unable to get past Castro's loyal and committed guards, who had made clear that they would take a bullet to protect their leader and Castro survived. Helms stated that President Kennedy, to whom he was obligated to report, should not be placed in the potentially embarrassing position of knowing about the intended assassination. Helms sought to rationalize his planned actions when ordering that veil of silence but his penchant for disguising the truth was later fully exposed when he was indicted for committing perjury before a committee of the United States Senate.

Events were moving quickly and in each instance the CIA's position was being compromised. At the end of September 1963, Kennedy established a method to communicate with Soviet leader Nikita Khrushchev in secret thus excluding his own State Department as well as the CIA. Less than two weeks later he issued a memorandum stating that within the next three months the withdrawal of American troops would begin and that in two years almost all American personnel would be home. On November 18, Kennedy spoke in Miami and said that if Cuba became no longer "a weapon in an effort dictated by foreign powers to subvert the other American republics" then there could be a new relationship between the United States and Cuba. Within forty-eight hours Castro responded saying that he hoped that Kennedy would be reelected and might become the greatest president of the United States by understanding that capitalist and socialists can coexist in peace even in the Americas. On November 21, just before leaving for the trip to Texas after reading the reports of Americans killed and wounded in Vietnam, Kennedy stated that the policy would be changed since, "Vietnam is not worth another American life."

On November 22 Fidel Castro was meeting with Jean Daniel, the founder and editor of *Le Nouvel Observateur*, the prominent magazine with the largest circulation of any general information weekly in France. Daniel had met with President Kennedy the month before and was taking to Castro the president's words of support for the Cuban revolution and his hopes for rapprochement to Premier Castro. Castro warmly accepted Kennedy's interest in a new relationship. During their luncheon meeting in Varadero Beach, Cuba, Castro and Daniels heard of the assassination. Fidel Castro, no doubt fearing that those who had often tried to kill him were responsible for the death of the American president, said, "Everything is changed. Everything is going to change."

President Truman's nightmare had become a reality. The intelligence-gathering unit he had created had become a policy-making force that conducted its independent operations without regard for the position of the president. The CIA was able to circumvent JFK's less than enthusiastic protectors and Kennedy was executed by an experienced murder incorporated group run by a part of his own government.

Castro's prediction unfortunately proved to be historically accurate. From a nation espousing a Good Neighbor policy during the administration of Franklin Roosevelt, calling for reciprocal exchanges with Latin American countries, to Kennedy's reaching out to Cuba, the United States has become the fearful but no longer feared Colossus to the North. Our relations with Cuba have deteriorated since November 22. Countries in our hemisphere have elected leader after leader hostile to our administrations. Some have entered into alliances with those who oppose our national interests.

Instead of the peace for all time Kennedy envisioned, we have had never-ending wars since his death. While we devote half of our annual budget to wars, past and present, China has rivaled our economic capabilities and in some instances surpassed us, and this century is still very young. At the time of Kennedy's assassination there were approximately 18,000 "advisors" in Vietnam, and plans were made to bring them home. After his death 500,000 Americans were sent to Vietnam, and more than 50,000 died there.

And now in many countries American men and women in uniform die each day.

The Central Intelligence Agency has its own air force and brags that it effectively kills more of the enemy than does the United States Air Force.

The leaders of the CIA have never been held accountable for their crimes.

Not even for their part in the assassination of an American president.

The Fourth Branch

At the conclusion of a trial, attorneys for the parties make closing arguments to the jury. Here there has been no trial, just an indictment. The court will instruct the jurors that the remarks of counsel are not evidence. The lawyers often respond by explaining the purpose of the summation.

After a trial, or even a book, the lawyer or author, in this case both the same person, may seek to assemble the many pieces of evidence into a logical, coherent and persuasive mosaic that resembles a completed jigsaw puzzle. As the segments unite and integrate the conundrum is resolved and the role and place of each bit of evidence, testimony, and documents becomes clear. Only when the elements are evaluated in context and taken together with other facts does the case emerge and become decipherable.

Long before we reach that point during a trial, in fact at the very outset of that journey, the court in all federal and state proceedings has already explained to the jurors that the indictment is not proof of anything or, in legalese, that it has no probative value. Its sole purpose is to serve as the vehicle that brings the accusations made by the prosecutors to the triers of fact, the members of the jury.

An indictment in a book can, of course, have no more weight or resolute posture than one in a criminal trial. It brings to your attention and for your consideration numerous issues and questions, allegations and facts.

We start with the understanding that no indictment and no argument is the equal of a verdict by jurors who may have resolved the issues to their satisfaction beyond a reasonable doubt. We act here in the absence of a serious inquiry by the Department of Justice, an agency that has failed to act appropriately. In a democracy that is our right as well as our obligation.

Now let us see together what picture emerges as we examine the evidence, not in the manner of poseurs who consider a television program to be a trial or who serve as assets for intelligence organizations, but as citizens who respect our laws, rules and traditions and do not wish to see them further traduced. This then is the case against the Central Intelligence Agency for the assassination of President John F. Kennedy.

Motive is not an element of a crime. Nevertheless, an understanding of the defendant's motivation, while proof of nothing, may provide a useful context in which to examine the facts. *Cui bono*, a Latin adage, is traditionally defined by the lawyer's standard reference tool, *Black's Law Dictionary*, as "For whose good; for whose use or benefit." Wikipedia accurately adds that it is "used either to suggest a hidden motive or that the party responsible for something may not be who it appears to be."

On April 29, 1962, President Kennedy invited the Nobel Prize winners of the Western Hemisphere to dinner at the White House. He said, "I think this is the most extraordinary collection of talent, of human knowledge, that has ever been gathered together at the White House, with the possible exception of when Thomas Jefferson dined alone." Of course, the president, known for his charm and wit, was being facetious. In founding our exceptional democracy Jefferson acted in concert with the most remarkable men in our history including Adams, Madison and Hamilton as well as Washington and Tom Paine, Paul Revere and James Monroe, as well as Thomas Mifflin and Nathaniel Gorham, each of whom served as president of the Continental Congress. Likely the most brilliant and certainly the most innovative was Benjamin Franklin. Before the American Revolution these men were farmers, scholars, writers, tradesmen, one a silversmith, and many were merchants or real estate investors. Some had impressive educational experience including degrees in medicine or theology, some were lawyers who had been trained at the Inns of Court in London, while others, including Washington and Franklin, were self-taught or gained knowledge through serving as apprentices.

All made a unique contribution to the history of the world, for they created a democracy with checks and balances designed for both the present and the future with the hope of ensuring a fair and lasting experiment.

It was comprised of three separate but equal branches of government. The legislative branch, the United States Congress, was designed to have two houses. No new law could be made unless they both agreed upon its concept and its precise language. It still would not become law unless the executive branch, the president, signed it into law. If he declined to do so there was yet another path the legislature could pursue. They could pass it over the president's veto if two-thirds of its members voted to do so.

The new law could be challenged by anyone who felt threatened or harmed by its provisions by asking the court system, the third branch of government, the judicial system, led by the Supreme Court of the United States, to declare that it was violative of the principles established in the United States Constitution, our founding document.

Since our founders knew that they did not possess sufficient knowledge to look into the future, they provided a method to amend the sacred Constitution through a difficult path that required the consent of most of the representatives of the states and the nation.

One house of the legislative branch was given the responsibility to initiate funding laws, the other, the power to declare war. No war could be both declared and financed unless both houses agreed. The president, who was by law also the commander in chief of the armed services, was in charge of directing the war, but he alone could neither initiate it nor provide funds for it.

To guarantee the right of the people to make changes, every member of one house of the legislature was required to face election each two years to remain in office. To provide stability, only one-third of the members of the other house faced election every two years with each member serving for six years. The president could be reelected every four years, and while there were no term limits, the first president, who likely could have been a president for life, retired after two terms, and for decades that tradition was honored by his successors and later was enacted into law.

The members of the judicial branch were appointed by the president; but they could not become federal judges, either trial judges or appellate judges or justices of the Supreme Court, without the consent of the United States Senate. As a prophylactic attempt to isolate them from political interference, they each served for life, but they could, after a legislative trial, be removed from office for serious misconduct.

Everywhere one looked one saw the intricate workings of the minds of the geniuses who designed our three-branch government, each acting independently on its own but all also requiring acts in accord with each other.

Our system of governance has been traduced by the emergence of a fourth branch, the Central Intelligence Agency; a branch which repudiates legislative limits, ignores presidential edicts, and refuses to respond to the decisions of the judiciary. Unlike the other branches, mandated by the founders to be cooperative with the Congress, the president, and the court system, the CIA alone has insisted upon and created its own rules that exempt it from seeking collaboration with the legally authorized branches of government.

Presidents and vice presidents have been impeached and prosecuted for relatively minor improprieties and crimes when compared with those committed by the CIA. Members of Congress have been censured, prosecuted and imprisoned for transgressions of less significance than those committed by the CIA. Judges have been removed from office for noncriminal conduct. Yet the CIA, which has engaged in acts of unspeakable depravity, operates beyond the reach of the law. Richard Helms, who committed a number of the most egregious criminal acts, was not prosecuted until he blatantly lied to Congress while under oath. After he was indicted, he was permitted to plead to a lesser count, received a suspended sentence and a $2,000 fine, which was paid by "friends" of the CIA. In every state of the United States and in federal prisons as well, there are prisoners who have been convicted of perjury in less serious matters and who are serving substantial sentences. In contrast, the CIA officials responsible for serious crimes leave office with their honors, medals, awards and their pensions intact.

If citizens bring outrageous conduct by the CIA to the attention of the relevant congressional committees and an investigation ensues with orders to provide the telling documents, the CIA refuses to produce the crucial documents and instead orders the destruction of the documents so that the full nature of its transgressions may never be known. No CIA director or leader has ever been punished for these violations of the law although they were exposed by committees of the United States Senate under the leadership of Sen. Frank Church and Sen. Edward Kennedy.

Presidents have asserted that the CIA establishes its own policies and refuses direct orders from the president. It has become the most powerful force in the nation. Members of the Congress, including those who sit on intelligence oversight committees, have no clue as to the plans of the CIA. Those who appropriate funds for the agency have no idea how the funds will be expended in the future or how previous funds were spent.

Almost a month to the day after President Kennedy was assassinated, Harry S. Truman, the president who organized the CIA, wrote that he had expected it "to operate as an arm of the president." He said that he expected the CIA to restrict its activities to analyzing intelligence reports from various groups including "the departments of State, Defense, Commerce, Interior and others (that) are constantly engaged in extensive information gathering and have done excellent work." President Truman wrote that he "never had any thought" when he established the CIA "that it would be injected into peace time cloak and dagger operations."

Truman added that "complications and embarrassment" that the United States has experienced "are in part attributable to the fact that this quiet intelligence arm of the president has been so removed from its intended role that it is being interpreted as a symbol of sinister and mysterious foreign intrigue." President Truman concluded that "I, therefore, would like to see the CIA be restored to its original assignment as the intelligence arm of the president" and that the CIA's "operational duties be terminated." He concluded, "There is something about the way the CIA has been functioning that is casting a shadow over our historic position and I feel that we need to correct it."

In the half century since then, the CIA was never restored and restricted to its original assignment. Instead its powers, its reach, and its independent operational aspects increased to the point where the United States now has two separate air forces. In the past the air forces of each branch of the military were merged for tactical and strategic reasons into one unit, and our nation had for the first time a United States Air Force. However, the CIA has since developed its own air force and now openly competes with the U.S. Air Force for bombing strikes in Afghanistan and claims that it is more effective than its rival.

On the very day that I write these words, March 18, 2011, *The New York Times* reported that missiles launched by the CIA in northwest Pakistan struck a meeting of local people gathered to settle a dispute. "The attack, a Pakistani intelligence official said, killed 26 of the 32 people present." The *Times* added that "attacks by American drones are immensely unpopular in Pakistan and have been a rallying point for anti-American sentiment." One resident, the *Times* reported, said, "It will create resentment among the locals and everyone might turn into suicide bombers."

While Truman became the first president alarmed by its actions, he was not the last chief executive to express concern. As the unbridled power of the CIA grew, administrations refused to act to constrain it either through allegiance to the agency (George H.W. Bush, for example, had been its director before he became president) or through fear, just as no president was willing to ask for J. Edgar Hoover's resignation as director of the FBI although his misconduct over a period of almost half a century was well known. Both intelligence groups maintained potentially embarrassing files and alliances with important members of the Congress and each administration was, of course, comprised of ambitious politicians.

One young and principled leader told us that all things were possible and then was determined to act. John Kennedy decided to end the war in Vietnam, and after dismantling the CIA he intended to create an intelligence agency similar to the one Truman thought he had initiated, one that would gather information and neither conduct operations nor make policy. The new group was to be led by his brother, then the attorney general, Robert Kennedy. In Langley, where the agency was devoted to power and terrified that its dark secrets might become public knowledge and its leaders prosecuted, alarm metamorphosized into a near stampede. That frenzy gave way to devising a plan to assassinate the president, but only after a scheme to lead investigators to another suspect had been put into place.

As we have seen, Helms led the effort to sabotage Kennedy's efforts at rapprochement with Cuba. Kennedy was then constrained to open a secret channel to Khrushchev in the Soviet Union in order to exclude the CIA from further efforts to interfere with and doom his foreign policy initiatives. Kennedy's instructions to Henry Cabot Lodge, the United States ambassador to Vietnam, about ending the war were not delivered due to CIA opposition to its contents.

In October 1963, according to two reputable journalists, Arthur Krock in *The New York Times* and Richard Starnes, the Kennedy White House considered the CIA's growth like "a malignancy" that President Kennedy might be unable to "control." The White House had concluded that "If the United States ever experiences an attempt at a coup to overthrow the government it will come from the CIA."

The next month, in an act that the CIA likely considered self-defense, the agency, which had assassinated tens of thousands of its perceived enemies from village leaders to heads of state, assassinated President Kennedy before he could take action against it. In a criminal case where the defendant is prosecuted for murder, the last words of the victim on the crucial question are often admissible.

Richard Nixon also felt the sting of the CIA. He had insisted that the Watergate episode involved the actions of the CIA and asked the agency for assistance. The CIA through Helms, its deputy director in charge of illegal actions, refused to assist the embattled president who was facing impeachment.

H. R. Haldeman, the chief of staff of the White House, wrote that Nixon had told him, "Well, we protected Helms from one hell of a lot of things." [135] According to Haldeman, Nixon suggested "the involvement of Hunt as a lever" and that "it would be very detrimental to have this thing go any further." According to Haldeman, Nixon "gazed out of the window, then turned to me: 'When you get the CIA people in say, "Look, the problem is that *this will open up the whole Bay of Pigs thing again.*"'"

Haldeman said that just before he met Helms, "Nixon expanded on this theme: 'Tell them if it gets out, it's going to make the CIA look bad, it's going to make Hunt look bad, and it's likely to blow the whole Bay of Pigs, which we think would be very unfortunate for the CIA.'" Nixon and Helms both knew of E. Howard Hunt's involvement in the assassination of President Kennedy.

Nixon then sent Haldeman to meet with Helms. Haldeman explained in his book what transpired.

So we had failed in our one previous attempt to obtain CIA cooperation, and now in Ehrlichman's office on June 23, 1972,

135. H.R Haldeman, *The Ends of Power* (Time Books, 1978). All references in this section to Nixon and Haldeman and to Haldeman and Helms are based upon statements made by Haldeman in his cited book.

the CIA was stonewalling again. "Not connected." "No way." Then I played Nixon's trump card. "The president asked me to tell you this entire affair may be connected to the Bay of Pigs, and if it blows up, the Bay of Pigs may be blown . . . "

Turmoil in the room, Helms gripping the arms of his chair leaning forward and shouting, "the Bay of Pigs had nothing to do with this. I have no concern about the Bay of Pigs."

Silence. I just sat there. I was absolutely shocked by Helms' violent reaction. Again I wondered, *what was such dynamite* in the Bay of Pigs story? Finally, I said, "I'm just following my instructions, Dick. This is what the president told me to relay to you."

Haldeman then discussed that Nixon had been sending a message in code to Helms since "in all of those Nixon references to the Bay of Pigs, he was actually referring to the Kennedy assassination." The violent eruption by Helms when he learned that the president was threatening to reveal that the CIA had assassinated President Kennedy demonstrates without question that Helms clearly understood the coded message.

Haldeman went on to write, "After Kennedy was killed the CIA launched a fantastic cover-up." He wrote as well, "In a chilling parallel to their cover-up at Watergate, the CIA literally erased any connection between Kennedy's assassination and the CIA."

No president except Kennedy had acted upon Truman's advice that the CIA's actions were detrimental to a democracy and had to be restrained. When Lyndon B. Johnson became president as the result of the murder, he demonstrated that he understood its meaning. From less than 20,000 advisors in Vietnam and very few American deaths there, his escalation began at once. In time 500,000 troops were sent to what was no longer a little war and more than 50,000 Americans died there. Johnson allowed the CIA to have its greatly expanded war and to increase its range of power.

Johnson appointed a commission to investigate the assassination and although its formal title was The President's Commission on the Assassination of President Kennedy, he later stated that he did not believe its central conclusion that Oswald was the lone assassin and that he did believe there had been a conspiracy to assassinate President Kennedy. Lawyers for the Warren Commission later stated that they had been misled by the CIA about the facts. The CIA also refused to provide relevant documents to the Warren Commission even when requested to do so. The CIA had achieved status as a major branch of the government and declined to operate cooperatively with the three other branches.

The available evidence proves that in late September and early October 1963, weeks before the assassination, the CIA had made plans to provide documentation that Lee Harvey Oswald was the lone assassin. The agency had chosen the victims, Kennedy and Oswald, for the crime that had not taken place, demonstrating beyond conjecture that it was the architect of the murder. Choosing the proposed culprit, for a crime that has not occurred, leaves little doubt about its sponsor.

The entire complex plan to blame Oswald for a crime that he did not commit, a crime that had not even taken place when the CIA began to lay a trail that would inexorably lead to an innocent man, involved cables to Mexican police authorities, instructions from the CIA to its Mexico City assets in the police department there to arrest and silence a witness at the Cuban embassy, a citizen of Mexico, who would not accept the false CIA legend and subsequently the use of demagoguery to present a false legend to the Warren Commission as fact. Each action by the CIA, including its destruction of its own files when an inquiry began, is a building block in the case against the CIA for its part in the assassination.

Under the direction of one of the highest-ranking CIA officials, David Atlee Phillips, based in Mexico City, an elaborate scheme was devised. Oswald, it was said, journeyed to Mexico City to meet with the KGB official at the Soviet embassy there, an official who, the CIA stated, was responsible for assassinations and acts of terror in the Western Hemisphere. Oswald then went to the Cuban embassy in Mexico City so that it could be said that he was arranging for a flight to Cuba from Mexico after he killed the president. The CIA, it would assert, had photographs of Oswald at the Soviet embassy and taped recordings of his discussions with the Soviets there. A tame Warren Commission accepted the story and stated that the story provided adequate motivation for the murder.

In fact Oswald had never been to Mexico City, as the evidence reveals. The CIA had no photograph of Oswald at the Soviet embassy or anywhere else in Mexico City. The tape recording of "Oswald" speaking to personnel at the Soviet embassy was proven to be a CIA fabrication. The voice of the man claiming to be Oswald was not Lee Harvey Oswald; it was the voice of an imposter chosen by the CIA. The FBI agents who interviewed Oswald agreed that his voice was not on the recording.

After he had committed perjury before the House Select Committee on Assassinations, David Phillips, the mastermind of the CIA scheme to implicate Oswald, stated publicly that Oswald had not visited Mexico City.

The evidence, all of it including eyewitness accounts, medical testimony, photographs and motion picture films, shows that the fatal shot came from behind a wooden fence on the grassy knoll. It also demonstrates that two men were on the sixth floor of the depository building where a rifle was planted and later discovered.

A man, likely the assassin, was emerging from behind the fence when a Dallas Police officer pointed a weapon at him as the likely suspect. Two men, strangers to the book depository, were seen leaving that building and were also stopped and questioned. Each of the three men escaped arrest by providing legitimate Secret Service credentials and each stated that he was in fact a Secret Service agent.

The Secret Service is part of the Department of the Treasury, which prints millions of documents each year including our paper money. It did not prepare the credentials for the Secret Service White House detail for November 22 and November 23. The Secret Service also confirmed that the only agents in Dallas were those in the motorcade; none were behind the fence and none were at the book depository.

Sidney Gottlieb was the director of a top secret group within the CIA engaged in methods that rivaled the Nazi concentration camp experiments, certainly not in scope or reach, but similar in depravity. He murdered Americans in the United States and tortured Vietnamese prisoners of war and then executed them and burned their bodies to cover his crimes. He prepared and carried poisoned pills to kill a head of state and originated plans to kill other leaders of their own countries. He never engaged in pure science. Each of his actions was devoted to some secret and illegal mission.

How did the men acquire the credentials that provided a free pass for them? Those credentials were prepared and distributed by Gottlieb, the CIA's leading expert for planning and executing the assassinations of heads of state.

Postscript

There is more than sufficient evidence for the attorney general of the United States and for United States attorneys serving in various jurisdictions to impanel a grand jury and consider asking for an indictment of the CIA and its leaders.

The failure of nerve and the lack of devotion to principle are all that prevents those sworn officers of the court from acting in accordance with the law and their obligations.

If all that is now required is an accusation—I accuse.

ML

An Open Letter to the President

Hon. Barack Obama

President of the United States
The White House
Washington, D.C.
August 17, 2011

Dear Mr. President:

In my most recent book I have published the words of President Truman written one month after the assassination of President Kennedy. He stated that the Central Intelligence Agency, which he had organized as an intelligence-gathering vehicle had become operational and policy making and had therefore imperiled the functioning of our democracy. He asked that it be reformed. At the time of President Kennedy's death the CIA had been actively involved in one war; it is presently operational in three wars.

However, I wish to bring to your attention its fourth, less-heralded war, the CIA's effort to limit the First Amendment rights of authors to write and our people to read views that differ from the orthodox CIA analysis of important matters. The CIA has its own website and it presents its positions there. In addition, from the shadows, utilizing its covert assets in the news media throughout the nation and overseas, it has prevented books from being published and has instructed feature writers and book reviewers what to write about books it does not favor. In *Last Word* I have published those explicit, and previously top secret, CIA documents that I retrieved through actions in the United States District Court for the District of Columbia under the Freedom of Information Act.

Perhaps the enormity of the CIA efforts was best summarized by David Atlee Phillips who served as chief of all operations for the CIA in the Western Hemisphere with the rank of GS18, the highest rank in the CIA not requiring executive appointment.

He publicly stated at a conference at the University of Southern California, "I regret the attempts by the CIA to destroy Mr. Lane." But the efforts of the CIA were not focused entirely upon me as other authors offering dissenting views were also targeted.

In my view and perhaps in yours as well, the First Amendment remains the single most important sentence in the documents that founded this democracy. Organizations acting in secrecy to traduce its teachings are a threat to what we believe in.

The CIA is an executive agency, and I request that you instruct that agency to cease and desist from its ongoing efforts to interfere with the rights of Americans in America to write and to read. It is well beyond their charter, but above all it is subversive of all that we stand for. I also request that you direct the attorney general, a man for whom I also have the greatest respect, to monitor and enforce that order. We are entitled to transparency in government, and if I am asked if I think we can achieve that I would reply, "Yes, we can."

Respectfully submitted,
MARK LANE

Appendix

The Commission's Omissions
The George De Mohrenschildt Story
by Mark Lane (1965)

[I wrote this in 1965 when I was writing Rush to Judgment. I decided against publishing it since it seemed somewhat speculative. It is published here for the first time since it is now clearly supported by other evidence.]

It has no doubt occurred to the reader prior to reaching this point that I offer no theories as to the identity of those who assassinated President Kennedy. I refrain from doing so merely because I have been unable to secure sufficient factual information upon which to soundly base a conclusion. Any attempt to suggest candidates for the role of conspirators would be an effort to deal in speculation and conjecture, an area thoroughly preempted by the commission.

In analyzing the commission's failure to fully explore obvious leads, I do not wish to create the impression that I anticipate that a valid inquiry along those lines would reveal the assassin's identity. Such an investigation, however, would have answered questions that at this time remain open.

The commission expended more than one million dollars in amassing data. It secured, or caused to be secured, upwards of twenty-seven thousand interviews and re-interviews, some so peripheral to the issues as to be absurd. In those circumstances no defense seems appropriate to explain its extravagant omissions. During April 1963, Lee and Marina Oswald, and their infant daughter resided in New

Orleans (W.C.R.. p. 114). On November 22, 1963, Lee Oswald lived in Dallas and was employed in a building directly on the route of the presidential motorcade. The building in which Oswald worked was located strategically at the site of a sharp curve, requiring the presidential limousine to reduce its speed considerably, thereby offering the president as a better target.

Lee Oswald did not decide to move to Texas. That decision was made by another. Lee Oswald did not seek out employment in the book depository building. That decision was made by another. Lee Oswald did not decide to separate from his wife and find quarters in Dallas. That decision was made by another.

When we determine that none of those now historic decisions could have been made without the assistance and activity of a gentleman named George S. De Mohrenschildt, we are quite naturally curious to learn more about him.

The commission made some startling discoveries regarding Mr. De Mohrenschildt, but was reluctant to share its information with readers of its report.

Mr. De Mohrenschildt testified that he was "in a controversial business," an "international business" (Vol. 9, p. 169). His testimony revealed that he graduated from a Polish military academy in 1931. His father, he explained, had been the "marshall of nobility of the Minsk Province" under the czar and part of the Russian government as the "elected representative of the landowners to the government" (Vol. 9, p. 169). His brother was "a ferocious anti-Communist" who served in the Russian Imperial Navy (Vol. 9, p. 176). The brother was sentenced to death by the Soviets, but the Polish government "exchanged him against a Communist," (Vol. 9 p. 176) De Mohrenschildt explained. Counsel for the commission asserted that Mr. De Mohrenschildt's cousin, who taught him how to make "documentary movies," was accused of being a "German spy. They made an exchange." (Vol. 9 p. 182) Mr. De Mohrenschildt, himself, chose a different life. He made an extensive study of "the economic influence of the United States on Latin America" (Vol. 9, p. 178) before arriving in America. He entered the United States just one year before the beginning of World War II (Vol. 9, p. 179). He allegedly was an insurance salesman (Vol. 9, p. 179) but admitted that he did not sell "a single policy" (Vol. 9, p. 180). Agents of the United States government seized Mr. De Mohrenschildt for photographing or sketching the United States Coast Guard Station at Aransas Pass (Vol. 9, p.185). Mr. De Mohrenschildt conceded that men from the FBI (commission counsel indicated that another governmental agency was involved in the incident) "came out of the bushes, and they said, 'You are a German spy.' " (Vol. 9 , p. 186). Mr. De Mohrenschildt testified that after that experience he proceeded to Mexico (Vol. 9 p. 186) .

Life in Mexico was no more tranquil, for there he was declared persona non grata and expelled from the country (Vol. 9, p. 187). Commission counsel was well prepared for interrogating Mr. De Mohrenschildt. A very thorough research job had been accomplished before Mr. De Mohrenschildt appeared as a witness. At one point the lawyer who questioned him for the commission astounded De Mohrenschildt by refreshing his recollection as to where his grandfather had been born and what business he was in. De Mohrenschildt, amazed, answered "I will be darned. I didn't know that." (Vol. 9, p. 183). Therefore, the very specific and probing questions asked by counsel very likely provide some clues to the vast store of data compiled by the government about Mr. De Mohrenschildt. Since the commission's lawyer had inadvertently left all of his preparatory work documents in a taxi when alighting at the commission office that morning, the grasp of the subject matter is all the more impressive.

After Mr. De Mohrenschildt stated that he had been expelled from Mexico during World War II, he was asked "While in Mexico you engaged in no espionage for anybody?" (Vol. 9, p. 187).

The question was assuredly most irregular unless the commission had some basis to suspect that the proper answer might be in the affirmative.

Mr. De Mohrenschildt stated that he was followed back to New York from Mexico by agents of the FBI. (Vol. 9, p. 188). Sometime thereafter Mr. De Mohrenschildt met and married the daughter of a United States State Department official (Vol. 9, p. 192–4). He then went to Texas and became active with the oil interests there (Vol. 9, p. 196). He then moved to Dallas (Vol.9 p. 198). From Dallas he became interested in international oil trusts.

Mr. De Mohrenschildt associated himself with a Cuban oil development "during the Batista days" (Vol. 9, p. 183). His assignment, he said, was to go to Texas and attempt "to contact the oil companies in regard to purchases of oil" (Vol. 9, p. 184).

After the war ended Mr. De Mohrenschildt became an agent of the United States government. He was sent to Yugoslavia by the International Cooperation Administration (ICA) "as an oil and gas specialist" (Vol. 9, p. 202) although his academic training was woefully meager in that area.

If the government hoped that Mr. De Mohrenschildt would serve as a goodwill ambassador in order to cement relations between the American and Yugoslavian people, they could not have been other than disappointed by his conduct. Alas, Mr. De Mohrenschildt began sketching again (Vol. 9, p. 270). This time, from a boat, he drew pictures of the fortifications surrounding the island where Marshal Tito generally retreated for vacations. The Yugoslavian guard fired upon Mr. De Mohrenschildt. "And they kept on shooting at me. And the bullets were hitting the water right around us—until we were away out into the sea" (Vol. 9, p. 270). After returning from his mission in Yugoslavia, Mr. De Mohrenschildt said he was debriefed by agents of the FBI or CIA (Vol. 9, p. 235). He returned to Yugoslavia again on a private business venture (Vol 9, p. 212). In 1957 Mr. De Mohrenschildt went to Ghana. The cover that he "chose" was that of a "philatelist." (Vol. 9, p. 211) Counsel asked him why he chose a cover and Mr. De Mohrenschildt explained that: "That was a trick, because . . . we did not want to let it be known to Shell Oil Co. that I was a consulting geologist." (Vol. 9, p. 211)

Counsel pressed the point: "Don't you think Shell Oil Co. would know that George De Mohrenschildt was an oil geologist? "

Mr. De Mohrenschildt cryptically replied, in explanation: "Well, we didn't want it to be known, anyway, because I even didn't go through— I didn't spend any time in Accra."

For "almost a year" (Vol. 9, p.211) De Mohrenschildt dropped out of sight. He finally emerged in Guatemala on the very day that the CIA-trained troops embarked from that country to invade Cuba at the Bay of Pigs.

Mr. De Mohrenschildt explained that he had taken a 5,000 mile walk for the past year (Vol. 9, p. 217). The walk, which Mr. De Mohrenschildt said he shared with his wife, took them through impenetrable "jungle" since they did not "follow any road." (Vol. 9, p. 215) Consequently it is impossible to confirm the story of the strange stroll by calling upon witnesses along the way.

One's admiration for Mr. De Mohrenschildt's fortitude and courage in undertaking such a remarkably arduous journey is increased when one uncovers facts relating to his health. During World War II he was rejected for service and classified as 4F since the doctors "found I have high blood pressure." (Vol. 9, p. 181)

Counsel raised the question of the Bay of Pigs invasion when inquiring about Mr. De Mohrenschildt's sudden appearance in Guatemala:

"Wasn't that about the time of the Bay of Pigs invasion?" (Vol. 9, p. 215)

Mr. De Mohrenschildt conceded that it was, adding that he "didn't know anything about it" (Ibid). The trip finally ended, Mr. De Mohrenschildt said, at the Panama Canal, where he then consulted with the U.S. ambassador there (Vol. 9, p. 216).

After the trip the De Mohrenschildts went to Haiti to visit a man who "used to be a very wealthy man in Russia—also involved in the oil industry in Russia, and in Czarist Russia . . . And I started preparing my contract with the Haitian government" (Vol. 9, p. 217).

The contract with Haitian dictator Duvalier, for more than a quarter of a million dollars, was consummated before De Mohrenschildt testified. The commission report refrained from informing its readers of Mr. De Mohrenschildt's outstanding career.

It was only with the most severe understatement that the commission, in its sole sentence devoted to assessing Mr. De Mohrenschildt's bizarre background, concluded, "De Mohrenschildt frankly admits his provocative personality" (W.C.R., p. 283).

Among Mr. De Mohrenschildt's domestic accomplishments was his ability to rapidly befriend Lee Oswald. Said the commission, "George De Mohrenschildt . . . was probably as close to the Oswalds as anyone else during their first stay in Dallas . . . "(W.C.R., p. 418). Mr. De Mohrenschildt's testimony is replete with his concern for association with those of "good family background" and great wealth, perhaps an acquired characteristic passed down from his father, a former marshall of nobility. Whatever the cause, Mr. De Mohrenschildt made plain to the commission on many occasions that he cultivated only those of sufficient social status. Odd that Oswald, the penniless son of a divorced day laborer, qualified for De Mohrenschildt's special attention.

It was De Mohrenschildt who introduced the Oswalds to the elite Russian émigré community in Dallas. (Vol.9 1:243) It was De Mohrenschildt who gave a party for the Oswalds to which he invited Ruth Paine (Vol. 9, p. 257). Mrs. Paine at once developed a "nice relationship" with Marina Oswald at the party (Vol. 9, p. 258). Mrs. Paine later drove to New Orleans and, in Lee Oswald's absence, brought Mrs. Oswald to her home in Irving, Texas, where they both remained until Nov. 22, 1963. Mrs. Paine herself put the Oswald belongings in her automobile. If a rifle was placed in the Paine garage, it was Mrs. Paine who put it into her own automobile and Mr. Paine who took it out and placed it in the garage, for when Oswald subsequently arrived he carried only a little suitcase, not large enough to contain the weapon.

And it was Mrs. Paine who secured a position for Oswald at the book depository, the building from which the commission argues Oswald fired the fatal shot.

And it was Mrs. Paine who housed Marina and her children at her home in Irving, Texas, but refused to permit Lee Oswald to live there, thereby causing Oswald to secure a room in Dallas.

After the Oswalds were originally settled in Dallas, Mr. De Mohrenschildt testified that he sought them out. He found them through the good offices of Max Clark. Said De Mohrenschildt, "Max Clark probably told me that Marina is there" (Vol. IX, p. 260). Max Clark was in some way connected with the FBI (Vol. IX, p. 235) and an "ex-colonel in the air force," (Vol. 9, p. 238) said De Mohrenschildt.

De Mohrenschildt and George Bouhe visited Marina one day while Oswald was not home after Bouhe had informed De Mohrenschildt that "he had checked with the FBI." (Vol. 9, p. 235).

Bouhe told De Mohrenschildt that it was his intention "to take Marina away from Oswald very soon—not for himself, but to liberate her from Oswald." (Vol. 9, p. 240).

Together Bouhe and De Mohrenschildt accomplished that objective. According to De Mohrenschildt, Bouhe said, "We have to take this girl away from him,' and this is one of the things that prompted us to take Marina and the child away from Oswald." (Vol. 9, p. 240). When asked why he physically took Marina away from her husband, De Mohrenschildt responded, "Now, I do not recall what actually made me take her away from Lee" (Vol. 9, p. 232).

De Mohrenschildt and his wife were the only witnesses, other than Marina, who claimed that they observed a rifle in the Oswald home (Vol. 9, p. 249).

Several days after the attempt upon the life of General Walker, the De Mohrenschildts visited the Oswalds. The commission solemnly reported, "During the visit, Jeanne De Mohrenschildt saw the rifle and told her husband about it." Without any knowledge of the truth (the truth, in the commission's view, being that Oswald was responsible for that attempted assassination), De Mohrenschildt jokingly intimated that Oswald was the one who had shot at Walker (W.C.R., p. 724).

Mr. De Mohrenschildt, accused of being a spy by two separate governments and an agent, according to his own testimony, for three others, certainly did manage to stumble into odd happenings. While the commission asserted its version of that event, Marina, who was present at the time, offered another view.

"I know that De Mohrenschildt had said that the rifle had been shown to him, but I do not remember that" (Vol. 1, p. 14).

De Mohrenschildt testified that it was only after the rifle was displayed by Marina that he "jokingly" brought up the Walker incident. Marina, on the other hand, said that De Mohrenschildt raised that subject the moment he saw Oswald and before he even would have had an opportunity to view the rifle in the closet:

"De Mohrenschildt—as soon as he opened the door, he said to Lee, 'How could you have missed, how could you have missed him?'" (Vol. 5, p. 619).

The decision not to probe further into De Mohrenchildt's association with the events of November 22 was arrived at quite deliberately. A minority among those charged with making that decision felt the matter was worthy of intensive investigation, given De Mohrenschildt's extraordinary background and his association with events related to bringing Oswald to Dallas and placing him in the book depository building. The majority took the position that it was the commission's role to dispel the doubts that existed regarding a possible conspiracy, not to create new ones. The decisive factor in the determination to allow the matter to escape further scrutiny was De Mohrenschildt's alleged "associations that led right up to the White House, to President Johnson's associates in oil interests in Texas."

The commission's decision to explore no further, while unsound from an investigatory view, was consistent with its understanding of its tasks, since its preconception that Oswald was the lone assassin precluded the necessity of looking further. For Oswald was the assassin and he acted alone.

Historians, no doubt, will devote many volumes to the commission's omissions. Here, as an example of the ample virgin terrain, we have just touched upon one.

Acknowledgments

In Gratitude

Thank you, the Charlottesville Gang. Sue Herndon, an excellent writer and critic who also became an expert on MKULTRA and who helped to organize the massive research documents and the manuscript. Professor Emeritus Paul Gaston taught American history at the University of Virginia and was among the first to read the manuscript and offer insights and extraordinary encouragement. The support of Bonnie Herndon, another writer and critic, was important. We all live down the block from Thomas Jefferson's Monticello, and I think that was a factor.

The contributions of my wife, Trish, are indispensable once again. She remains the best editor I have ever worked with.

The last members of the group are Giselle, probably the smartest of us all, a beautiful all-black German Shepherd, and Squash, an orange cat who is the most gentle and loving member of the gang.

There are authors whose works have provided information and analysis and I am grateful to them. They include:

- John Marks and his historic work both in securing information and in writing *The Search for the "Manchurian Candidate:" The CIA and Mind Control*.
- Abraham Bolden, a courageous and patriotic American, for his contributions and for his book, *The Echo from Dealey Plaza*.
- James W. Douglass, for his kindness to me in sharing information, and for his book *JFK and the Unspeakable*.
- Alexander Cockburn and Jeffrey St. Clair, for their book, *Whiteout: The CIA, Drugs and the Press*.

And of course, for Google and Wikipedia, the indispensable research tools.

At the outset there were student volunteers from all over the nation who joined with us in New York and later in Washington, D.C.

They asked not what their country could do for them but what they could for their country, and by their tireless work they answered their president's call.

Hundreds of ordinary people, teachers, housewives, businessmen, and authors became extraordinary citizen investigators and joined in the effort to obtain greater transparency from their government. Some became life long friends and supporters including Peter Tomasino, researcher, analyst, and business executive, and Pauley Perrette of NCIS-TV fame (Abby) who became the director and producer of the documentary film Citizen Lane soon to be opening at film festivals and maybe at a theatre near you.

With the development of the Internet, voices previously silenced could be heard and heeded. New means of communication helped to shape the Arab Spring and an international and spontaneous cry for democracy and the truth. In our own country it created a means for exchange and a call for the release of previously suppressed information about unsolved national questions. Among haunting questions were efforts to settle properly doubts about the death of our president. Websites were created and decades later a new generation of Americans were engaged. We are all indebted to those who have given life to serious efforts to explore serious questions for they honored the First Amendment. No doubt the founders never even dreamed of the possibility of the Internet, with the possible exception of Benjamin Franklin, but they knew that all forms of inquiry, those familiar and creations yet to come, must be free and untrammeled if democracy is to thrive. They knew that suppression and coverup was the dark way of tyranny and transparency the way of light. I urge you to join the discussion by checking out maryferrell.org, Spartacus.schoolnet.com .uk/JFK.htm, educationforum.com's JFK debate, Brent Holland's radio show at brenthollandshow.com and Len Osanic's Black Ops Radio at blackopradio.com.

And there are others who agreed to be tribunes of the people including Harvey Levin and TMZ-TV and Harvey's TMZ website.

It is customary to thank your publisher whether it is deserved or not. It this case it is most appropriate, in fact mandatory. Those who labor at Skyhorse Publishing deserve our respect and gratitude, for this has not been an easy book to publish in the United States in the year

2011. Its lessons are all too clear and its meaning unambiguous. Thank you, Tony Lyons, Herman Graf and Jennifer McCartney.

I have run out of superlatives just when I was most in need of them. But words are inadequate to express my appreciation for Bob Tanenbaum's heroic introduction. When the country's best former prosecutor (also presently among its most successful authors) says kind things about a defense lawyer, we note that we have achieved something. I predict that many may obtain this book to read his opening remarks.

Mark Lane may be contacted at marklane.com